EUROPEAN STANDARDISATION OF SERVICES AND ITS IMPACT ON PRIVATE LAW

With the New Approach, the EU has incorporated European standardisation in its regulatory approach to improve the free movement of goods. Such a New Approach does not exist for services. Nevertheless, a significant number of European services standards have been made.

This book focuses on European standardisation of services and its impact on private law. Two services sectors are analysed: the healthcare sector and the tourism sector. The core chapters of the book contain a number of case studies based on empirical research in these sectors.

The first part discusses how European services standards interact with existing legal regulation at the European and national level. It is shown that, at the European level, there is no clear legal framework in which European services standards are adopted. This has an impact on their application in private law, which is the main theme of the second part of the book. Moreover, there is a real risk that European services standards create obstacles to free movement. This will prevent their successful application in private law.

Volume 68 in the Series Modern Studies in European Law

Modern Studies in European Law

Recent titles in this series:

What Form of Government for the European Union and the Eurozone?
Federico Fabbrini, Ernst Hirsch Ballin and Han Somsen

The UK and European Human Rights: A Strained Relationship?
Edited by Katja S Ziegler, Elizabeth Wicks and Loveday Hodson

The European Union in International Organisations and Global Governance: Recent Developments
Edited by Christine Kaddous

Nudge and the Law: What Can EU Law Learn From Behavioural Sciences?
Edited by Alberto Alemanno and Anne-Lise Sibony

Fundamental Rights in EU Internal Market Legislation
Vasiliki Kosta

Uniformity of Customs Administration in the European Union
Kathrin Limbach

The Impact of Union Citizenship on the EU's Market Freedoms
Alina Tryfonidou

Equal Citizenship and Its Limits in EU Law
Päivi Johanna Neuvonen

European Law on Unfair Commercial Practices and Contract Law
Mateja Durovic

The European Union's External Action in Times of Crisis
Edited by Piet Eeckhout and Manual Lopez-Escudero

The Legitimacy of Family Rights in Strasbourg Case Law: Living Instrument or Extinguished Sovereignty?
Carmen Draghici

Strengthening the Rule of Law in Europe: From a Common Concept to Mechanisms of Implementation
Edited by Werner Schroeder

The Pluralist Character of the European Economic Constitution
Clemens Kaupa

Exceptions from EU Free Movement Law
Edited by Panos Koutrakos, Niamh Nic Shuibhne and Phil Syrpis

For the complete list of titles in this series, see
'Modern Studies in European Law' link at
www.hartpub.co.uk/books/series.asp

European Standardisation of Services and its Impact on Private Law

Paradoxes of Convergence

Barend van Leeuwen

• HART •
PUBLISHING
OXFORD AND PORTLAND, OREGON
2017

Hart Publishing
An imprint of Bloomsbury Publishing Plc

Hart Publishing Ltd
Kemp House
Chawley Park
Cumnor Hill
Oxford OX2 9PH
UK

Bloomsbury Publishing Plc
50 Bedford Square
London
WC1B 3DP
UK

www.hartpub.co.uk
www.bloomsbury.com

Published in North America (US and Canada) by
Hart Publishing
c/o International Specialized Book Services
920 NE 58th Avenue, Suite 300
Portland, OR 97213-3786
USA

www.isbs.com

HART PUBLISHING, the Hart/Stag logo, BLOOMSBURY and the Diana logo are trademarks of Bloomsbury Publishing Plc

First published 2017

British Library Cataloguing-in-Publication Data
A catalogue record for this book is available from the British Library.

ISBN:	HB:	978-1-50990-833-2
	ePDF:	978-1-50990-834-9
	ePub:	978-1-50990-835-6

Library of Congress Cataloging-in-Publication Data

Names: Leeuwen, Barend van, author.

Title: European standardisation of services and its impact on private law : paradoxes of convergence / Barend van Leeuwen.

Other titles: European standardization of services and its impact on private law

Description: Oxford [UK] ; Portland, Oregon : Hart Publishing, 2017. | Series: Modern studies in European law ; volume 68 | Includes bibliographical references and index.

Identifiers: LCCN 2016046244 (print) | LCCN 2016046775 (ebook) | ISBN 9781509908332 (hardback : alk. paper) | ISBN 9781509908356 (Epub)

Subjects: LCSH: Service industries—Law and legislation—European Union countries. | Civil law—European Union countries—International unification. | International and municipal law—European Union countries.

Classification: LCC KJE6819 .L44 2017 (print) | LCC KJE6819 (ebook) | DDC 343.2407/8—dc23

LC record available at https://lccn.loc.gov/2016046244

Typeset by Compuscript Ltd, Shannon
Printed and bound in Great Britain by Lightning Source UK Ltd

Acknowledgements

This book is based on PhD research conducted at the European University Institute in Florence. The research was funded by the European Research Council under the European Union's Seventh Framework Programme (FP/2007–2013). I am grateful to Catherine Barnard, Stefan Grundmann and Carla Sieburgh for the constructive comments on my thesis. Their comments have helped enormously in developing my thesis into this book.

The EUI is a unique institution and it was a privilege to have been a part of this stimulating community. I am happy that, in addition to the institutional *esprit* of the EUI, I have been part of a research team: the ERC-ERPL project team. I am grateful to the team's leader, Hans Micklitz, for his inspiring supervision, his never-ending curiosity and his constant availability. Thanks also to Yane Svetiev for his guidance and advice. It was great to share an office with my friends Marta Cantero Gamito, Guido Comparato, Lucila De Almeida, Betül Kas and Heikki Marjosola. I miss our discussions and lunches in the mensa of Villa Schifanoia. I am grateful to Rossella Corridori and Beate Hintzen for the excellent administrative assistance.

Thomas Roethe was a great help in conducting and analysing the interviews for my research. We were a good team together and I am grateful for his support of my arguments based on medical professionalisation. I very much enjoyed our various trips across Europe. Catherine Barnard made it possible for me to spend one term in Cambridge as a Visiting Researcher at the Centre for European Legal Studies. Thanks to my old college, Trinity College, for providing accommodation. In Cambridge, Amy Ludlow and William Flowers were almost like a host family to me, for which I am grateful.

This book has been completed in Groningen. After ten years abroad, my integration in the Netherlands could not have been easier thanks to my new colleagues at the University of Groningen.

Finally, I would like to thank my parents, Roeland and Marie-Anne, my sister Claar, and my brother Otto. Met jullie als fundament was en ben ik "steeds op reis en altijd thuis" (Vasalis).

Contents

Table of Cases

I. COURT OF JUSTICE OF THE EUROPEAN UNION

Alphabetical

Numerical

II. NATIONAL COURTS

i. France

ii. Germany

iii. The Netherlands

iv. Sweden

v. United Kingdom

II. NATIONAL COURTS

a. France

b. Germany

c. The Netherlands

d. Sweden

e. United Kingdom

1

Context and Methodology

THIS INTRODUCTORY CHAPTER sets out the context and methodology of the book. The book has been written in the context of a research project on European Regulatory Private Law. The first part of this chapter introduces the general background to the research project and its methodology. The second part links the general project methodology to the methodology of this book. The third part provides an outline of the book's structure.

I. THE CONTEXT: EUROPEAN REGULATORY PRIVATE LAW

A. The European Regulatory Private Law Project

In early 2015, the European Commission ('Commission') withdrew its Proposal for a Common European Sales Law ('CESL').[1] The withdrawal could be regarded as the conclusion of a period of intensive debates about the relationship between the EU and private law. In the 2000s, various attempts were made to identify a common set of private law principles which could be used to develop a European Civil Code.[2] Although these attempts were strongly encouraged by the Commission, most of the projects were the product of academic discussion. Their focus was primarily on the traditional areas of private law in the Member States—contract law and tort. The intention to develop a European Civil Code was not dissimilar to the project of a European Constitution, which failed after it had been rejected by referenda in France and the Netherlands. After the publication of the Proposal for a CESL in 2011, several national Parliaments indicated their objection to the proposal.[3] Therefore, it is clear that it remains difficult and controversial to attempt to harmonise private law at the European level.

[1] Proposal for a Regulation of the European Parliament and of the Council on a Common European Sales Law, COM(2011) 635 final.

[2] For the background, see H Micklitz, 'The Visible Hand of European Regulatory Private Law' (2009) 28 *Yearbook of European Law* 3, 4.

[3] See M Heidemann, 'European Private Law at the Crossroads: The Proposed European Sales Law' (2012) 20 *European Review of Private Law* 1119, 1121.

In 2011, a new research project on European Regulatory Private Law was started at the European University Institute in Florence.[4] The main aim of the project was to fundamentally rethink the interaction between the EU and private law. The focus on a European Civil Code is too much orientated on the past. While many of the continental Member States adopted a civil code as part of their nation-building projects, the EU has not followed the same logic. If nation-building was one of the primary aims of the Member States in the nineteenth and early twentieth centuries, the key focus of the EU has always been on building an internal market.[5] From that perspective, the EU provides a good example of the transformation from the nation state to the market state.[6] Private law has been used as a tool for the construction and completion of this internal market. In the process of internal market-building, the EU has created its own type of private law: European Regulatory Private Law ('ERPL'). To identify and to analyse ERPL, it is not only necessary to look at contract law and tort, but also at other areas in which the EU has had an impact on private law. Therefore, the scope of ERPL is much broader than traditional private law—it includes areas such as labour law, consumer law, and regulated markets. Due to the close relationship between the building of the internal market and ERPL, the European legislator has played an important role in the expansion of ERPL.[7] However, it does not stop there—the Court of Justice of the European Union ('CJEU') has played an equally important role through its interpretation of secondary EU law and through its case law on the free movement provisions. As a result, to understand the impact of ERPL, it is crucial to adopt a perspective which is able to combine both EU law and private law. The interwoven nature of EU law and private law is one of the foundations of the ERPL project.

The starting point of the ERPL project is that ERPL constitutes an independent legal order—a 'self-sufficient' legal order—which interacts with national private law orders.[8] Two of the main driving forces behind ERPL are economisation and globalisation. Economisation means that private law is employed as a tool to structure the economy—to give shape to the internal market.[9] Its regulatory purpose is twofold: on the one hand it is necessary to shape the market; on the other hand it enables parties to participate in the market. In parallel to this process of economisation, a second process of politicisation can be identified.[10] In order to improve

[4] H Micklitz, 'Project Application: The Visible Hand of European Regulatory Private Law (ERPL)—The Transformation from Autonomy to Functionalism in Competition': http://blogs.eui.eu/erc-erpl/project-description.

[5] H Micklitz, above n 4, 2.

[6] H Micklitz and D Patterson, 'From the Nation State to the Market: The Evolution of EU Private Law as Regulation of the Economy Beyond the Boundaries of the Union?' in B van Vooren, S Blockmans and J Wouters (eds), *The EU's Role in Global Governance* (Oxford, OUP, 2013), 59–78.

[7] H Micklitz, above n 4, 5.

[8] ibid, 6.

[9] ibid, 2.

[10] ibid, 3.

the internal market, the EU has to a significant extent relied on new governance mechanisms, such as co-regulation and self-regulation. As a consequence, both the law-making and the application of private law have been politicised. In the EU, governance takes place through complicated transnational networks of public and private actors. These networks are genuinely horizontal—the traditional hierarchy between the State and private parties can no longer be maintained.[11] Private law has escaped the boundaries of the State.[12] The increased influence of private parties in new governance has also resulted in a need for more constitutionalisation of private law. Actors in new governance have to comply with basic principles of accountability and transparency.[13]

B. The Methodology of the ERPL Project

The ERPL has three fundamental methodological starting points. Firstly, the impact of ERPL can only be tested by looking at the interaction between ERPL and national private law. ERPL constitutes a self-standing legal order that interacts with national private law. Four patterns of interaction have been identified. Each of these patterns—also called 'parameters'—focus on a different kind of impact of ERPL on national private law systems. The four parameters are intrusion and substation,[14] conflict and resistance,[15] hybridisation[16] and convergence.[17] For all four parameters, the research analyses the interaction between ERPL and national private law. It starts with an analysis of ERPL at the European level. The next step is to trace the impact of ERPL on national private law. This book focuses on the parameter of convergence. The two-stage approach adopted by the ERPL project is also clearly visible in the structure of this book.

Second, the ERPL project adopts a broad definition of private law. Private law does not only include contract law and tort, but also anti-discrimination law, regulated markets, commercial practices, competition law, state aid and procurement law, standardisation of services, health and safety and food safety.[18] One of the

[11] K Ladeur, 'The State in International Law' in C Joerges and J Falke (eds), *Karl Polanyi, Globalisation and the Potential of Law in Transnational Markets* (Oxford, Hart Publishing, 2011), 397–418.

[12] R Michaels and N Jansen, 'Private Law Beyond the State? Europeanisation, Globalisation, Privatisation' (2006) 54 *American Journal of Comparative Law* 843.

[13] F Cafaggi, 'The Making of European Private Law: Governance Design' in F Cafaggi and H Muir Watt (eds), *The Making of European Private Law* (Cheltenham, Elgar Publishing, 2008), 289–352.

[14] See the contributions of J Smits, A Ottow and M Cantero Gamito in H Micklitz and Y Svetiev (eds), 'A Self-Sufficient European Private Law: A Viable Concept?', *EUI Working Papers LAW 2012/31*.

[15] See the contributions of G Comparato and H Muir Watt in H Micklitz and Y Svetiev (eds), 'A Self-Sufficient European Private Law: A Viable Concept?', *EUI Working Papers LAW 2012/31*.

[16] See the contributions of K Tuori and B Kas in H Micklitz and Y Svetiev (eds), 'A Self-Sufficient European Private Law: A Viable Concept?', *EUI Working Papers LAW 2012/31*.

[17] See the contributions of R Brownsword and B van Leeuwen.

[18] H Micklitz, above n 2, 21–28.

main claims of the ERPL project is that the impact of the EU on private law can best be identified in these newer and specialist areas of law rather than in traditional contract law and tort. It is in these areas that the regulatory intervention of the EU to shape the internal market through private law can most clearly be observed.

Third, the impact of ERPL can only convincingly be identified and analysed by adopting an empirical approach. The impact of ERPL cannot be tested only by looking at the academic literature, the legislation or the case law. Legal analysis has to be combined with empirical research to find out what is happening in practice. This empirical research will highlight many aspects of ERPL that would otherwise remain hidden to academic research. As a result, lawyers, regulators, judges and public bodies have been interviewed with a view to find out more about the interaction between ERPL and national private law. The analysis of the interviews has subsequently been incorporated in the legal analysis. The result is research which can be described as socio-legal research. It is not strictly empirical, but the results of the interviews have been incorporated in the analysis of case law and legislation. As such, the ERPL project combines (theoretical) legal analysis with empirical research.

The ERPL project ran from October 2011 to August 2016. In May or June of every year a workshop was organised to present the current state of the research. These annual meetings have resulted in the publication of a number of EUI Working Papers as well as a special issue of the European Review of Contract Law.[19]

II. METHODOLOGY

A. The Aim of the Book

This book analyses the parameter of convergence in the ERPL project. In the project application, convergence was described as 'a process of mutual approximation of the two different legal orders'.[20] These two legal orders are ERPL and national private law. The process of convergence does not directly lead to merged legal orders—'they still exist side by side, but they are drawing nearer to each other'.[21] As such, convergence has both a horizontal and vertical dimension. Firstly, it is a horizontal process of approximation between the national private law orders,

[19] H Micklitz and Y Svetiev (eds), 'A Self-Sufficient European Private Law: A Viable Concept?' *EUI Working Papers LAW 2012/31*; H Micklitz, Y Svetiev and G Comparato (eds), 'European Regulatory Private Law: The Paradigms Tested' *EUI Working Papers LAW 2014/04*; the contributions of H Micklitz, O Cherednychenko, Y Svetiev and A Ottow, H Marjosola and F della Negra in (2014) 10 *European Review of Contract Law*; G Comparato, H Micklitz and Y Svetiev (eds), 'European Regulatory Private Law—autonomy, competition and regulation in European private law' *EUI Working Papers LAW 2016/06*.

[20] H Micklitz, above n 4, 8.

[21] ibid.

which grow more closely to each other.[22] This process of convergence is encouraged by the intervention of ERPL. This intervention constitutes the vertical dimension of convergence.

The aim of this book is to analyse the impact of European standardisation of services on private law. Therefore, the two drivers of ERPL—economisation and politicisation—are clearly visible in its set-up. The starting point is that European standardisation of services takes place with the intention to improve the internal market for services. European services standards have to facilitate free movement of services. This constitutes the economisation aspect—European standardisation is used as tool for internal market-building. The politicisation aspect is that the internal market for services is not improved by harmonisation of legislation, but by European standardisation. European standardisation through the Comité Europeén de Normalisation ('CEN'), one of the main European standardisation organisations, is an important example of new governance in the EU. European standardisation has been given an important role in the construction of the New Approach to goods.[23] The New Approach provided a key role to private parties in the standard-setting process for products that manufacturers would like to place on the internal market. The starting point for this book is to investigate whether this approach could also be successful to improve the internal market for services. No normative position is taken on whether there should be convergence in private law through European standardisation. The aim is to analyse how convergence would work, and to evaluate the viability of convergence in private law through European standardisation. This includes an analysis of the reasons why convergence in private law would take place. However, this book does not seek to make a case for convergence in private law.

European standardisation of services provides a good example of self-regulation at the European level. It does not have a direct impact on private law. European services standards which have been made through European standardisation are not directly binding in law. They have to obtain binding force in law through a second step, such as their application in private law. The application of European services standards would bring national private law orders closer to each other. It would mean that European services standards would determine the obligations and liability of service providers in private law. As such, the book closely follows the methodology of the ERPL project. Convergence has two dimensions. The first dimension takes place at the European level—it is the European standardisation process. Therefore, the first part of this book focuses on the making of services standards at the European level and the legal framework in which these standards are made. However, this standardisation process is not sufficient in itself to increase convergence. As a result, the second part of the book looks at the application of European standards in private law—for example, in contract law or in tort. The link from ERPL to national private law is made in that part. The book

[22] W van Gerven, 'Private Law in a Federal Perspective' in R Brownsword et al (eds), *The Foundations of European Private Law* (Oxford, Hart Publishing, 2011), 337–51.

[23] See H Schepel, *The Constitution of Private Governance* (Oxford, Hart Publishing, 2005).

discusses various cases in which European standards were or could have been applied in private law. These cases were selected on the basis of their relevance for the first part of the book. In fact, most of time the cases followed directly from the analysis in the first part. In addition to the case studies, the second part analyses judgments from national courts. The book does not adopt a strict comparative approach. Most of the case studies in the first part came from France, Germany, the Netherlands and the United Kingdom. Therefore, these countries were also selected for more in-depth analysis of the case law on the application of European standards in private law. Moreover, they represent Member States with different legal backgrounds.

The two dimensions of convergence involve interaction between three elements: European standardisation, free movement of services and private law. For that reason, the main aim of this book is to investigate the relationship between European standardisation, free movement of services and private law.

B. The Selection of the Services Sectors

To analyse the potential of convergence in private law through European standardisation of services, two services sectors have been selected. These are the healthcare sector and the tourism sector. They have been selected by looking at the services sectors in which European standards have been or are being made through CEN. The focus is exclusively on European standardisation through CEN. This has been done to keep the research manageable, but also because CEN is a European standardisation organisation that has been integrated in the EU's governance of goods in the context of the New Approach. As such, it is particularly representative of ERPL. At the same time, it should immediately be acknowledged that European standardisation of services is a relatively new activity. European services standards have only really been adopted from the early 2000s. The result is that the list with European services standards which have been developed through CEN is still relatively short. As a result, this book will occasionally extend its focus to European standardisation of goods—especially when it comes to the application of European standards in private law.

The healthcare sector has been chosen because it is an interesting sector from the perspective of ERPL. Traditionally, the healthcare sector has been primarily regulated through public law at the national level. The EU does not have the competence to harmonise the delivery of healthcare services in the Member States. Nevertheless, the EU has had an impact on the healthcare sector—for example, through the application of the free movement provisions to the organisation and delivery of healthcare services at the national level. Furthermore, a few years ago, the EU adopted a directive to facilitate cross-border movement of patients.[24]

[24] Directive 2011/24/EU on the application of patients' rights in cross-border healthcare.

The key principle of the directive is that the Member States are still individually responsible for the delivery of healthcare services. However, this regulatory independence is affected by the application of the free movement provisions. In parallel to developments at the European level, there are also a number of important developments that directly affect healthcare services at the national level. A significant number of Member States have introduced elements of privatisation and competition in their healthcare systems. This has made patients—who were traditionally in a very hierarchical relationship to their doctor—much more like consumers. Moreover, the increased privatisation of healthcare services has made the role of private law in the regulation of healthcare services more important. In combination with the various developments at the European level, this means that there is scope for European standardisation and private law to play a role in the regulation of the healthcare sector.

The healthcare sector is compared with the tourism sector. There are important differences between the two sectors. The tourism sector has never been very strictly regulated by public law at the national level. Private law has always played an important role. Moreover, the EU has a number of competences in the field of tourism. It has also adopted legislation in this sector on the basis of its internal market competence. The most prominent example is the Package Travel Directive,[25] which grants a number of rights to consumers who conclude contracts for package travel. These rights have a direct impact on private law—they shape the contractual relationship between consumers and package travel providers. The EU is also working towards an EU policy on tourism to guarantee that Europe remains one of the most attractive tourist destinations in the world.[26] Another important reason to select the tourism sector was that the tourism sector is a genuinely European—or even international—sector. The whole concept of tourism is based on the idea that there should be cross-border movement of tourists and tourism service providers. As such, the internal market dimension of tourism services is obvious.

C. Interviews and Socio-Legal Research

One of the main aims of the ERPL project was to find out what the impact of ERPL is in practice. The analysis of legislation and cases has to be based on empirical research. For that reason, conducting interviews has played an important role in the research leading to this book. Four separate steps should be identified: firstly, the selection of interviewees; second, conducting the interviews; third, the

[25] Council Directive 90/314/EEC on package travel, package holidays and package tours. Now replaced by Directive (EU) 2015/2302 on package travel and linked travel arrangements.

[26] Commission Communication, 'Europe, the world's No 1 tourist destination—a new political framework for tourism in Europe' COM(2010) 352 final.

analysis of the interviews; and fourth, the incorporation of the interviews in the legal analysis. Each of these steps will now be explained in more detail.

Firstly, interviewees were selected on the basis of purposive sampling. They were chosen on the basis of their expertise or involvement in recent European standardisation projects, or in the application of European standards in private law. Most of the interviewees were representatives of organisations that were involved in European standardisation of services, stakeholders who were participating in European standardisation, and lawyers involved in cases in which European standards (potentially) played a role in private law. Occasionally, the interviewees were able to point to other persons who could be interesting to talk to. As a result, some of the interviews were the result of a 'snowball effect'. A total of about 20 interviews have been conducted. Efforts were made to ensure that the interviews took place in a sufficiently broad number of Member States, including a new Member State.

Second, the interviews were conducted in the period between 2012 and 2014. All of the interviews were conducted by the author. Furthermore, a sociologist participated in a number of the interviews. Before the interviews, the interviewees were given a list with potential topics for discussion. All of the interviews were open-ended. Although some indication had been given about the topics for discussion, there were no prepared questions or questionnaires. The interviews were general discussions in which the interviewees were offered an opportunity to present their opinion about European standardisation of services and its impact on private law. With the exception of one interview,[27] all interviews that are analysed in this book were recorded. More informal interviews were not recorded.

Third, all recorded interviews were analysed in co-operation with the same sociologist who had attended a number of the interviews. Before conducting the analysis, the author had listened to the complete recordings of the interviews at least five times. On that basis, key passages of the interviews were identified and were subsequently transcribed. An approach based on objective hermeneutics was used for the analysis of the interviews. Objective hermeneutics is an approach which has primarily been used in sociology.[28] It is very much based on an analysis of the transcripts of interviews—on the words that were spoken by the interviewees. The transcripts were read closely to identify their structures of meaning. A structure of meaning was an objective latent meaning that could only be discovered by analysing the words spoken by the interviewees. Once such a structure of meaning was identified, the rest of the transcript was read to see if other passages could be found that would possibly confirm the structure of meaning.

Fourth, the analysis of the interviews was subsequently incorporated in the legal analysis. Most of the chapters of this book contain two or three case studies based

[27] Interview with ECO (European Cleft Organisation) (Skype) on 14 March 2012.

[28] See J Reichertz, 'Objective Hermeneutics and Hermeneutic Sociology of Knowledge' in U Flick, E von Kardoff and I Steinke, *A Companion to Qualitative Research* (London, SAGE, 2004), 570–82.

on the interviews. Chapters two and eight do not contain case studies. Chapter two provides the theoretical background to the book, while chapter eight analyses the main conclusions. The case studies in chapter seven, in which two judgments of the CJEU are analysed, are not based on interviews. The analysis in chapter seven is based solely on the basis of the judgments of the CJEU[29] as well as an analysis of what happened before and after the cases. For the other chapters, the case studies present the information provided by the interviewees. Footnotes are used to indicate where a statement represents the narrative of an interviewee. With the exception of a few clarifications or observations, the main analysis of the interviews takes place in the sections immediately after the case studies. At that point, the interviews are used for the analysis of the legal framework.

This book is not strictly empirical. However, the empirical research constitutes one of its main foundations. The aim of this book is to present socio-legal research on the interaction between ERPL and national law. The interviews are used to assess and to evaluate the legal framework for European standardisation of services and the application of European standards in private law. The conclusions about convergence in private law through European standardisation are based on linking the empirical research with the legal framework. Therefore, this book has a strong empirical basis—it presents what is happening in practice, and it analyses how the legal framework should be evaluated in light of that practice.

III. THE STRUCTURE OF THE BOOK

A. The Macrostructure of the Book

This book closely follows the structure of the ERPL project. As such, it makes a connection between ERPL and national private law. To analyse the interaction between the two legal orders, the book starts with an analysis at the European level, where ERPL is made. The next step is to trace the impact of ERPL on national private law. This is where the perspective shifts from the European to the national level.

The book has four main parts. The first part (chapter two) provides the theoretical foundations on the basis of which the book is constructed. The concept of convergence is introduced as a two-stage process. It starts with European standardisation of services, which is followed by the application of European standards in private law. The second part (chapters three, four and five) focuses on the European level. The discussion of the European regulatory framework for standardisation is followed by an analysis of the making of European standards in the

[29] Case C-171/11 *Fra.bo SpA* v *Deutsche Vereinigung des Gas- und Wasserfaches eV (DVGW)—Technisch-Wissenschaftlicher Verein* ECLI: EU: C: 2012:453; C-367/10-P, *EMC Development v Commission*, ECLI: EU: C: 2011:203.

healthcare and tourism sectors. The third part (chapters six and seven) shifts the perspective from the European to the national level. It assesses how European standards are applied in private law—in particular, in contract and tort law. Furthermore, the impact of the free movement and the competition law provisions on the application of European standards in private law is discussed. In the fourth and final part (chapter eight), the viability of convergence in private law through European standardisation of services is evaluated. Two paradoxes of convergence are identified and analysed.

B. The Microstructure of the Book

Chapter two starts with a discussion of the theory of convergence in private law. The concept has featured frequently and prominently in the academic literature on the Europeanisation of private law. However, its precise scope and meaning remain unclear. Therefore, the first task of this book is to give a concrete meaning to convergence in private law. It then places this discussion about convergence in the broader regulatory framework for services in the EU.

Chapter three discusses the general legal framework for European standardisation and the extent to which European standardisation of services is embedded in that framework. It strongly argues that standardisation of services is different from standardisation of goods. Two important differences are highlighted: the substantive dimension and the legal dimension. From a substantive point of view, standardisation of services goes beyond standardisation of goods, in that it also seeks to standardise social interaction between service provider and recipient. The standardisation process is less scientific and technical. From a legal point of view, services standards have no clear role to play in the EU's regulatory framework for services. In the absence of a New Approach to services, the recent integration of European standardisation of services in the Standardisation Regulation 2012 appears to be cosmetic. Moreover, services standards are more likely to interact with existing legal regulation. As a result, it is important that European standardisation of services takes the legal framework in which the standards will be applied into account.

After this horizontal perspective on services, the book moves on to discuss European standardisation in two specific services sectors, ie the healthcare sector and the tourism sector. These two sectors are discussed in chapters four and five. Both chapters follow the same structure. They start by setting out the legal framework for the service at the European level. Firstly, the impact of primary EU law is analysed. Second, the impact of secondary EU law is discussed. This analysis is used to evaluate the potential role of European standardisation in private law. The European regulatory framework is then linked to national regulatory frameworks. In particular, the chapters focus on the interaction between public and private law in the regulation of healthcare and tourism services. After this, for each sector, two or three case studies are presented. These case studies are based on interviews.

Finally, in both chapters, the potential for European standardisation to play a role in the regulation of services in private law is evaluated.

Chapters six and seven focus on the application of European standards in private law, and the extent to which European standardisation can contribute to convergence in private law. Chapter six analyses the application of European review in contract law and tort, as well as the role of the Unfair Contract Terms Directive. The starting point of chapter seven is different: it discusses the extent to which the free movement and competition law provisions are used to review the provisions of European standards. This review could potentially prevent the application of European standards in private law. In both chapters, the book follows the same structure. Firstly, the analysis is framed from the perspective of convergence. Second, each chapter discusses two case studies. Third, the case studies are followed by an analysis of the potential for convergence in private law, and the potential impact of the free movement law and competition law on convergence.

Chapter eight, the concluding chapter, returns to the interaction between European standardisation, free movement of services and private law. It draws a number of broader comparisons between European standardisation in the health-care and tourism sectors. Three themes are highlighted: the parties who initiate European standardisation of services, the triggers for European standardisation of services and the impact of European standardisation of services on quality. The absence of a clear European regulatory framework for standardisation of services is linked to the lack of direct impact of European standards on private law. At the end of the book, two important paradoxes—'paradoxes of convergence'—are analysed. Some suggestions are made about how to resolve these paradoxes.

2

Convergence in Private Law, European Standardisation and Free Movement of Services

FOR A LONG time, the concept of convergence has had a prominent place in discussions about the European harmonisation of private law. This prominent position in the academic discourse does not mean that a general consensus about the meaning of convergence can easily be identified. Convergence is an open concept, which has been given different meanings in different contexts. Against this background, the aim of this chapter is threefold. First of all, it sets out the context of the main theoretical discussions about convergence in private law. The focus will be on the distinction between convergence through harmonisation and convergence through co-regulation or self-regulation. Secondly, the link between convergence and European standardisation will be made. The second part of this chapter will explain how convergence in private law through European standardisation would work. Convergence through European standardisation is introduced as a two-stage process. The first stage is the European standardisation process, and the second stage is the application of European standards in private law. The third part of the chapter makes the link from convergence and European standardisation to services. It will analyse how services are regulated by the EU, and what the potential impact of European standardisation of services on private law could be.

I. CONVERGENCE IN PRIVATE LAW: THE CONTEXT OF THE DISCUSSION

A. The Limits of 'top-down' Convergence in Private Law Through European Harmonisation

In the European context, the combination of the terms 'private law' and 'convergence' usually provokes very strong reactions. Without doubt, an important contributing factor to this controversy has been the work of Pierre Legrand, who has written extensively on the possibility of convergence of private law in the EU.[1] Basically, his argument is that harmonisation of legislation at the European level does not result in effective convergence of private law. As such, Legrand is critical of those who believe that the very introduction of a harmonised legal rule—convergence through harmonisation—is sufficient to realise convergence in the application of that rule. A sole focus on the transplantation of the rule would be too limited and would ignore the existence of very different legal cultures across the EU. The application of a rule cannot be considered without also looking at the legal culture in which the rule is received. This is exactly the main obstacle to convergence. According to Legrand, '[t]he meaning of the rule is, accordingly, a function of the interpreter's epistemological assumptions which are themselves historically and culturally conditioned'.[2] As a result, a common lawyer in the United Kingdom will still interpret a rule which has been harmonised at the European level completely differently from a civil lawyer in France. Although convergence might have been realised in the books—this is what Legrand calls a 'bookish' approach[3]—in practice the rule is still applied differently across the EU. One of the important foundations of Legrand's argument is the fundamental difference in approach between common lawyers and civil lawyers. That difference, well established in the legal education of lawyers, cannot be remedied by the mere introduction of a similar rule. As a consequence, Legrand emphasises cultural and sociological differences—legal rules are considered as (a manifestation of) culture. After all, '[e]ach English child is a common-law-lawyer-in-being long before she even contemplates going to law school'.[4] A similar—albeit more subtle—argument has been made by Hugh Collins, who wrote in 1995 that 'the habits of mind of lawyers in different legal systems, no doubt reinforced by rules of civil procedure, are too deeply ingrained to achieve practical uniformity in approach'.[5]

The simplicity of Legrand's 'no convergence' argument is also one of its pitfalls. While Legrand accuses his opponents—in particular, Alan Watson[6]—of a formalistic approach towards legal rule-making, he himself has adopted a rather primitive understanding of culture.[7] In effect, Legrand denies the possibility of

[1] P Legrand, 'The Impossibility of Legal Transplants' (1997) 4 *Maastricht Journal of European and Comparative Law* 111, and P Legrand, 'European Legal Systems Are Not Converging' (1996) 45 *ICLQ* 52.

[2] P Legrand, 'The Impossibility of Legal Transplants' (1997) 4 *Maastricht Journal of European and Comparative Law* 111, 114.

[3] ibid, 122.

[4] ibid, 115.

[5] H Collins, 'European Private Law and the Cultural Identity of States' (1995) 3 *European Review of Private Law* 353, 356.

[6] A Watson, 'Aspects of Reception of Law' (1996) 44 *American Journal of Comparative Law* 335.

[7] For a more nuanced perspective, see T Wilhelmsson, 'The Legal, the Cultural and the Political—Conclusions from Different Perspectives on Harmonisation of European Contract Law' (2002) 13 *European Business Law Review* 541, 548. See also G Helleringer and K Purnhagen (eds), *Towards a European Legal Culture* (Oxford, Hart Publishing, 2014). For a comparative law perspective, see M van Hoecke and M Warrington, 'Legal Cultures, Legal Paradigms and Legal Doctrine: Towards a New Model for Comparative Law' (1998) 47 *ICLQ* 495.

interaction between legal rules and (legal) culture. Although he is right to emphasise that harmonisation can never in itself be sufficient to create convergence in law across the EU, a process of harmonisation can set in motion a convergent development. The introduction of a legal rule at the European level could necessitate a cross-border dialogue about how the rule should be applied as consistently and uniformly as possible. Such an exchange could eventually result in some degree of convergence in the application of the rule. Certainly, it would be a gradual process, and the approximation of laws would only be the start, but the assertion that legal cultures themselves are not open to influences from other legal systems appears to be rather primitive. Legal cultures, as well as other cultural manifestations, are subject to cross-cultural exchange. Cultures may themselves develop in a convergent way. Furthermore, it should be noted that Legrand—as he himself is ready to acknowledge[8]—has presented very limited empirical evidence for his arguments.

Some of this empirical evidence has been provided by Gunter Teubner, who has discussed the reception and application of the concept of 'good faith' in English law.[9] Good faith was introduced in English law by the implementation of the Directive on Unfair Terms in Consumer Contracts.[10] By focusing on the subsequent implementation and application of that rule in English law, Teubner seeks to demonstrate that this 'foreign' rule, transplanted into English law through European harmonisation, had the effect of a 'legal irritant' in the English legal system.[11] No convergent effect was reached by the harmonisation of the rule and the English concept of good faith has developed in a very different way from the German concept, which was the original source that the EU had tried to transplant across the various jurisdictions of the EU Member States.[12] The irritation of the new rule did not result in convergence, but it rather created a new product which had little to do with the original intention of the process of harmonisation.[13] A similar empirical approach—but one which has focused on continental courts—has been taken by Leone Niglia, who has analysed the application and enforcement of private law directives in national courts.[14] In Niglia's argument, national courts have consistently refused or failed to comply with obligations imposed by directives. The cause of this 'non-Europeanisation of private law' can be found in the traditional patterns of co-operation between judges and law professors in most continental jurisdictions. As such, this provides a good illustration

[8] P Legrand, above n 2, 119.

[9] G Teubner, 'Legal Irritants: Good Faith in British Law or How Unifying Law Ends Up in New Divergences' (1998) 61 *MLR* 11.

[10] Council Directive 93/11/EEC on unfair terms in consumer contracts.

[11] G Teubner, above n 9, 12.

[12] See H Micklitz and N Reich, 'The Court and Sleeping Beauty: The Revival of the Unfair Contract Terms Directive' (2014) 51 *CML Rev* 771, 775–81.

[13] G Teubner, above n 9, 27–31. See also H Collins, above n 5.

[14] L Niglia, 'The Non-Europeanisation of Private Law' (2001) 4 *European Review of Private Law* 575.

of the importance of legal culture. Judges base their judgments on the way in which law professors have structured and analysed private law. Since law professors have not sufficiently taken the impact of directives on legal practice into account, it is not surprising that judges have not been able to successfully incorporate and apply directives in their judgments. Therefore, the solution should primarily come from academics, who should focus more on the impact of directives in national legal practice.[15]

In order to get away from the somewhat formalistic focus on harmonisation of legal rules,[16] Jan Smits has argued that it is better to focus on the decision-making process rather than on the outcome.[17] Convergence can also take place in the arguments which are being taken into account in the process of reaching a decision on a certain legal problem. As such, the decision-making process becomes the subject of convergence. According to Smits, 'the focus should be on identifying common sets of arguments that can be weighed in different ways in the various national jurisdictions'.[18]

Overall, what lessons can be learnt from these discussions, most of which took place in the 1980s and 1990s? Two points should be emphasised. First, convergence is an abstract term which has to be specified in a particular context. The discussion about convergence is not brought forward by general abstractions. Rather, it should be applied to specific cases, and it should receive its meaning through particular examples. Secondly, harmonisation, or approximation of laws, is but one strategy to increase convergence at the European level. While Legrand's criticism of the convergent potential of harmonisation might have been overstated, it is true that harmonisation of laws has its limitations. The 'top-down' nature of harmonisation, imposing a rule 'from above' at the European level, encounters certain obstacles to convergence. First of all, a European directive has to be implemented at the national level. It is already at this point that divergent developments might take place across the EU. Secondly, the national legislation which implemented a Directive has to be interpreted by national judges. At both stages, the implementation and interpretation stage, there is a risk that divergence might occur across the EU. As such, it is clear that harmonisation of legislation does not guarantee the consistent application of the rule. Therefore, it is useful to consider other strategies for convergence in law as an alternative to European harmonisation.

[15] ibid, 598–99.

[16] See also T Wilhelmsson, 'The Contract Law Acquis: Towards More Coherence through Generalisation?', *4th Europäischer Juristentag* (Wien, Manz, 2008), 111–53.

[17] J Smits, 'Contract Law in the European Union: Convergence or Not?' *Tilburg Institute of Comparative and Transnational Law Working Paper* No 2008/1. See also J Smits, 'Convergence of Private Law in Europe: Towards a New Ius Commune?' in E Örücü and D Nelken (eds), *Comparative Law: A Handbook* (Oxford, Hart Publishing, 2007) 219–40.

[18] J Smits, above n 17, 5.

B. 'Bottom-up' Convergence Through European Standardisation as an Alternative to European Harmonisation

One of the main proponents of alternative strategies for convergence at the European level has been Walter van Gerven. In particular, through the 'Ius Commune' Project,[19] Van Gerven has argued for more emphasis on 'bottom-up' convergence. By bottom-up convergence, Van Gerven means that the convergent effect would not derive from harmonisation, but rather from co-operation and co-ordination between the various national legal orders.[20] The advantages of such bottom-up convergence would be, first of all, that it would firmly root European law in the national systems and secondly, that it would realise convergence between the European legal order and the national orders.[21] As a result, it could potentially avoid primacy conflicts. Therefore, Van Gerven has argued for a kind of co-ordination through what he called the 'Open Method of Convergence'.[22] Essentially, he focuses on soft convergence which would establish itself as hard convergence through judicial practice. His primary example of such a strategy for convergence would be the doctrine of consistent interpretation.[23] As such, Van Gerven appears to rely primarily on the judiciary as the main actor in initiating and encouraging a process of convergence. The result of that convergence would be a more standardised application of private law rules across the EU. Therefore, the Open Method of Convergence could be described as a method of standardisation. The Open Method of Convergence is not too dissimilar from the 'free movement of ideas' supported by Thomas Wilhelmsson.[24] Similarly to Van Gerven, Wilhelmsson has argued that convergence can most effectively be realised through an exchange of legal ideas and doctrines. This strategy would increase convergence without eliminating legal pluralism in the EU. Moreover, it would be a suitable method regardless of one's chosen perspective on law—whether one has an economic, practical, academic or social engineering perspective on law.[25] However, an important condition for free movement of ideas to be effective is that lawyers across Europe have an open mind to receive ideas and approaches coming from other Member States.

Although the approach of Van Gerven has focused almost exclusively on the judiciary, this does not exclude the possibility of other actors instigating a

[19] See in particular, the Ius Commune Casebooks.

[20] W van Gerven, 'Private Law in a Federal Perspective', in R Brownsword et al. (eds), *The Foundations of European Private Law* (Oxford, Hart Publishing, 2011) 337–51.

[21] ibid, 342.

[22] ibid, 343. See also W van Gerven, 'Bringing (Private) Laws Closer to Each Other at the European Level', in F Cafaggi (ed), *The Institutional Framework of European Private Law* (Oxford, OUP, 2006) 37–78.

[23] ibid, 344–48.

[24] T Wilhelmsson, above n 7, 546.

[25] ibid, 547–52

process of convergence at the European level. One of these processes could be co-regulation or self-regulation. This is where European standardisation enters into the arena. It could exactly be one of the processes of soft co-ordination which Van Gerven refers to. European standardisation involves the voluntary making of European standards for goods and services by the sector itself. The standardisation process takes place at the European level, through the European standardisation organisation CEN, where national standardisation organisations are represented by national representatives. As such, it could be argued that European standardisation is very much like a 'top-down' process, which would result in the adoption of a European instrument that has to be applied at the national level. But this is not correct. The end-result of a European standardisation process, a European standard, is not legally binding in the 27 Member States. Although the precise legal status of the instrument is different in the 27 Member States,[26] the standard does not have any automatic binding force. As a consequence, unlike harmonisation, European standardisation does not impose a binding legal rule on all Member States. It is just the co-ordination of a 'soft law rule' which takes place at the European level. At the same time, an important difference with Van Gerven's strategy is that the actors in European standardisation are not necessarily lawyers. There is no guarantee that the link from European standardisation to law can easily be made. The effect of European standardisation in law is not as automatic as, for example, with consistent interpretation or judicial co-operation. Furthermore, as has been emphasised by Fabrizio Cafaggi,[27] parties involved in private regulation—such as European standardisation—do not necessarily have legal integration as one of their main objectives. They do not necessarily want to achieve harmonisation through private regulation. They do not necessarily seek to achieve co-ordination of (the application of) legal rules at the European level. As a result, for European standardisation to increase convergence it has to be successfully linked to the legal framework in which European standardisation are applied.

For European standards to be play a role in legal regulation, a subsequent step is necessary to make the link from a European standard to its convergent effect in law. This is where the link from European standardisation to private law is made. Private law provides a route to give binding effect to European standards. For example, European standards can be incorporated in contracts (as express terms), or they can be used by the judiciary to determine the required standard of care in a contractual dispute (as implied terms). Similarly, European standards can be used

[26] H Schepel, *The Constitution of Private Governance* (Oxford, Hart Publishing, 2005) 101–43. See also H Schepel and J Falke, *Legal Aspects of Standardisation of the EC and EFTA, Volume 1: Comparative Report* (Luxembourg, Office for Official Publications of the European Communities, 2000).

[27] F Cafaggi and A Janczuk, 'Private Regulation and Legal Integration: The European Example' (2010) *Business and Politics* 1, 21–23.

to determine the standard of care in tort cases, to decide whether or not liability in negligence can be established.[28] In these various ways, European standards could be applied in private law. The standards of care agreed through European standardisation would then become binding legal standards. If such a process took place in the various EU Member States, the standards of care throughout the EU would become more converged through the initial European standardisation process and the subsequent application of European standards in private law.

It is important to note that the subsequent application of European standards in national private law—through which the actual 'bottom-up' convergence takes place—is a voluntary process. The choice of service providers to incorporate a European standard in a contract or the choice of the judiciary to refer to a European standard in a negligence case is a voluntary decision. It would be based on the recognition that a European standard expresses the appropriate standard to be expected from service providers in private law. In addition, certification of service providers could take place on the basis of European standards. Such European standards will only be applied if they adequately reflect the standards that can be expected from a service provider. Consequently, convergence 'in practice' usually precedes convergence in law. The European standard must have been accepted as applicable by the sector itself. Convergence through the application of standards in private law is, as a result, closer to 'bottom-up' convergence than to 'top-down' convergence. A European standard, like any private standard, must have proved itself before it will be applied in law. This process is a combination of what Van Gerven has called soft co-ordination at the European level combined with voluntary (judicial) application and enforcement in private law at the national level.

In summary, this alternative strategy for convergence is essentially a two-stage process. Firstly, a European standard has to be developed through CEN. Second, that European standard has to be applied in private law. It should immediately be noted that such a strategy encounters problems that are not too different from harmonisation at the European level. However, it essentially involves one stage less than European harmonisation of legislation. While with harmonisation the national judge will always start with the national legislation which implements a European directive, this is not necessary for European standardisation. The national judge can directly rely on the European standard, for example to specify a duty of care. However, this does not mean that the European standard does not contain any concepts which are open to multiple interpretations at the national level. Furthermore, this alternative strategy assumes that the link between European standardisation and private law can easily be made. However, the extent to which private law is open to receive and apply European standards is something which will have to be tested in the next chapters. Before these

[28] A Ogus, 'Regulation of Services and the Public-Private Divide' in F Cafaggi and H Muir Watt (eds), *The Regulatory Function of European Private Law* (Cheltenham, Edward Elgar, 2009) 3–15, 9.

questions can be analysed in more detail, it is, first of all, necessary to discuss how convergence in private law through European standardisation works, what it means and why it would occur. This is what will be done in the next section of this chapter.

II. CONVERGENCE IN PRIVATE LAW THROUGH EUROPEAN STANDARDISATION

A. How Would Convergence in Private Law Through European Standardisation Work?

In this part of the chapter, convergence in private law through European standardisation will be defined more precisely. After explaining how convergence in private law would work, the focus will be on the questions of why convergence takes place and how convergence can be tested.

Convergence in private law through European standardisation involves a two-stage process: firstly, the standard-making process at the European level; second, the application of these standards in private law at the national level. Both stages are necessary for a process of convergence in private law through European standardisation to take place. The first step is the standardisation process at the European level. The European standardisation process will be discussed in more detail in the next chapter, but it necessarily involves a meeting of minds of the stakeholders in a particular sector. The term 'stakeholders' is very broad and general. In the context of European standardisation, the stakeholders are all parties which would be affected by the adoption of a European standard in that sector. This will inevitably include the businesses in a particular sector, or their professional associations, but also consumers, the State and non-profit organisations. One of the challenges for European standardisation is to make the European standardisation process more inclusive and to include as many stakeholders as possible. The stakeholders from various Member States—not necessarily all Member States—meet at the European level to identify a set of common standards which are subsequently incorporated in a European standard. For services standards, for example, these standards usually focus on the qualifications of service providers and on the process of service provision. A European standard is always based on consensus between all parties that are taking part in the standardisation process.[29] As a result, the first convergent effect is taking place at the European level in the standardisation process through regulation of the concept of quality of care. The parties will have to agree on a common definition of what constitutes the minimum level of care required from a service provider. Once a European standard has been

[29] The European Standardisation Organisations have adopted the World Trade Organisation's principles in the field of standardisation. The concept of consensus is also defined in Annex II of Regulation 1025/2012 of the European Parliament and of the Council on European standardisation.

adopted, it will contain a set of standards that have to be fulfilled by producers or service providers. The standard is then published by the national standardisation organisations.[30] This concludes the first stage of the process of convergence.

The second stage of the process of convergence is the application of the European standard in private law. To be able to assess the ability of European standardisation to realise convergence in private law as an alternative to legal harmonisation, the application of European standards in law is crucial. The fact that the standard has now been set as the professional standard through a European process of self-regulation does not automatically mean that it will also be set as the legal standard to be expected from service providers in private law. Although it could be argued that there would frequently be market pressure for service providers to comply with a particular standard, that pressure alone is not sufficient to realise convergence in law. This does not exclude the possibility that market pressure could lead to the 'voluntary' application of the standard in contractual relationships. As a consequence, for the second stage of the process of convergence, a decision is necessary to apply the European standards—to put their provisions into practice. This decision does not necessarily have to be express—it can start with the application of the standards in practice. Such application in practice would subsequently encourage the application of the standards in private law. However, the simple adoption of a European standardisation is never sufficient to increase convergence in private law—the convergence has to result from the application of the standards in practice. A distinction should be made between the application of European standards in contract law and in tort law. There are basically two groups of actors who could encourage convergence through the application of European standards. The first group would be the stakeholders themselves, who could apply European standards in contract law. This could be a contract between a service provider and service recipient, but also between service providers and their association of service providers.[31] The incorporation in contract law would mean that the contracts expressly provided that the service provider complies with the standards of care as set out in a European standard. Another possibility would be for stakeholders to create a certification body, which would check that service providers complied with a European standard. This is often also a (quasi-)contractual relationship. In tort law, stakeholders could refer to European standards to defend themselves against liability claims. The European standard would be used as a benchmark to demonstrate compliance with the required standard of care in tort.

As an alternative, the judiciary could be relied on to give binding force in private law to European standards. This could be as an implied term of the

[30] The European Standardisation Organisations do not own copyright in European standards. The standards are sold by the national standardisation organisations who own the copyright.

[31] For example, compliance with a European standard could be required for membership of an association of service providers.

contract, or simply in determining the contractual standard of care to be expected from the service provider. In both situations, the European standard would be used to specify—or concretise—the required duty of care in private law. A similar process could occur in a tort case. The judge could refer to a European standard to determine what standard of care is owed by a service provider to a service recipient. For example, in medical negligence cases, the standard could assist in an assessment of the required standard of care of a medical practitioner. In most cases an expert would be required to give evidence, but this expert could use the European standard to give an indication to the court of the standard of care which is expected from a medical practitioner. Again, therefore, it would be the stakeholders themselves who would refer the judiciary to the European standard and invite the judiciary to give binding force to the European standard in private law.

To conclude, this second stage is necessary to complete the process of convergence in private law. The application of European standards in practice provides a bridge from the adoption of European standards to their harmonising impact on private law. One of the questions which will have to be answered is whether this two-stage 'bottom-up' strategy can result in an effective application of European standards in private law. Such a strategy for convergence will only be effective if two problems can be overcome. Firstly, the judiciary will use certain criteria for deciding whether or not to adopt the European standard as the required standard of care in contract or tort. The European standardisation process, and the standard itself, will have to fulfil these criteria before they can be applied and enforced in private law.[32]

Secondly, the judicial application of a standard means that the standard will have to be interpreted. This is where Legrand's 'no convergence' argument becomes relevant again. What is the difference between interpreting a legislative instrument which has been adopted to implement a European directive and interpreting the provisions of a European standard? Two differences can be identified. Firstly, with harmonisation through directives, the judge will be basing his decision primarily on the national implementing legislation. A risk of divergent interpretation could already flow from the simple fact that the European legislation had to be implemented in national law. Second, the source of interpretation will be a European standard which has been agreed by stakeholders in the sector. It is a self-regulatory instrument which has not been drafted by lawyers, but which has been agreed by the stakeholders in a particular sector. As such, the language could be presumed to be somewhat different from legal instruments, such as directives. The substance of the standard could be more technical, and more adapted to the particular requirements of the specific sector that has developed the European standard.

[32] H Schepel, above n 26, 345.

B. Why Would Convergence in Private Law Through European Standardisation Occur?

Independent from the question of how a process of convergence in private law through European standardisation would occur, it is another matter to analyse why such a process has to take place. What are the reasons to attempt to increase convergence between legal orders? Roger Brownsword has distinguished four different reasons to increase convergence between legal orders: political reasons, economic/efficiency reasons, health and safety reasons and moral reasons.[33] Within the European context, it is clear that convergence through harmonisation has primarily served the purpose of building an internal market. The foundations of that internal market are not only built on economic and efficiency reasons, but also on a very strong political conviction of integration through free movement.[34] It is in that light that the various directives which have affected national private law should be considered. Although they are mainly based on economic and efficiency reasons, consumer protection can ultimately be considered as a tool to build a more effective and efficient internal market.

Through the adoption of various directives, for example on unfair terms in consumer contracts, private law is made an instrument—is 'instrumentalised'—to realise a better-functioning internal market. As a consequence, convergence in private law becomes a strategy to improve the internal market. A recent and prominent example of the instrumentalisation of private law is the Proposal for a Regulation on a Common European Sales Law ('CESL'), published by the European Commission ('the Commission') in October 2011.[35] The fundamental assumption on which this proposal is based is that unification of national sales laws will result in more cross-border activity. It is assumed by the Commission that the uncertainty of not knowing a foreign legal system is an obstacle to the use of cross-border transactions.[36] Therefore, the aim of the instrument is to remove that obstacle by creating the possibility of a CESL which is accessible to all parties and effectively removes a transaction from the specific national legal regime in which it takes place. Despite the fact that the application of the Regulation is of a voluntary nature, in that parties can choose to opt-in and make the Regulation applicable to their transaction, the CESL represents an attempt to realise an ultimate form of convergence—a European legal framework that would effectively replace the use of national legal systems. The convergence would arise from the application of the CESL in practice. Harmonisation would be achieved not through legislation but

[33] R Brownsword, 'Convergence: What, Why, and Why not?' in H Micklitz and Y Svetiev (eds), 'A Self-Sufficient European Private Law—A Viable Concept?' *EUI Working Paper Law* 2012/31, 77–82.

[34] Commission White Paper, 'Completing the Internal Market', COM(85) 310 final.

[35] Proposal for a Regulation of the European Parliament and of the Council on a Common European Sales Law, COM(2011) 635 final.

[36] ibid, 2–4.

through the practical impact of the CESL on business transactions.[37] After strong opposition from a number of national parliaments, the Commission decided to withdraw the proposal for the CELS in June 2015.

Although the focus of the CESL was on the free movement of goods, private law can similarly be instrumentalised to increase the free movement of services. However, services in the EU have primarily been regulated through free movement law. Article 56 on the Treaty of the Functioning of the European Union ('TFEU'), which provides for the right to free movement of services, was used to remove obstacles to the free movement of both service providers and service recipients.[38] Certain requirements imposed on service providers or recipients by Member States were eliminated if they were discriminatory or prevented access to the market for service providers or recipients coming from another Member State. As such, the focus of the regulation of services through the free movement of services was on negative integration.[39] In this process, obstacles to the functioning of the internal market for services have gradually been removed. However, there has been little positive integration, for example through harmonisation, to replace national regulation of services by a European equivalent. A distinction should be made between regulated markets, in which the EU has encouraged liberalisation through very precise and technical harmonisation, and horizontal services more generally. For regulated markets which were previously under State control, such as telecom and energy, the EU has adopted standards through legislation.[40] This has not happened for all other services. In these service sectors, European standardisation could then go one step further and make a positive case for which requirements should be imposed on service providers. As a consequence, it would be closer to positive integration.

The next question is whether European standardisation has any specific purpose which harmonisation of legislation would not have, or whether it is also simply being instrumentalised as a tool for internal market-building? This links back to another argument made by Brownsword, namely whether convergence takes place 'for the sake of convergence'—because compatibility is considered to be necessary—or because we believe that convergence might actually be a good thing.[41] Article 26 of the Services Directive 2006 ('the Services Directive') encourages the use of various voluntary European regulatory tools to increase the compatibility of services, with the aim to encourage free movement of both service

[37] V Reding, 'The Next Steps Towards a European Contract Law for Businesses and Consumers', in R Schulze and J Stuyck (eds), *Towards a European Contract Law* (Munich, Sellier, 2011) 9–22, 16.

[38] V Hatzopoulos, *Regulating Services in the European Union* (Oxford, OUP, 2012) 97–145.

[39] ibid, 99.

[40] M Cantero, 'Towards the Self-Sufficiency in European Regulatory Private Law (I)—the Case of European Telecommunications Services Law' in H Micklitz and Y Svetiev (eds), 'A Self-Sufficient European Private Law—A Viable Concept?', *EUI Working Papers, LAW 2012/31*, 165–94.

[41] R Brownsword, above n 33, 78. See also W van Gerven, 'A Common Law for Europe': The Future Meeting the Past' (2001) *European Review of Private Law* 485.

providers and services recipients.[42] Standardisation is mentioned as one of the tools in Article 26(5). From the wording of the section, we could simply conclude that this is all about compatibility and, therefore, about convergence for the sake of convergence. However, Article 26 is part of a section on the quality of services, and the quality of services is also expressly mentioned as one of the purposes of standardisation.[43] Consequently, it is not just convergence for the sake of convergence. It is assumed in Article 26 that convergence through standardisation will also improve the quality of services, which will in turn be an incentive for more cross-border movement of service recipients. However, as will become clearer in the next chapters, the relationship between European standardisation and quality of services is complicated and requires further analysis.

Overall, it would be too simple to argue that convergence in private law through European standardisation has the efficiency of the EU internal market as its sole objective. Improving the quality of services is a second important objective. It is intended that the improved quality of services should again make the EU internal market more efficient. However, it would not only make the EU internal market for services more efficient, it would also raise the quality of service provision at the national level. As such, national service recipients should also benefit from the convergence without having to access cross-border services. This will become more obvious when the various examples of European standardisation initiatives in the healthcare and tourism sectors are analysed.

C. What Does Convergence in Private Law Through European Standardisation Mean?

A distinction should be made between the substantive impact of convergence in private law through European standardisation and its procedural impact. Focusing on European standardisation of services, a European standard would define the substantive standards to be expected from service providers. The various elements that are used to define the required quality of a particular service are given a common European meaning. If these standards were applied in private law, the substantive requirements of the duty of care in contract or tort would be defined by reference to a common European standard and would, as a result, become more converged. By way of example, the following elements of the service process are frequently standardised in European standards:[44]

(i) Education/training requirements: the standard could identify the required level of training which service providers should have completed before

[42] Directive 123/2006/EC of the European Parliament and of the Council on services in the internal market.

[43] See Chapter V, Quality of Services of the Services Directive. See also Recitals 97–102.

[44] The elements are based on the categories used by H Micklitz, 'The Service Directive: Consumer Contract Law Making via Standardisation', in A Colombi Ciacchi et al (eds), *Liability in the Third Millennium (Liber Amicorum Gert Brüggemeier)* (Baden-Baden, Nomos, 2009) 439–64, 451.

they can provide a particular service. Moreover, it could provide how much training is necessary for a particular part of the service.

(ii) Facilities: the standard could prescribe which facilities should be available to service recipients and which facilities are suitable for which (part of the) service. Furthermore, the standard could identify the materials or devices to be used in the provision of the service.

(iii) Communication/information: the standard could set out what information should be given to the service recipient before the contract is concluded and the service is provided. This could extend to information which has to be given during the service process, as well as after the service has been provided.

(iv) The service provision itself: the standard could provide which specific elements a service process has to provide.

(v) After-care and complaints: a standard could oblige service providers to have a complaint mechanism in place. Moreover, it could set out the requirements imposed on a service provider after the actual service has been delivered.

(vi) Monitoring of quality: monitoring of quality is an important element of the regulation of quality of care of service providers. The standard could specify how the quality of the service should be monitored, for example through internal or external visitation or through certification.

This process of substantive convergence in the elements of the service provision will also have a spill-over effect on the substantive meaning of certain private law concepts. For example, a European standard could have an impact on the concept of competence in private law. Similarly, the standard could have an impact on the availability of a particular remedy in private law if it provided that a particular remedy should or should not be available.

From a procedural point of view, the very existence of a European standard might also have a convergent impact on private law. It could be that the existence of a standard would result in a presumption that compliance with the standard is required. As such, a breach of any of its provisions would automatically result in liability in private law. This would mean that the traditional obligation of a service provider would be construed as an *obligation de résultat*—the obligation to satisfy or fulfil the requirements of the standard—rather than an *obligation de moyens*, which is usually required for service contracts.[45] As a result, this could mean that once a breach of the European standard has been established by a claimant in a contract or tort case, the burden of proof would shift to the service provider to establish that there has not been a breach of the duty of care. The service provider would then have to justify why he breached the European standard without breaching the duty of care in private law.[46] Again, if European standardisation

[45] H Micklitz, 'Reform des Werkvertragsrechts?' (1984) *ZRP* 239.

[46] This would be similar to, by way of example, the fact that medical practitioners are expected to comply with professional medical standards and have to justify a possible departure from the requirement of a standard. This is called the 'comply or explain' principle.

were to have such an impact, this would mean that European standardisation would have a convergent effect on the determination of liability in private law.

D. How Could Convergence in Private Law Through European Standardisation be Tested?

If convergence through standardisation was all about the efficiency of the internal market for services, it could simply be tested by counting the number of service recipients or service providers who move to another Member State to receive or provide services as a result of the adoption of a European standard in a particular sector. Such an approach would have to develop a strategy to test and determine the causal link between the adoption of a standard and the free movement of service recipients or providers. This would be quite problematic, since many initiatives for European standardisation take place in sectors in which there is already a significant amount of cross-border movement. It cannot automatically be assumed that the adoption of a European standard would necessarily increase the amount of cross-border movement. Because it is difficult, if not impossible, to define one unitary test for convergence through European standardisation, a test with two limbs will be adopted. The test closely follows the process of convergence in private law through European standardisation as it has been developed in the sections above:

(i) How many European standards are being adopted? In which sectors are European standards being adopted?
(ii) Are these European standards subsequently applied and enforced in private law at the national level?

As can be seen from the two limbs, the first part of the test is more quantitative than qualitative. The explanation for that choice is rather simple: without any European standards, there would never be any convergence in private law through European standardisation, because the European standards which are needed to increase that convergence are missing. The focus of this first part of the test is necessarily on the standard-making at the European level, and at standardisation through CEN. In chapter three, the European legislative framework for standardisation of services will be set out. Chapters four and five will analyse the making of European standards in the healthcare and tourism sectors.

The second test is the more qualitative assessment. This requires an assessment of what happens with a European standard once it has been adopted. If it is never used or referred to in private law disputes—which could be either in contract or in tort—there would not be any convergence in private law. However, it is insufficient to look only at case law. A case-law focused approach should be combined with looking at contracts in which a European standard has been implemented or is referred to. This is an alternative way of giving legal effect to a European standard in private law. Similarly, European standards might be applied in certification schemes. The key issue for the application of European standards in private law is that there has to be a direct link between the adoption of European services standards and the liability of service providers in contract law or tort. This is closely linked to the procedural dimension of convergence explained above. European standards only increase convergence in private law if the provisions of European standards have an impact on the determination of liability of service providers in contract law or tort. Otherwise, European standards would not have any legal effect and would not be effectively enforced in private law. This means that European standards must be applied as the required standard of care in contract or tort. This, and the role of the Unfair Contract Terms Directive ('UCTD'), will be analysed in chapter six. Furthermore, it is important that European standards comply with the requirements which are imposed by EU law. Free movement law and competition both impose requirements on European standards. If the standards are not compatible with these requirements, there is a risk that they will not be applied in private law. As a result, compliance with the free movement provisions and the competition law provisions becomes a condition for convergence. This will be discussed in chapter seven.

The second part of the test will therefore have to involve an assessment of the application of European standards in private law. This requires an analysis of the extent to which European services standards have an impact on the determination of liability of service providers in private law. Furthermore, European services standards have to comply with the requirements that are imposed by EU law before they can be successfully applied in private law. In conclusion, for convergence in private through standardisation to occur, both stages of the test have to be fulfilled. By following the process from the standard-making to the application in private law, it will be possible to make a realistic assessment about the potential of European standardisation to increase convergence in how a particular service is regulated in private law.

III. THE REGULATION OF SERVICES BY THE EU, ITS IMPACT ON PRIVATE LAW AND THE ROLE OF EUROPEAN STANDARDISATION

A. Free Movement of Services Under Article 56 TFEU

So far, this chapter has discussed European standardisation in general, without focusing on services in particular. At this point in the chapter, the link from European standardisation to services will be made. First of all, it will investigate to what extent the case law of the Court of Justice of the European Union ('the CJEU') has resulted in convergence in how services are regulated across the EU. The second step will be to see to what extent secondary EU law, and in particular the Services Directive, has had a convergent impact. Furthermore, the impact of these two levels of service regulation—primary and secondary EU law—on private law has to be discussed. This discussion will open up the possibility to analyse the possible role and impact of European standardisation on the regulation of services through private law and its interaction with primary and secondary EU law.

From the very first cases on the free movement of services, as provided in Article 56 TFEU, the focus of the CJEU has been on the removal of restrictions to the free movement of services created by Member States. As Jukka Snell and Mads Andenas have pointed out,[47] the identification of a restriction, which necessarily has to have cross-border impact and has to have an effect which is more than *de minimis*, has enabled the CJEU to assume the competence to regulate. Once such a restriction has been identified, the burden shifts to the national regulator to justify the restriction by some overriding reason in the public interest. Concerns about the quality of a service could be such an overriding reason. This public interest is closely linked to the protection of service recipients and consumers, which appears to be one of the major justifications accepted by the CJEU in the field of services.[48] In addition to the identification of such an overriding reason of public interest, the restriction must also be proportionate. This requires an assessment of the suitability and necessity of the restriction.[49]

If the CJEU finds that a restriction cannot be justified or is disproportionate, the Member State in question will be required to remove it. The restriction will not be replaced by a European solution imposed by the CJEU, but the Member State will rather be forced to accept the regulatory choice made by the Member State of origin. This would be most obvious for cases in which the defendant Member State raised quality of care concerns as a justification for the imposition of a restriction. It would not exactly be mutual recognition in the way it has been introduced for the free movement of goods, but it could have a similar result. If a restriction to free movement of services imposed by a Member State cannot be justified, the outcome might very well be that it has to recognise and accept the regulatory measure of another Member State. This is particularly important for (technical) standards for products or services.[50]

How this works in practice can best be illustrated by an example.[51] The German regulator of tourist guides refuses permission for a Dutch tourist guide to provide tourist guide services to a group of Dutch tourists in Berlin. The basis for the refusal is that the guide has not undertaken the same amount of training as a German tourist guide, because the Dutch training for tourist guides is significantly shorter than the German training. Therefore, there is a risk, according to the German regulator, that Dutch tourists will be misinformed about the many

[47] J Snell and M Andenas, 'Exploring the outer limits: restrictions on the free movement' in M Andenas and W Roth (eds), *Services and Free Movement in EU Law* (Oxford, OUP, 2002) 69–139, 83.

[48] V Hatzopoulos, above n 38, 153.

[49] C Barnard, *The Substantive Law of the EU: The Four Freedoms* (Oxford, OUP, 2013) 177–92.

[50] Case C-45/87 *Commission v Ireland (Dundalk Water)* ECLI: EU: C:1988:435.

[51] There have been a number of cases on tourist guide qualifications, which will be discussed in ch 5 on tourism services: Case C-154/89 *Commission v France (tourist guides)* ECLI: EU: C:1991:76; Case C-180/89 *Commission v Italy (tourist guides)* ECLI: EU: C:1991:78; Case C-198/89 *Commission v Greece (tourist guides)* ECLI: EU: C:1991:79; Case C-375/92 *Commission v Spain (tourist guides)* ECLI: EU: C:1994:109.

highlights of Berlin. The CJEU might find that this constitutes a restriction on the freedom of the Dutch tourist guide to provide services abroad. If Germany cannot justify the restriction, the final outcome is that it has to accept that the Dutch training is sufficient. The result would be some sort of indirect mutual recognition. For future cases, it would be useful for the German and Dutch authorities to have a discussion about the training requirements with a view to avoid future litigation. Moreover, the German regulator would be required to look more precisely at the Dutch training requirements. The negative integration instigated by the CJEU could then be a trigger for European standardisation to enable regulators to agree on a set of European standards.

The example above is based on the recognition of qualifications of a service provider. It is not difficult to find an example that is more directly linked to the quality of a service provider. A Dutch patient travels abroad to receive healthcare services in an Austrian private clinic. He subsequently applies to his Dutch healthcare insurer for reimbursement of the costs of the treatment. The Dutch insurer investigates the Austrian clinic and concludes that the treatment was of such low quality that it refuses to compensate the Dutch patient for this treatment. If this restriction to the free movement of the patient to receive healthcare services abroad was found to be justified, it would mean that the Dutch insurer's interpretation of quality of care prevails over that of the Austrian clinic. However, again, it does not mean that the CJEU attempts to define a common European concept of quality of healthcare. Negative integration tells parties what they cannot do, but it does not provide a positive solution.

So far, one could argue that this tool of removing obstacles is more of a procedural solution than a substantive solution. Quality of care is used as a negative concept—a lack of quality can be employed as a justification for imposing a restriction on the free movement of service providers or recipients. Implicitly, however, the CJEU's decisions in the examples given above also express a more substantive judgment about the quality of the service provided (or the quality of the training of the service provider). For example, in the case of the Dutch tourist guide, if the CJEU holds that the restriction cannot be justified, it implicitly finds that the Dutch tourist guide training is of sufficient quality and has to be accepted as appropriate by the German authorities. However, what the exact meaning of the minimum quality level is can only be identified through litigation or through an exchange between regulatory authorities. This is a time-consuming and expensive process. Furthermore, there is a risk that the constant removal of obstacles might lead to a race to the bottom, and that the pressure of regulatory competition—and the risk of litigation—forces national regulators to adopt the lowest possible level of quality regulation.[52] This was exactly the fear in certain Member States after

[52] S Deakin, 'Regulatory Competition after *Laval*' (2008) 10 *Cambridge Yearbook of European Legal Studies* 581. See also N Reich, 'Competition between Legal Orders: A New Paradigm of EC Law?' (1992) 29 *CML Rev* 861.

reading the first draft of the Services Directive. The debate on the risks of regulatory competition in the EU was revived after the controversial decisions of the CJEU in *Viking*[53] and *Laval*.[54]

What does the case law of the CJEU mean from the perspective of convergence? Clearly, the ability of the case law to bring the various regimes that regulate services at the national level closer to each other is limited. The CJEU is no legislator—the tool of identifying and eliminating restrictions to free movement of services does not enable it to substitute its own regulatory solution. It simply provides a mechanism whereby one national regulator has to accept and recognise the solution of another. If the regulatory solution is not of satisfactory quality, the CJEU will find the imposed restriction justified. As such, the CJEU effectively performs some sort of quality test of the national regulation of a particular service. The outcome of this test could lead to a process of mutual exchange of regulatory solutions. However, in most services sectors it would seem unlikely that this mere exchange would lead to sufficient consensus to adopt a common solution and would enable an onwards development from negative integration to positive integration. Although the negative integration approach—focusing on the removals of obstacles to free movement—could pave the way for positive integration, which according to Snell and Andenas would be the logical next step,[55] in fact the political will or legal competence to move to positive integration might be absent. This will be discussed later with regard to the healthcare sector, in which there is no legal competence to adopt harmonising measures on quality of healthcare, and the tourism sector, in which some limited harmonisation has taken place but in which there is limited political consensus to define quality of care issues at the European level. The result of this lack of competence or political opposition is that regulatory diversity is preferred, and that negative integration will continue to be employed as the main regulatory strategy.

In addition to the limited impact on convergence of service regulation in general, the convergent impact of Article 56 TFEU in private law has also been minimal. The main reason for this is that for a long time the free movement provisions have not been applied to private law relationships. Traditionally, while the free movement provisions could be relied on directly by individuals to challenge restrictions on free movement imposed by the State, it was not possible for individuals to challenge restrictions imposed by private parties. For that reason, Article 56 TFEU was not considered to have horizontal direct effect. In 1974, the CJEU already created an exception to this rule in *Walrave and Koch*:[56] the conduct

[53] Case C-438/05 *International Transport Workers' Federation and Finnish Seamen's Union v Viking Line ABP et al* ECLI: EU: C:2007:772.

[54] Case C-341/05 *Laval un Partneri Ltd v Svenska Byggandsarbetareförbundet et al* ECLI: EU: C:2007:809.

[55] J Snell and M Andenas, above n 47, 83.

[56] Case C-36/74 *Walrave and Koch v Association Union cycliste internationale et al* ECLI: EU: C:1974:140.

of private parties who are involved in collective regulation in the exercise of their legal autonomy can be caught by the free movement provisions. However, this still covers quite a limited category of parties. The question as to what extent 'simple' contracts between private parties can be subject to review by the CJEU remains unclear. At the moment, the impact is minimal.[57] It could be argued that after *Laval* it is clear that Article 56 TFEU has full horizontal direct effect, but such a statement would not do justice to the complicated facts of this case and the role of the Swedish State in the background of the legal dispute.[58] Nevertheless, it is clear that the suggestion of Advocate General Poiares Maduro, who argued in his Opinion in *Viking*[59] that it should be the effect of private parties' actions on the EU internal market rather than the public or private status of parties which should determine the applicability of the free movement provisions, will have an impact on the development of the case law and will broaden the scope of application of the free movement provisions to private parties. The public or private status of parties is no longer decisive for the applicability of the free movement provisions, but rather the impact of their actions on the EU internal market.[60]

The gradual extension of the horizontal application of Article 56 TFEU means that the free movement provisions might have a more significant impact on the relationship between service providers and consumers.[61] Nevertheless, this impact will mainly be on a case–by–case basis.[62] Because the main focus of Article 56 TFEU remains on the removal of obstacles to free movement, the extent to which it has potential to have a harmonising impact on private law is restricted. Convergence through negative integration has its limitations. The next question is then whether the adoption of the Services Directive has had more impact on private law.

B. The Services Directive 2006

The Services Directive is without doubt one of the most controversial legislative instruments adopted by the EU in the last decade. The underlying motivation to propose a legislative instrument on the free movement of services was that services play a major role in the European economy. However, the internal market for

[57] G Davies, 'Freedom of movement, horizontal effect, and freedom of contract' (2012) *European Review of Private Law* 805.

[58] B van Leeuwen, 'An illusion of protection and an assumption of responsibility: the possibility of Swedish State liability after *Laval*' (2012) 14 *Cambridge Yearbook of European Legal Studies* 453.

[59] Opinion of Advocate General Poiares Maduro in *Viking*, above n 53, ECLI: EU: C:2007:292.

[60] H Schepel, 'Constitutionalising the Market, Marketising the Constitution, and to Tell the Difference: On the Horizontal Application of the Free Movement Provisions in EU Law' (2012) 18 *European Law Journal* 177, 187.

[61] A Hartkamp, *European Law and National Private Law* (Deventer, Kluwer, 2012), 48–53.

[62] See, eg: Case C-251/83 *Eberhard Haug-Adrion v Frankfurter Versicherungs-AG* ECLI: EU: C:1984:397.

services in the EU was not functioning as well as the internal market for goods. The choice was made for a horizontal instrument that would cover all services. The initial Bolkestein draft provided that service providers only had to comply with the regulatory requirements imposed by their home Member State—the Member State of establishment. As such, it introduced the 'country of origin' principle—a very strong version of mutual recognition. The proposal of the country of origin principle provoked strong opposition, in particular in France.[63] After a period of intensive debate,[64] the final version of the Services Directive contained a much less strong version of mutual recognition—the mere recognition of a right to freely provide and receive services in another Member States—with an extensive list of justifications for limitations to that right.[65]

Moreover, a number of services sectors were removed from the scope of the Directive. Healthcare services are no longer covered by the Services Directive.[66] The idea was that the healthcare sector needed a specific legislative solution and was not suitable for a horizontal instrument.[67] The solution came five years later, when the Directive on the application of patients' rights in cross-border healthcare was finally adopted.[68] To fully understand the impact of the Services Directive, it is necessary to briefly outline the various sections and to discuss the possible impact of the Services Directive on the regulation of services in private law.

Essentially, the Services Directive consists of three sections. The first is a section on administrative simplification.[69] The procedures for service providers who want to provide services in another Member State and for those who want to establish themselves in another Member State have to be simplified. In addition, Member States have to create central 'Points of single contact' where all relevant information for service providers can easily be obtained.[70] As such, the focus of this section is on the efficient and transparent exchange of information by administrative authorities.

The second section reiterates the rights of service providers who want to establish themselves on a permanent basis in another Member State.[71] It focuses on authorisation schemes, and the conditions for a lawful authorisation scheme, and prohibited requirements, which cannot be imposed by national regulators

[63] E Grossman and E Woll, 'The French Debate over the Bolkestein Directive' (2011) *Comparative European Politics* 344.

[64] J Flower, 'Negotiating European Legislation: the Services Directive' (2007) 9 *Cambridge Yearbook of European Legal Studies* 217.

[65] Articles 16–18 of the Services Directive.

[66] Article 2(2)(f) of the Services Directive.

[67] For more background, see W Gekiere, R Baeten and W Palm, 'Free movement of services in the EU and health care', in E. Mossialos et al (eds), *Health Systems Governance in Europe* (Cambridge, CUP, 2010) 461–508, 497.

[68] Directive 24/2011/EU of the European Parliament and of the Council on the application of patients' rights in cross-border healthcare.

[69] Chapter II Administrative Simplification, Articles 5–8 of the Services Directive.

[70] Article 6 of the Services Directive.

[71] Chapter III Freedom of Establishment for Providers, Articles 9-15 of the Services Directive.

on service providers from other Member States. This section closely followed the CJEU's case law on the freedom of establishment.[72] It was also a relatively uncontroversial section of the Services Directive.

The third and most important section focuses on the right to provide services and receive services in another Member State.[73] This is where we still find a somewhat diluted version of the 'country of origin' principle, with a long list of derogations and case–by–case justifications.

By looking at these three main sections of the Services Directive, it would seem that an approach of negative integration combined with administrative cooperation remains crucial to the regulation of services in the EU. However, there is a fourth section which provides for measures on the quality of services. A significant part focuses on information requirements imposed on service providers.[74] The section appears to be a combination of left-overs from the other sections. However, from the perspective of convergence through European standardisation, Article 26 is of significant importance.

Article 26

Policy on quality of services

1. Member States shall, in cooperation with the Commission, take accompanying measures to encourage providers to take action on a voluntary basis in order to ensure the quality of service provision, in particular through use of one of the following methods:
   (a) certification or assessment of their activities by independent or accredited bodies;
   (b) drawing up their own quality charter or participation in quality charters or labels drawn up by professional bodies at Community level.

2. Member States shall ensure that information on the significance of certain labels and the criteria for applying labels and other quality marks relating to services can be easily accessed by providers and recipients.

3. Member States shall, in cooperation with the Commission, take accompanying measures to encourage professional bodies, as well as chambers of commerce and craft associations and consumer associations, in their territory to cooperate at Community level in order to promote the quality of service provision, especially by making it easier to assess the competence of a provider.

4. Member States shall, in cooperation with the Commission, take accompanying measures to encourage the development of independent assessments, notably by consumer associations, in relation to the quality and defects of service provision, and, in particular, the development at Community level of comparative trials or testing and the communication of the results.

[72] C Barnard, 'Unravelling the Services Directive' (2008) 45 *CML Rev* 323, 359.
[73] Chapter IV Free movement of Services, Articles 16–21 of the Services Directive.
[74] W Roth, 'Freier Dienstleistungsverkehr und Verbraucherschutz' (2007) 24 *Verbraucher und Recht* 161.

5. Member States, in cooperation with the Commission, shall encourage the development of voluntary European standards with the aim of facilitating compatibility between services supplied by providers in different Member States, information to the recipient and the quality of service provision.

Unlike the other provisions in the Services Directive, Article 26 constitutes an attempt to encourage substantive regulation of the quality of services at the European level. This would go further than mutual recognition—it would be a development from negative integration towards positive integration. The various mechanisms referred to in Article 26 all go some way towards defining qualitative criteria for the provision of services.[75] The aim would be to make services more compatible and of a higher quality. This would not necessarily result in a reduction of the regulatory diversity of services, as the standards would only provide for a minimum level of care, but it would mean that there was Europe-wide agreement on the minimum quality standards to be expected from service providers. In addition, the measures would be a voluntary means of working towards higher quality. As such, the service recipient who is receiving services in a cross-border context is better protected and also better informed about the quality of service providers in other Member States.

A number of points should be made about Article 26. Firstly, all regulatory tools in Article 26 are voluntary. They focus on soft convergence at the European level. There is no direct legal obligation on service providers and Article 26 does not have anything to say about the subsequent application of this soft convergence in (private) law. As such, the co-ordination at the European level is a very soft kind of co-ordination. Secondly, although the mechanisms referred to in Article 26 are voluntary, it appears to impose an obligation on Member States to encourage such voluntary initiatives. The question is how far this obligation would go. Could the Commission start infringement proceedings if Member States failed to encourage the processes set out in Article 26? That raises another important question: would the obligation imposed on the Member States mean that the European standards were still 'voluntary'? This could transform the 'bottom-up' nature of the standardisation process into something which would be closer to 'top-down' convergence.

Thirdly, the increased involvement of Member States in the standardisation could transform the soft law character of European standards. The development from pure self-regulation towards something which looks more like co-regulation could result in a hybrid instrument with more legally binding status than a purely self-regulatory standard. This could be useful for the subsequent application of the standard in private law. However, it could also mean that, again, the standardisation process would become more 'top-down' in nature and that the standard would look more like legislation than self-regulation. Moreover, it could mean

[75] T Ackermann, 'Das Informationsmodell im Recht der Dienstleistungen' (2009) 17 *Zeitschrift für Europäisches Privatrecht* 230.

that the European standard would play a more prominent role in public law rather than in private law. The main question that remains is what role Article 26 of the Services Directive is going to play in practice. It is clear that very few Member States have actively implemented Article 26.[76] Nevertheless, standardisation is now on the list of regulatory strategies as one of the tools to increase the compatibility of services and the quality of those services.[77]

For the impact of the Services Directive on convergence in private law in general, it should be noted that the obligations in the Services Directive are primarily imposed on States. Any questions about the extent to which the Services Directive could have horizontal direct effect, and could be applicable to disputes in private law, seem to be mainly theoretical.[78] The obligations imposed in the Services Directive primarily have to do with administrative formalities and requirements that are imposed on States or quasi-public regulators. In that respect, Article 4(7) of the Services Directive copies the formula used in *Walrave and Koch* to justify the application of the Services Directive to professional bodies or organisations which adopt rules.[79] Although this could result in private law disputes between service providers and these professional bodies, the overall impact of the Services Directive on convergence in private law is limited. For that reason, the role of European standardisation of services, as a third level of service regulation which would be additional to, but also interacting with, Article 56 TFEU and the Services Directive, will now be discussed.

C. European Standardisation of Services and its Impact on Private Law

Unlike Article 56 TFEU and the (main parts of) the Services Directive, European standardisation actually makes a positive case for what the quality of a particular service should be. It takes mutual recognition to the next level—instead of recognising national regulatory solutions, a single European regulatory solution is imposed. Such positive integration would mean that the diversity of national regulatory solutions is replaced by a European solution that provides the required standard of care. However, the European standard would not be the only acceptable standard. European standardisation only aims to introduce minimum quality criteria—it seeks to identify a common set of standards with which all service providers should comply. The standards cannot be compared with maximum harmonisation. The introduction of a number of similar

[76] See the Comparative Report in U Stelkens, W Weiss and M Mirschberger (eds), *Implementation of the EU Services Directive: Transposition, Problems and Strategies* (The Hague, Asser, 2012).

[77] For a more optimistic perspective, see H Micklitz, 'Regulatory Strategies on Services Contracts', in F Cafaggi and H Muir Watt (eds), *The Regulatory Function of European Private Law* (Cheltenham, Edward Elgar, 2009) 16–61, 53.

[78] M Schauer, 'Contract Law of the Services Directive' (2009) 4 *European Review of Contract Law* 1.

[79] Article 4(7) of the Services Directive.

minimum quality criteria should guarantee a minimum level-playing field for services in the EU. This level-playing field should increase the safe movement of service recipients within the EU and guarantee a minimum standard of care in all 27 Member States. This means that there is no complete 'equalisation' of the standard of care provided, but simply that providers are required to comply with a European minimum standard. Competition and diversity above that minimum standard remains possible.

Roger Brownsword has identified three types of convergence: soft convergence, medium convergence and hard convergence.[80] Soft convergence would be an optional or default rule, medium convergence would be the creation of a mandatory minimum standard and hard convergence would a mandatory rule which would also be the maximum. The process of convergence in private law through European standardisation of services cannot easily be classified as belonging to one of these three categories. The standardisation process at the European level can be described as soft convergence. The subsequent application of the standard in law can be described as a mandatory minimum standard, since a European standard would be given binding effect in law. However, the incorporation in law would still be optional—either by the stakeholders through incorporation in contracts, or by the judiciary in contract or negligence cases. The fact that the standard would acquire binding status as a result of the application in law does not detract from the fact that it was a voluntary choice to refer to the standard. However, if European standards are applied in private law, for example in tort law, they are essentially upgraded from soft convergence to medium convergence—after all, a mandatory minimum standard is identified.

The link from European standardisation of services to private law can more easily be made than for Article 56 TFEU and the Services Directive. This is partly because European standardisation of services, although it is to some extent embedded in a European legal framework, has not been integrated in a European regulatory approach. As a consequence, European standardisation of services cannot rely directly on EU law to provide binding effect to European standards. Therefore, the role of private law becomes even more important. However, the fact that European standards only provide for a minimum standard of care could have a detrimental impact on their application in private law. If they are only minimum standards, it might be that both the judiciary and stakeholders prefer to adopt higher standards of care.[81] The result of the process of soft convergence at the European level might be lower than the traditional national standard, with the result that the national courts and stakeholders would continue to enforce national standards. Nevertheless, it would still be helpful in that situation to be able to refer to a minimum standard which can be expected from a service provider. Furthermore, in certain Member States in which there are fewer quality standards in particular services

[80] R Brownsword, above n 33, 78–79.

[81] A Ogus, above n 28, 13–14.

sectors, a European standard could help to fill gaps. This could be particularly important for the new Member States in Eastern Europe. At the same time, certain Member States might not be used to apply private standards to regulate the expected standard of care of service providers—not even in private law. The material scope of self-regulation of the quality of services, what could be described as the margin of operation of self-regulation, varies among the EU Member States. As a consequence, the potential for convergence in private law through European standardisation will depend on how broad the margin of operation of self-regulation is, and to what extent public regulation—and public law—leaves a role for private regulation to regulate aspects of the service provision process.[82] In Member States in which the provision of services is more strictly regulated by public law, the potential for European standardisation to have a convergent effect in private law is more limited.

Furthermore, the extension of the application of Article 56 TFEU to private parties will have an impact both on the European standardisation process and on the subsequent application of European standards in private law. It has implications both for standard-making bodies and for private parties who apply European standards in private law. Private regulation through contract law or through certification can now be challenged under the free movement provisions. This means that European standardisation, as a third level of European regulation, would become subject of supervision under the first level of regulation. In the recent case of *Fra.bo*,[83] the CJEU held that the provision on free movement of goods was applicable to a German private certification organisation. Although it could be argued that a decisive factor in this case was the fact that German legislation had provided that goods certified by this organisation could be lawfully bought on the German market, the judgment opens the door to the application of the free movement provisions to certification organisations more generally.

The judgment of the CJEU in *Fra.bo* means that standardisation and certification activities can be scrutinised under the free movement provisions. Furthermore, there is a close link to the relationship between European standardisation and free movement of services. The horizontal direct effect of the free movement provisions means that an indirect obligation to comply with free movement law is imposed on stakeholders who are participating in European standardisation. This will indirectly improve the quality of European standards from the perspective of free movement law. If they do not do so, private parties are less likely to apply the standard in private law relations, since they could be held responsible for possible breaches of free movement law in the provisions of the European standard.

[82] A Ogus, above n 28, 9.

[83] Case C-171/11 *Fra.bo SpA v Deutsche Vereinigung des Gas- und Wasserfaches eV (DVGW)—Technisch-Wissenschaftlicher Verein* ECLI: EU: C:2012:453.

A European standard which contained provisions in breach of the free movement of services would not be enforced in private law. As a result, Article 56 TFEU puts indirect pressure on parties involved in European standardisation to comply with the free movement provisions.

IV. A PRELIMINARY CONCLUSION

This chapter has essentially gone through three steps to set the scene for the rest of the book. First, the theoretical background has been discussed. Secondly, that background has been applied to this book by introducing the concept of convergence in private law through European standardisation. Thirdly, the role of European standardisation of services in the broader framework of the regulation of services at the European level has been discussed.

At the start, the theoretical frame on the basis of which the book has been constructed was set out. In light of the strong criticism of the potential of European harmonisation to bring about a convergent effect in the application of a rule in private law, it is realistic and helpful to consider alternative strategies for convergence in private law through European processes. European standardisation could be such a process.

The second step was then to define convergence in private law through European standardisation. It is a two-stage process—firstly, the European standardisation process; second, the application of the European services standards in private law. The application of European services standards will usually be voluntary. It can be done either by a services sector itself, or by the judiciary. European standardisation of services and private law are combined to improve the internal market for services. At the same time, the application in private law also means that the quality of services at the national level is improved, even in the absence of a cross-border dimension. The fact that European services standards would set out minimum standards means that the convergence would be of a relatively soft nature. It could also mean that the willingness of stakeholders and courts to apply European standards at the national level would be less if national standards were significantly higher.

European services standards are adopted in a European legal framework for the regulation of services. Services have primarily been regulated through Article 56 TFEU and through the Services Directive. In effect, European standardisation could then be described as a third 'layer' of regulation. European standardisation, unlike regulation through Article 56 TFEU and the Services Directive, has the potential to encourage a development from negative integration to positive integration and could also have a real impact on private law. At the same time, however, European standardisation interacts with Article 56 TFEU, which means that any European standardisation initiatives have to comply with the free movement of services. Whether or not European standardisation of services can have a real impact on private law—and have a convergent effect—depends on the extent to which European standards are tailored to be applied and enforced in (national) private law.

Therefore, it is now necessary to look in detail at the European standardisation process for services to understand how the process works and how European standardisation is embedded in the European legal framework for services. This is what will be done in the next chapter.

3

The Legal Framework for European Standardisation of Services and the Role of Private Law

THIS CHAPTER ANALYSES the legal framework for European standardisation of services. It starts with an outline of the various EU instruments that regulate standardisation at the European level. The relationship between the New Approach, the Services Directive and the new Standardisation Regulation will be analysed. The next step is to make a link from the European legal framework to private law. This also involves an analysis of the standardisation process and its legitimacy from a governance perspective. Finally, the last part will provide the perspectives of some key players in European standardisation of services. It will be shown that CEN, ANEC and the European Commission all have different views about the role of European standardisation in the internal market for services.

I. THE EUROPEAN LEGAL FRAMEWORK FOR STANDARDISATION OF SERVICES

A. The New Approach and Directive 98/34 on Technical Standards

While the European Commission ('Commission') has always been the motor to improve the internal market for goods and services within the EU, the CJEU has without a doubt played an equally pivotal role.[1] Its judgment in *Cassis de Dijon*[2] paved the way for further integration in the field of free movement of goods through the principle of mutual recognition. National product requirements came under the immediate supervision of the CJEU. This opened up the possibility of regulatory intervention at the European level. However, the road towards positive integration remained difficult and slow. For that reason, the Commission decided

[1] L Azoulai and R Dehousse, 'The European Court of Justice and the Legal Dynamics of Integration' in A Menon et al. (eds), *Oxford Handbook of the European Union* (Oxford, OUP, 2012) 350–64.

[2] Case C-120/78 *Rewe-Zentral AG v Bundesmonopolverwaltung für Branntwein* ECLI: EU: C:1979:42.

to adopt an alternative strategy to increase the free movement of goods, which was called the New Approach.[3] With this New Approach, the Commission developed a regulatory framework in which legislative instruments and European standards, developed through European standardisation, were to interact.[4]

European standardisation was not invented for the purposes of the New Approach. The European standardisation organisations had already existed for some time, and at the national level standardisation had existed for much longer. The Committee Européen de Normalisation ('CEN') was established in Brussels in 1975.[5] It became a private, non-profit association established under Belgian law. It was founded primarily to transpose at the European level international standards which had been developed through the International Standardisation Organisation ('ISO').[6] As such, CEN was dependent on and relying on the national standardisation organisations. This situation has not really changed. Although CEN has an important function in the communication with the European institutions and in the co-ordination of standardisation initiatives among national standardisation organisations, CEN is still a relatively small organisation compared to some of the national standardisation organisations.

The New Approach provided an enormous boost to European standardisation through CEN. It was started in parallel with attempts by the Commission to obtain more insight in national standardisation activities and to create greater transparency in the EU internal market. This was attempted with the Information Directive,[7] which provided that Member States had to notify the Commission of any technical specifications, regulations and standards. This Directive resulted in a series of cases on the possible horizontal direct effect of directives.[8] However, the exchange of information was not sufficient to overcome problems with market integration and to encourage a development from negative towards positive integration. As a result, the Commission decided to go one step further with the New Approach, which was integrated in the legal framework by updating the Information Directive to the new Directive 98/34/EC on Technical Standards ('Technical Standards Directive').[9]

The idea behind the New Approach is quite simple—the EU adopts legislation with the 'essential requirements' with which products have to comply before they

[3] Council Resolution on a new approach to technical harmonization and standards (85/C136/01).

[4] For a detailed analysis of the New Approach, see H Schepel, *The Constitution of Private Governance* (Oxford, Hart Publishing, 2005) 63–67.

[5] See www.cen.eu/about/Pages/default.aspx.

[6] H Schepel, above n 4, 101–02.

[7] Council Directive 83/189/EEC laying down a procedure for the provision of information in the field of technical regulations and standards.

[8] Case C-194/94 *CIA Security v Securitel* ECLI: EU: C:1996:172; Case C-226/97 *Lemmens* ECLI: EU: C:1998:296; Case C-443/98 *Unilever v Central Food* ECLI: EU: C:2000:496. See S Weatherill, 'Compulsory Notification of Draft Technical Regulations: The Contribution of Directive 83/189 to the Management of the Internal Market' (1996) 16 *Yearbook of European Law* 129.

[9] Directive 98/34/EC laying down a procedure for the provision of information in the field of technical standards and regulations and of rules on Information Society services.

can be placed on the European market.[10] The specific technical requirements are later laid down in European standards developed through CEN. CEN has been granted a monopoly to develop these standards. It is asked by the Commission to start working on a European standard through the issuance of a 'mandate'.[11] After the European standard has been adopted and has been published, a reference to the standard will be published in the Official Journal of the European Union ('OJEU'). The Commission is responsible for the publication of the reference to the standard in the OJEU. This publication of the reference will trigger a 'presumption of compliance': after the publication it is presumed that goods that comply with the requirements of the European standard also comply with the essential requirements of the Directive. There is no legal requirement to comply with the European standard—at least, not *stricto sensu*. However, if producers of goods decide to comply with another standard, the burden is on them to prove that they also fulfil the essential requirements of the Directive. As such, European standardisation has been granted a highly advantageous position in the New Approach. It should be noted that the complete European standard does not have to be published in the OJEU—it is only the reference to the standard that is published. The copyright of the standards remains with the national standardisation organisations, which will sell the standards as products. The Member States and the Commission can also object to a European standard before a Standing Committee set up under the New Approach.[12] The ground for objection must be that the developed European standard does not satisfy the essential requirements as set out in the Directive.[13] If the objection procedure is started, the publication of the reference to the standard has to be delayed. The Standing Committee then has to provide an opinion on the standard. However, it remains the decision of the Commission whether or not to finally publish the reference. It has been argued that after *Fra.bo*[14] European standards are now open to judicial review[15]—also for their compliance with the essential requirements—which means that the CJEU could start to have a more important role in the review of standards in the New Approach.[16] In a recent preliminary reference made by the Irish Supreme

[10] Council Resolution of 7 May 1985, above n 3, 2–3.

[11] General Guidelines for the Cooperation between CEN, CENELEC and ETSI and the European Commission and the European Free Trade Association of 28 March 2003 (which replaced the guidelines of 13 November 1984) (2003/C91/04).

[12] Article 5 of the Technical Standards Directive.

[13] If a Member State does not object to the standard, it has to accept that goods which comply with the European standard satisfy the essential requirements and can be placed on the market: Case C-470/03 *AGM COS.MET v Suomen valtio and Tarmo Lehtinen* ECLI: EU: C:2007:213.

[14] Case C-171/11 *Fra.bo SPA v Deutsche Vereinigung des Gas- und Wasserfaches EV* ECLI: EU: C:2012:453.

[15] H Schepel, 'Case C-171/11, *Fra.bo SPA v Deutsche Vereinigung des Gas- und Wasserfaches*' (2013) 9 *ERCL* 186, 191.

[16] See C Joerges, 'Scientific Expertise in Social Regulation and the European Court of Justice: Legal Frameworks for Denationalized Governance Structures' in C Joerges, KH Ladeur and E Vos (eds), *Integrating Scientific Expertise in Regulatory Decision-Making: National Traditions and European Innovations* (Baden-Baden, Nomos, 1997), 295–323.

Court,[17] the key question is whether the CJEU has the jurisdiction to interpret and review the provisions of European standards adopted under the New Approach. In his Opinion, Advocate General Campos Sanchez-Bordonna provided a positive answer.[18] He used three main arguments: firstly, the use of the New Approach should not compromise the CJEU's jurisdiction to give preliminary rulings; second, the Commission exercises a significant amount of control over the standardisation process; third, after *Fra.bo*, standardisation activities come within the scope of EU law and this should also apply to the activities of CEN.[19] The CJEU has not yet delivered its judgment.

Advocate General Campos' emphasis on the power of the Commission in European standardisation is not uncontroversial. The set-up of the New Approach leads to a complicated process of interaction and co-operation between the Commission and CEN. How their co-operation should be defined remains unclear. Egan has analysed the co-operation under the agency theory.[20] However, it has been argued that the co-operation between the Commission and CEN does not fulfil the requirements of the *Meroni*[21] doctrine developed by the CJEU.[22] This is mainly because of the extent to which the Commission actually controls the substance of the work of CEN. It could be argued that, now that European standards are starting to come under review of the CJEU,[23] this would be a development towards stricter compliance with the *Meroni* requirements.[24] In any event, it is clear that the Commission and CEN are highly dependent on each other in the New Approach. As it is always the Commission that issues mandates and that initiates the start of European standardisation in the New Approach, it has an interest in ensuring that the European standardisation process does not take too long. After all, if European standardisation were to take many years the Commission could just as well have chosen the legislative route. However, European standardisation is also quite a complicated process, which involves continuous interaction between the European and the national level. Despite the interdependency between the Commission and CEN, the Commission has on several

[17] Case C-613/14 *James Elliott Construction Limited v Irish Asphalt Limited* preliminary reference made by the Irish Supreme Court on 30 December 2014.

[18] Opinion of Advocate General Campos in *James Elliott*, above n 17, ECLI: EU: C:2016:63.

[19] ibid, paras 42–61.

[20] M Egan, 'Regulatory strategies, delegation and European market integration' (1998) 5 *Journal of European Public Policy* 485. See also M Egan, *Constructing a European Market: Standards, Regulation and Governance* (Oxford, OUP, 2003) ch 7.

[21] Case C-9/56 *Meroni*, ECLI: EU: C:1958:7. See, for a discussion of the current application of *Meroni*, T Tridimas, 'Community Agencies, Competition Law, and ECSB Initiatives on Securities Clearing and Settlement' (2009) 28 *Yearbook of European Law* 216.

[22] H Schepel, above n 4, 225–27. See also C Daelemans, 'The Legitimacy and Quality of European Standards: The Legitimation of Delegation of Powers and Standard-Setting Procedures' in C Joerges, KH Ladeur and E Vos (eds), *Integrating Scientific Expertise in Regulatory Decision-Making: National Traditions and European Innovations* (Baden-Baden, Nomos, 1997) 257–71, 264.

[23] R van Gestel and H Micklitz, 'European Integration through Standardisation: How Judicial Review is Breaking Down the Club House of Private Standardisation Bodies' (2013) 50 *CML Rev* 145.

[24] H Schepel, above n 4, 227.

occasions complained about the slow pace of CEN's standardisation activities. The first signs of irritation were already visible in 1990, when the Commission published a Green Paper with strong criticism of the very nature of the European standardisation process.[25] The majority of the criticism was not really taken any further by the Commission, but its unease with some of fundaments of European standardisation has remained.

Before the reform of European standardisation in 2012, the Technical Standards Directive provided the legal framework for European standardisation as part of the New Approach. Its key provisions will be briefly summarised. Articles 2–4 of the Directive deal with the obligation for national standardisation organisations to inform the Commission and the other standardisation organisations of initiatives for a new standard.[26] The next part establishes a Standing Committee, which has to be consulted when the European Commission wants to provide a mandate to CEN to start working on a standardisation initiative.[27] Finally, a standstill obligation is imposed on national standardisation organisations when a European standardisation process is started.[28] In such cases, all national standardisation processes that are in the same area as the European standardisation process, or that might be incompatible with the European standardisation process, have to be stopped. This standstill obligation is closely related to the agreement between the national standardisation organisations and CEN.[29] Once a European standard is adopted, the national standardisation organisations are obliged to transpose the standard as a national standard. Furthermore, they are required to remove existing national standards which are incompatible with the adopted European standard. These obligations do not exist for standards which have been adopted through ISO.

With the New Approach, European standardisation always starts with a mandate from the Commission. As such, this type of European standardisation could be described as 'top-down' European standardisation—it is initiated at the European level. Two different types of mandates should be distinguished: 'programming mandates', which invite one of the European standardisation organisations to develop a proposal for a European standard in a particular area, and 'standardisation mandates', which effectively contain a concrete proposal for a European standard. Although it is in theory possible for CEN to refuse to start a European standardisation process mandated by the Commission, this has never happened.[30] CEN's administration is funded almost entirely by the Commission. The initiation of a European standardisation process means that the national standardisation

[25] Commission Green Paper on the Development of European Standardization: Action for Faster Technological Integration in Europe, COM (1990) 456 final.

[26] Articles 2–4 of the Technical Standards Directive.

[27] Articles 5–6 of the Technical Standards Directive.

[28] Article 7 of the Technical Standards Directive.

[29] General Guidelines, above n 11.

[30] Interview with CEN (Brussels) on 4 April 2012.

organisations have to co-operate at the European level to work on the requested European standard. However, there is also a lot of European standardisation that takes place outside the scope of the New Approach. It is still possible for initiatives for European standardisation projects to be initiated through the national standardisation organisations. Such bottom-up European standardisation can be initiated by stakeholders at the national level. The majority of European standardisation processes are still started in this way.[31] Finally, it is also possible that the Commission asks CEN to start working on a standard without the standard being used for the New Approach. The Commission could then simply see a role for a standard as a supplementary tool to legislation which it is preparing.

Overall, this means that three categories of European standards should be distinguished:

(i) European standards mandated by the Commission under the New Approach;
(ii) European standards mandated by the Commission in support of a policy or legislative instruments outside the New Approach;
(iii) European standards developed at the request of one of the national standardisation organisations.

Various directives have been adopted under the New Approach,[32] and although it is clear that the New Approach is not without its own problems, it has certainly had a significant impact on the free movement of goods within the internal market. Free movement of services has always remained the less successful younger brother, despite the fact that services account for around 70% of the GDP.[33] The New Approach has not been copied for services. This does not exclude the possibility that certain services which are intrinsically tied to products could be indirectly covered by the New Approach. However, in general, the New Approach has only been applied to products. This means that, in the field of services, only two types of European standards can be identified—standards mandated by the Commission in support of a policy or European legislation outside the New Approach and standards initiated by stakeholders through the national standardisation organisations. Overall, the number of services standards has been much lower than for goods and services standards have only started to be developed from a much later date.[34]

From the mid-1990s onwards, the Commission has taken an active interest in European standardisation of services. Similarly, around that period, CEN

[31] Recent statistics show that 80% of the European standards developed by CEN have not been published in the OJEU. These are either European standards mandated by the Commission outside the New Approach or European standards developed at the request of the national standardisation organisations: ftp://ftp.cencenelec.eu/EN/AboutUs/InFigures/CEN-CENELEC_StatPack2014-Q2.pdf.

[32] For an up-to-date list, see http://ec.europa.eu/growth/single-market/european-standards/harmonised-standards/rss_en.xml.

[33] Recital 4 of the Services Directive.

[34] H Micklitz, *Services Standards: Defining the Core Consumer Elements and their Minimum Requirements*, Study Commissioned by ANEC, Brussels, April 2007, 81–89.

started to actively promote its activities in various services sectors. However, in the absence of a New Approach to services, the function of European services standards remained unclear. Nevertheless, the Commission was of the opinion that European standardisation of services could, in principle, play an important role in removing obstacles to free movement of services within the EU. Therefore, it issued a mandate to CEN in 1996 to start work on a European standard for postal services.[35] This was a good example of a sector in which European standardisation was considered as part of the toolbox to promote and accelerate the liberalisation of postal services in the EU. However, the standardisation process was not based on the legal framework for European standardisation. Although the Commission claimed to act on the basis of a specific directive on postal services, the legal framework for European standardisation at that time did not expressly provide for services standardisation.

This was still the case in 2003 when the Commission issued a programming mandate to CEN to develop a work programme in the field of services.[36] This resulted in a report issued by CEN in 2005, in which it outlined its strategy for services.[37] CEN outlined the existing work in the services sector and proposed to take a more detailed approach to certain specific topics in the services sector which were suitable for European standardisation. CEN's report was followed by a new programming mandate issued by the Commission to CEN in July 2005.[38] The focus of this mandate was on various aspects of services which could be standardised at the horizontal level—ie for services in general. CEN produced various feasibility studies on aspects of services standardisation in the course of 2007 and 2008.[39] These studies finally resulted in the CHESS study, which outlined a general strategy for horizontal services standardisation.[40] Its main focus was on the creation of one horizontal standard which would cover various sub-aspects of the service provision process.

The CHESS study was not very positively received among stakeholders in the various services sectors.[41] It was generally believed that one horizontal standardisation project would not be sufficiently tailored to particular services sectors. As a result, the Commission initiated a period of reflection on the purposes and

[35] M/240 Mandate to CEN for standardisation in the field of postal service and equipment of 15 March 1996.

[36] M/340 Programming mandate addressed to CEN, CENELEC, and ETSI in the field of services of 10 October 2003.

[37] CEN, Final Report on European Commission Mandate M/340 in the field of services, 15 March 2005.

[38] M/371 Second programming mandate addressed to CEN in the field of services of 25 July 2005.

[39] See www.cen.eu/work/areas/services/Pages/default.aspx.

[40] CEN, *CEN's Horizontal European Services Standardization Strategy, CHESSS Feasibility Study* of July 2008.

[41] Interview with DG Enterprise of the European Commission (Brussels) on 29 November 2012. See also J Graz, 'International Standards and the Services Economy' in C Joerges and J Falke (eds), *Globalisation and the Potential of Law in Transnational Markets* (Oxford, Hart Publishing, 2011) 209–29, 226.

usefulness of European services standardisation. This period of reflection has now resulted in a new mandate issued to CEN in January 2013.[42] This programming mandate invites CEN to assess the possibility of European standards for a number of specific topics related to services. The standards would be separate and would no longer be part of one general horizontal services standard. The mandate was already being prepared by the Commission before the coming into force of the Standardisation Regulation, which will be discussed in detail below. The Commission relied on Article 26(5) of the Services Directive as the legal basis for the mandate.[43] Therefore, the role of the Services Directive in European standardisation of services should now be discussed.

B. The Services Directive 2006: Towards a New Approach to Services?

As has already been mentioned in the first chapter, the Services Directive has a section on the quality of services. Article 26(5) mentions standardisation as a voluntary regulatory tool in the services sector. However, there is no clear intention behind the reference to European standardisation in Article 26. European standardisation is not embedded in the structure of the Services Directive—it does not provide a legal framework in which the adopted services standards will play a role. The only thing the reference in Article 26 does is to indicate that European standardisation could be one of the tools to improve quality of services at the European level. It is certainly not part of a New Approach to services—there is no reason to believe that the standards adopted as a result of Article 26(5) are intended to provide substance to essential requirements in directives on the safety of services. In fact, it cannot even be said that European services standards are adopted as a result of, or on the basis of, Article 26(5). Contrary to the position of the Commission, it does not actually provide a legal basis for the Commission to issue mandates to the standardisation organisations. It simply provides an obligation on the Member States to encourage voluntary standardisation initiatives for services in co-operation with the Commission. This is still some way from a legal basis on which mandates for European standardisation can properly be based. Furthermore, it does not create a link from regulation through standardisation to legal regulation. The role that European standards will play in the legal regulation of services remains dependent on their application in law. This is where private law could and perhaps even has to play an important role.

Furthermore, the obligation imposed on Member States does not seem to be an enforceable obligation:[44] 'Member States, in cooperation with the Commission,

[42] M/517 Mandate addressed to CEN, CENELEC and ETSI for the Programming and Development of Horizontal Service Standards of 24 January 2013.

[43] ibid, 1.

[44] For the implementation of Article 26 in the various Member States, see U Stelkens, W Weiss and M Mirschberger (eds), *Implementation of the EU Services Directive: Transposition, Problems and Strategies* (The Hague, Asser, 2012).

shall encourage the development of voluntary standards'.[45] Is this an obligation which could be enforced through, for example, infringement proceedings if Member States systematically failed to encourage European standardisation of services? And how far would the 'encouragement' have to go? Would the Commission normally have to take the initiative or would the co-operation with Member States be more horizontal? Overall, for its lack of specificity, Article 26(5) could best be described as an expression of policy—a policy tool. This is confirmed by the Commission's Handbook on the Implementation of the Services Directive. According to the Commission, 'Article 26 provides for a framework for voluntary quality-enhancing measures which will have to be encouraged by Member States in cooperation with the Commission'.[46] The obligation in Member States is not very strict, because '[t]here are different means for Member States to encourage such measures, such as awareness campaigns, organisation of workshops and conferences, funding of programmes and projects, etc. The Commission will use its best efforts to support such measures and to spread best practice among Member States'.[47] As a consequence, the Commission appears to interpret the obligation in Article 26(5) as an obligation to use best efforts. It does not require a result from the Commission or the Member States. In other words, compliance with the obligation is not tested by counting the number of European services standards that have been adopted.

If Article 26(5) did impose an obligation on Member States to encourage the making of European services standards, this would have the potential to change the character of European standardisation of services. In effect, such an obligation would add a fourth category of European standards to the categories set out above: European standards mandated by the Member States. This could potentially make European standardisation of services more co-regulatory. Moreover, it would make European standardisation of services more of a top-down process. However, even if Article 26(5) did impose such an obligation, its significance should not be overestimated. It would only mean that there would be a European drive to make more services standards. Article 26(5) would not control the process itself—beyond its aim, which should be the improvement of the quality of services—and it would certainly not have any impact on the role that the standards would play after their adoption. It is silent about the legal effect of European services standards. It has already been argued that Article 26(5) does not create an enforceable obligation for Member States to encourage the making of European services standards, but even if it did, its importance would be restricted to the initiation of European standardisation of services.

To conclude, the Services Directive 2006 does not integrate European standardisation in the European legal framework for services regulation. European

[45] Article 26(5) of the Services Directive.

[46] European Commission, Handbook on the Implementation of the Services Directive, http://ec.europa.eu/internal_market/services/docs/services-dir/guides/handbook_en.pdf, 47.

[47] ibid, 47.

standardisation remains somewhat on the side line of services regulation, as a possibility to be considered and encouraged by Member States and the Commission. Moreover, it does not in any way signify a development towards something like the New Approach. This has no doubt to do with the fact that the Commission has not yet entirely made up its mind about the desirability of European standardisation of services. Nevertheless, it is faced with the reality that services standards are being made. Therefore, it has decided that services standardisation should at least be integrated in the legal framework for European standardisation. The right occasion to do this came with the publication of the Standardisation Package in 2011.[48] The main element of this package was the proposal for a Regulation on standardisation which would amend and/or repeal some of the existing Directives and Decisions on European standardisation.[49] One of the key aims of the Regulation was to bring services standardisation within the scope of these instruments. As such, the next section will focus on the extent to which the Standardisation Regulation has an impact on European services standardisation.

C. The Standardisation Regulation 2012

The Standardisation Regulation was approved by the European Parliament in September 2012 and came into force in January 2013.[50] A quick look at the Standardisation Regulation immediately shows that services have now become fully integrated in the framework for standardisation. Article 1 explains that the Regulation provides rules for the co-operation between the European and national standardisation organisations in the field of standardisation of products and services in support of Union legislation and policies.[51] Services are now incorporated in the standardisation regime and the Standardisation Regulation thus provides a legal basis for mandates for services standards. Such standards can be adopted in support of the EU's policy to improve free movement of services. At the moment, however, there are no EU legislative instruments on services that provide for a role for European standards. The Standardisation Regulation does not change that situation. It remains to be seen whether, in the future, the EU will adopt instruments in the field of services that leave the quality requirements of that particular service to be regulated by European standards.

The emphasis of the Standardisation Regulation is on transparency and inclusiveness. As such, the Commission was clearly concerned that European

48 Commission Communication, 'A strategic vision for European standards: Moving forward to enhance and accelerate the sustainable growth of the European economy by 2020' COM(2011) 311 final.

49 European Commission, ' Proposal for a regulation of the European Parliament and of the Council on European standardisation' COM(2011) 315.

50 Regulation 1025/2012 of the European Parliament and of the Council on European standardisation.

51 Article 1 of the Standardisation Regulation.

standardisation under the New Approach—which, after all, is a quasi-legislative process—would be sufficiently legitimate and transparent. The Standardisation Regulation contains a number of efforts to improve these points. The European and national standardisation organisations are required to publish work programmes at least once a year, so that it is clear in which areas work is being undertaken at the European and national level.[52] This should help standardisation organisations to make a realistic assessment of the need for and desirability of a particular standardisation project. Furthermore, the Standardisation Regulation imposes obligations on the European and national standardisation organisations to circulate draft versions of standards among each other. They then have to ensure that there is a possibility for all relevant parties to comment on the draft.

There is also more emphasis on the possibility for relevant stakeholders to participate in European standardisation. The European standardisation organisations are obliged to encourage and facilitate the appropriate representation of all relevant stakeholders.[53] The nature of this obligation is again rather soft and difficult to enforce. The same applies to the obligation to encourage the participation of SMEs in European standardisation.[54] There has been a long and ongoing discussion about the ability of SMEs to participate in European standardisation.[55] SMEs do not usually have the financial, administrative and technical means to participate effectively in European standardisation processes.[56] As a result, there is a risk that European standardisation is dominated by large businesses that have the means to participate in the process. However, while the Standardisation Regulation might seem to improve the situation for SMEs, it does not actually give them anything which they did not already have. Standardisation organisations are encouraged to apply special rates to SMEs and to publish summaries of standards on their website. However, the real core of the problem is not addressed—for copyright reasons SMEs are not given free access to participate in European standardisation processes and they are not given free access to European standards. From the point of view of the structure of European standardisation, this makes perfect sense, since any changes would undermine the solvability of the whole system. It should be noted that the standardisation organisations are dependent for their funding on the Commission and on stakeholders who participate in European standardisation. Finally, Member States are also obliged to encourage

[52] Article 3 of the Standardisation Regulation.

[53] Article 5 of the Standardisation Regulation.

[54] Article 6 of the Standardisation Regulation.

[55] H de Vries et al., *SME access to European standardization: Enabling small and medium-sized enterprises to achieve greater benefit from standards and from involvement in standardization*, Rotterdam School of Management, Erasmus University Rotterdam, August 2009. This study was requested by CEN. In May 2013 CEN organised a conference on the role of SMEs in European standardisation: www.cencenelec.eu/news/events/Pages/EV-2013-08.aspx.

[56] Interview with Chairman of Dutch Mirror Committee for Aesthetic Surgery Services (Goes) on 29 December 2012 and Interview with HOTREC (Brussels) on 29 November 2012.

the participation of public authorities in European standardisation of goods under the New Approach.[57]

The next section of the Standardisation Regulation focuses on the procedure for mandates to be issued by the Commission. Here, two key changes should be emphasised. First of all, it is now expressly stated that the Commission can only issue mandates for European standardisation in areas that come within the competence of the EU.[58] This means that, for example, it is not possible for the Commission to issue a mandate for healthcare services, as they fall outside the competence of the EU. This is something which had been actively lobbied for by certain sectors, amongst which is the healthcare sector.[59] Secondly, the European Parliament has been given the possibility to object to a European standard adopted under the New Approach.[60] This is clearly an attempt to provide more democratic legitimisation to the New Approach. It remains to be seen to what extent the European Parliament will actively scrutinise European standards and to what extent it will be able to comment on rather technical questions of whether certain product standards fulfil the essential requirements of a particular directive.[61]

In conclusion, the Commission can now issue mandates for the development of services standards on the basis of the Standardisation Regulation. This means that services standards mandated by the Commission fall within the scope of the Regulation. However, importantly, 'bottom-up' initiatives for European services standards, where the initiative comes from stakeholders at the national level through one of the national standardisation organisations, remain outside the scope of the Standardisation Regulation. As such, they are not adopted in any regulatory framework[62] and it remains the responsibility of the stakeholders to give a role to the standard in the legal regulation of services at the European or national level. The Standardisation Regulation has no impact on such standardisation projects.

D. Certification in the New Approach and Outside a European Framework

European standardisation under the New Approach is closely linked to certification. The New Approach is not just structured around the standard-making process. It includes a system that organises the enforcement of compliance with the European standard. Once a European standard has been adopted

[57] Article 7 of the Standardisation Regulation.

[58] Article 10(1) of the Standardisation Regulation.

[59] Interview with UEMS and CPME (Warsaw) on 19 February 2013.

[60] Article 11(1) of the Standardisation Regulation.

[61] J Pelkmans, 'The New Approach to Technical Harmonization and Standardization' (1997) 25 *Journal of Common Market Studies* 249, 260.

[62] Because they primarily provide policy objectives, the General Guidelines for the Co-operation between CEN, CENELEC and ETSI and the European Commission and the European Free Trade Association of 28 March 2003 (2003/C 91/04) cannot properly be regarded as a regulatory framework.

and its reference has been published in the OJEU, it is presumed that producers whose goods comply with the requirements of the European standard also comply with the relevant directive. The starting point of the New Approach is that the manufacturers of the goods have to declare that their goods comply with the European standard. This can be done by affixing the 'CE mark' on their products. For certain categories of products, this is essentially a formalised kind of self-certification. The manufacturer is required to complete a dossier and to sign a declaration stating that the goods comply with the relevant directive. For these products, there is no involvement of external parties. For potentially more dangerous products, the involvement of an external party, which has to check that the goods comply with the European standard, is required. This procedure is called a conformity assessment procedure. It is a kind of certification, which has to be done by a 'notified body', a certification body that has been notified to the Commission by the Member State in which it is established. Except for the most dangerous types of products, it does not normally require an inspection of the products. The conformity assessment procedure is primarily based on an inspection of the manufacturer's paper work, which has to indicate how and from what material the products are made.

Most of the notified bodies are private certification bodies, but some of them are public bodies.[63] If the goods are found to be in conformity with the European standard, they will be allowed to carry the CE marking. Notified bodies must have been accredited themselves and Member States are responsible for ensuring that notified bodies are sufficiently qualified to perform conformity assessments.[64] Once products with a CE mark have been placed on the market, market surveillance is carried out by national public supervisory agencies.[65] Despite the involvement of a third party in the form of a notified body, it remains a fundamental tenet of the New Approach that producers themselves bear individual responsibility for ensuring that their goods comply with the European directives. This has resulted in difficulties with liability issues if goods are found to be defective. More particularly, it is unclear to what extent notified bodies, whose 'stamp of approval' is necessary for manufacturers before they can place goods on the market, can be held liable if products which have passed the conformity assessment procedure turn out to be defective.[66] The key issue is that with the New Approach, the EU has regulated the *ex ante* aspects of the marketisation of goods in the EU, while liability issues as a result of a failure to comply with the legal requirements imposed

[63] JP Galland, 'The Difficulties of Regulating Markets and Risks in Europe through Notified Bodies' (2013) 3 *European Journal of Risk Regulation* 365, 368.

[64] See, in the context of medical devices, Commission Implementing Regulation (EU) No 920/2013 on the designation and the supervision of notified bodies under Council Directive 90/385/EEC on active implantable medical devices and Council Directive 93/42/EEC on medical devices.

[65] S Singh, 'What is the Best Way to Supervise the Quality of Medical Devices? Searching for a Balance Between ex-ante and ex-post Regulation' (2013) 4 *European Journal of Risk Regulation* 465–77.

[66] B van Leeuwen, 'PIP breast implants, the EU's New Approach for goods and market surveillance by notified bodies' (2014) 3 *European Journal of Risk Regulation* 338.

by the New Approach have not been regulated at the European level.[67] The Product Liability Directive[68] could assist to a certain extent, but it only provides for liability of the producer or importer.[69] This makes it difficult for claimants to decide against whom to bring a case in circumstances where it is not possible to bring a case against the producer.[70] The complicated interaction between private and public parties in the New Approach makes it difficult for victims of defective products to decide who to hold responsible for production failures. This has become particularly evident after the PIP breast implants scandal, which will be discussed in detail in chapter six.

Certification on the basis of European standards is not limited to the New Approach. European services standards, which have necessarily been adopted outside the New Approach, can also be used for certification. In fact, many European services standards are made with a view to facilitate some kind of certification. For example, tourist guides could get certification to certify that they comply with the European standard for Tourist Guide Training.[71] Often, European standards are used to set the entry level for providers who want to offer services. Certification with European standards fulfils an *ex ante* regulatory function—in order to be allowed to join the club, one has to pass the examinations based on the requirements of the European standard.[72] In some cases, these associations have themselves been certified, which means there is third-party certification. In other cases, there is no certification or accreditation of the examining body.[73] As a consequence, there is no control on the professional associations to verify to what extent they actually comply with the European standards in their examination activities. The scope of the use for European services standards for certification activities is not very broad. More importantly, there is very limited external involvement from the standard-making to the certification. The European standards are effectively made by the same organisations that are applying the standards for the purposes of certification, and that are also doing the certification themselves.

It is important to note that such certification does not take place in the context of a legal framework established by the EU. Unlike certification under the New Approach, which has made certification a legal requirement before goods can be distributed across the EU, this kind of certification is entirely voluntary from the EU's perspective. The EU has not provided any legal effect to such certification. Its main function is to improve the marketisation of products or services. In general, the fact that a product or service provider has been certified does not create any

[67] ibid.

[68] Council Directive 85/374/EEC on the approximation of the laws, regulations and administrative provisions of the Member States concerning liability for defective products ('the Product Liability Directive').

[69] Articles 1 and 3 of the Product Liability Directive.

[70] Interview with UK barrister (London) on 28 January 2014.

[71] Interview with the Guild, ITG and APTG (London) on 21 January 2014.

[72] ibid.

[73] ibid.

enforceable legal rights between service provider and consumer on the basis of which consumers can require a particular kind of service or product.[74] As a result, its impact on private law, and the possibility of convergence in private law, is also limited. This will be discussed in more detail when the PIP breast implants case study is discussed in chapter six.

II. EUROPEAN STANDARDISATION OF SERVICES AND PRIVATE LAW

A. Standardising Goods and Services: Similar or Different?

After having discussed the legal framework in which European standardisation of services takes place, this section will now discuss in detail how the European standardisation process works. One preliminary issue has to be addressed first. This is the question to what extent standardisation of goods and standardisation of services can be considered to be similar activities. Two dimensions will be highlighted—the substantive and the legal dimension.

From a substantive point of view, services standards address a different concern from product standards. With standardisation of goods, the main focus is on the compatibility of the technical requirements for products. This is a quasi-scientific exercise, which is of a very technical nature.[75] For product standards adopted under the New Approach, these technical requirements have to be in accordance with the essential requirements laid down in the Directive. The result is that the standards which are adopted look very technical and are focused on the sizes and materials of a particular product.[76] The issues that have to be dealt with in the standardisation process are restricted to what is required to provide substance to the essential requirements that have already been laid down in legislation. As a consequence, the set-up of the New Approach restricts the margin of operation of stakeholders to the more technical and scientific issues. Although an agreement on these issues requires a common opinion about the required quality of products, the discussion remains at a very technical level. This is different from standardisation of services. Although the aim of services standardisation will also be compatibility, this compatibility is achieved not so much by defining sizes and materials of products, but rather by agreeing on a common definition of the quality of a

[74] H Schepel and J Falke, *Legal Aspects of Standardisation of the EC and EFTA, Volume 1: Comparative Report* (Luxembourg, Office for Official Publications of the European Communities, 2000), 237–38.

[75] E Vos, 'Market Building, Social Regulation and Scientific Expertise: An Introduction' in C Joerges, KH Ladeur and E Vos (eds), *Integrating Scientific Expertise in Regulatory Decision-Making: National Traditions and European Innovations* (Baden-Baden, Nomos, 1997) 127–39. See also KH Ladeur, 'The Integration of Scientific and Technological Expertise in the Process of Standard-Setting according to German Law', in the same volume 77–100.

[76] H Micklitz, 'The Service Directive: Consumer Contract Law Making via Standardisation', in A Colombi Ciacchi et al. (eds), *Liability in the Third Millennium (Liber Amicorum Gert Brüggemeier)* (Baden-Baden, Nomos, 2009) 439–64, 454.

service. It involves standardisation of the social interaction between service provider and customer.[77] This requires a discussion which is much more dominated by cultural and personal preferences, and which is also significantly less scientific than product standardisation. It means that it might be more difficult to agree on a common definition of what quality means at the European level. Furthermore, in the absence of scientific evidence as a basis for standardisation of services, the discussion on the standards is inevitably less technical and more politicised.[78] As a result, it is more difficult to agree on European standards for services.

The Commission is not convinced about this difference. In the preambles of the Standardisation Regulation, it is stated that 'the delineation between goods and services is becoming less relevant in the reality of the internal market'.[79] As a result, 'it is not always possible to clearly distinguish standards for products from standards for services'.[80] The reason why the distinction is not deemed to be very important is that it is foreseen that many services standards will contain significant parts which are focused on products.[81] According to the preambles, they 'should primarily focus on services linked to products and processes'.[82] As a consequence, it would seem that the standardisation of services mandated under the Standardisation Regulation would be very much restricted to a particular kind of services, namely those for which products play a key role or which are closely linked to the provision of products. A simple and common example would be the tying of installation or maintenance services linked to the sale of a machine. In such cases, there would be a combination of a product and services and the standardisation would aim at standardising both aspects of the same 'package'.

Secondly, the legal dimension should be discussed. Here, the most significant difference is between standards mandated under the New Approach and non-mandated standards. The legal role of standards mandated under the New Approach is clear. They are intended to provide the technical standards that are necessary to specify the essential requirements. Compliance with the standard raises a presumption of compliance with the Directive. As such, the European product standard has a clear role to play in the legal regulation of products. These mandated standards could also play a role in private law. The New Approach does not have a direct impact on the role that mandated standards play in private law. In that respect, there does not seem to be a significant difference with European standards which have been adopted outside the New Approach. How-

[77] ibid.

[78] On the politicisation of European standardisation in the context of the New Approach, see C Frankel and E Hojbjerg, 'The constitution of a transnational policy field: negotiating the EU internal market for products' (2007) 14 *Journal of European Public Policy* 96.

[79] Preamble 10 of the Standardisation Regulation.

[80] ibid.

[81] For a discussion of the 'commodification' of services, see P Verbruggen, 'The Impact of Primary EU Law on Private Law Relationships: Horizontal Direct Effect under the Free Movement of Goods and Services' (2014) 22 *European Review of Private Law* 201, 211.

[82] Preamble 11 of the Standardisation Regulation.

ever, it is important to realise that European standards adopted under the New Approach have been given a clear public law mandate. The fact that they are made in a European regulatory framework means that they have been given a stamp of approval by the EU. This is likely to have an impact on their application in private law at the national level. There can be no doubt that European standards adopted under the New Approach represent the technical standards with which products have to comply. The whole regulatory framework is constructed in such a way that European standards adopted through CEN represent the technical standards for products. For services standards, there is no such European regulatory framework. There has not been a similar legitimisation by the EU of the standardisation process and the standards have not been produced in a regulatory framework which is directed and controlled by the EU. As a result, it is likely that national courts will be stricter in their scrutiny of non-mandated standards.

Moreover, the fact that standardisation of services regulates social interaction means that services standards are more likely to interact with legal regulation than product standards.[83] For example, European services standards can interact with (European) legislation on qualifications, facilities or information requirements. If tourist guide associations want to adopt a European standard on the training requirements for tourist guides in Europe, they have to think about how this standard would interact with the Professional Qualifications Directive 2005.[84] If medical associations want to adopt a European standard for Aesthetic Surgery Services, which frequently involves the provision of cross-border healthcare, they have to make sure that the European standard is compatible with the information requirements imposed by the Cross-Border Healthcare Directive 2011.[85] European standardisation of services does not only result in a politicisation of the standardisation process, it similarly results in what could be described as a process of legalisation of European standardisation. Standardisation of services does not take place in a narrowly defined vacuum—it constantly interacts with existing legislation. This imposes quite a burden on stakeholders involved in standardisation—they have to be aware of the legal framework in which they are operating and they have to take it into account in the standardisation process. A failure to do so would mean that the European standards would not be compatible with existing European legislation. This would make their application in private law less likely and less successful.

In conclusion, it can be said that there are significant differences between European standardisation of goods and services. These differences have a particular impact on the interaction between European standards and the legal framework in which they are adopted. As such, the extent to which they can play a

[83] H Micklitz, above n 76, 454–55.

[84] Directive 2005/36/EC of the European Parliament and of the Council on the recognition of professional qualifications.

[85] Directive 2011/24/EU of the European Parliament and of the Council on the application of patients' rights in cross-border healthcare.

role in private law is also likely to be affected by their status as mandated or non-mandated standards. Before the role of European services standards in private law can be discussed, it is necessary to look at the standardisation process in more detail.

B. The Interaction Between the European and the National Level in European Standardisation

The European standardisation process involves a complicated interaction between the European level and the national level. How does a European standardisation process begin? For standards mandated by the Commission, the mandate will be received at the European level by CEN. With mandates, the procedure remains much more at the European level than with non-mandated standards. CEN is required to consult stakeholders and after a period of consultation the mandate is sent to CEN's Technical Board for a decision.[86] The Technical Board is CEN's main management body. It consists of the President and/or Vice President of CEN as well as representatives of each of its members. CEN currently has 33 members—the 28 EU Member States, Turkey, Macedonia and the three EEA members (Switzerland, Norway and Iceland). After it has received the mandate, taking into account the position of the stakeholders and CEN, the Technical Board will take a decision on whether or not to accept the mandate.

The procedure is slightly more complicated for non-mandated standards.[87] For such standardisation projects, the proposal will have to be submitted through one of the national standardisation organisations. This is irrespective of the question whether the proposal is submitted by a national stakeholder or a European stakeholder, such as an association of companies or professionals. It is not necessary to submit a proposal through the standardisation organisation in the country where the stakeholder is based—they have the option to choose which standardisation organisation they would like to use to submit the proposal. This is an important tactical decision, because if the proposal is accepted the national standardisation organisation which submitted it will act as secretariat to the standardisation process.[88] Various standardisation organisations have developed expertise in particular areas. For example, the Austrian standardisation organisation ASI is very active in the healthcare sector, while the German standardisation organisation DIN has developed particular expertise in the tourism sector. This is often because these sectors are considered to be successful at the national level. Austria is proud

[86] CEN Resolution BT 20/2004, BT C75/2009 and BT C127/2010. See http://ftp.cen.eu/BOSS/Flowcharts/Production_Processes/Proposal%20for%20new%20work%20through%20a%20mandate.pdf.

[87] See ftp://ftp.cen.eu/BOSS/Flowcharts/Production_Processes/Proposal%20for%20new%20work%20using%20form%20A.pdf.

[88] Interview with ECO (Skype) on 14 March 2012 and interview with ASI (Vienna) on 12 November 2012.

of its healthcare system and believes that its knowledge and expertise could also be used at the European level.[89] European standardisation is then regarded as a strategy to extend that success to the European level. It is also closely connected to what employees of the national standardisation organisations believe will be useful projects for European standardisation.[90]

When a proposal has been submitted to CEN by a national standardisation organisation, CEN will consult its members. This means that the proposal is sent to all national standardisation organisations, which then have to consult with the relevant stakeholders. This period of consultation has to be concluded within three months of the submission of the proposal. This usually means that national standardisation organisations have to organise a meeting where stakeholders can provide comments on the proposal. They are completely free to decide who to invite to this meeting, but they are bound by the WTO Code of Good Practice.[91] As a result, they are obliged to do their best to consult as widely as possible among all (potentially) relevant stakeholders. However, in the end, they have very little influence on who turns up at the consultation meetings.[92] Although there is an obligation to consult as broadly as possible, there is no obligation that certain parties must actually provide their views on the proposal, or that certain parties must participate in the standardisation process. During the national consultation meeting a decision will be taken on whether or not the proposal should be supported and on whether or not the national standardisation organisation would be willing to actively participate in the standardisation process.

After this period of consultation, all national standardisation organisations have to vote at the European level. For a proposal to be accepted, two-thirds of the votes cast—it is possible to abstain—have to be in favour of the proposal. Moreover, at least five of the members have to commit to actively participate in the standardisation process.[93] As such, a European standardisation process can start with only five national members actively participating in the process. If a national standardisation organisation casts a negative vote, it is expected to provide reasons or comments. It is also possible to express 'fundamental disagreement' with a proposal. If one of the members expresses fundamental disagreement, the proposal has to go to the Technical Board of CEN for a final decision. Otherwise, the proposal is accepted and the work on a European standard can start.

[89] Interview with ASI (Vienna) on 12 November 2012.

[90] Interview with NEN (Delft) on 12 April 2012.

[91] Code of Good Practice for Standardization of the WTO Technical Barriers to Trade agreement, www.wto.org/english/docs_e/legal_e/17-tbt_e.htm.

[92] Interview with NEN (Delft) on 11 April 2012.

[93] By Resolution BT C75/2009, BT approved that both of following criteria are to be met for acceptance of such proposal for new work:

- A two-thirds majority of the votes cast (abstentions not counted) are in favour of the proposal;
- Five (or more) Members express commitment to participate.

To start a European standardisation process, a Technical Committee ('TC') will be created. Each of the national standardisation organisations willing to participate have to create 'mirror committees', which closely scrutinise the European process and send representatives to the TC. Membership of the mirror committees is open to parties who are interested to participate and who are willing to pay the costs of participation. Again, there are no formal rules on which parties should definitely participate in the mirror committees. The national standardisation organisations are dependent on the fees of participants to be able to survive financially.[94] Although they may apply lower fees to non-profit organisations or research institutes, the basic principle is that the members of the mirror committees have to collectively bear the costs of the European standardisation process. There are no separate costs for the involvement of CEN, which is funded almost exclusively by the Commission.

The TC will be chaired by a chairperson, who is usually nominated by the standardisation organisation that is responsible for the secretariat. The structure of the standardisation process means that European standardisation is not a very supranational process. There is constant interaction between the national and the European level. Certain members of the TC might not be able to take decisions at the European level due to disagreement among the members of the national mirror committee. This might act as an obstacle to effective decision-making at the European level. It is difficult for members of the TC to 'rise above' national interests which have an impact on the European standardisation process. When work on a European standard has been started, national standardisation organisations are no longer allowed to initiate new standardisation projects on the subject of the standard and they also have to stop national standardisation processes on the subject.[95] This is called the 'standstill obligation', already referred to above.

The standardisation process is completely confidential. All documents related to the standardisation process, as well as the names of those participating in the process, remain confidential. The TC will have to agree on the draft content of the European standard. This is the only moment when the process opens its doors to the public. After agreement has been reached on the draft standard, the 'CEN Enquiry' will be started. The draft standard is then sent to the national standardisation organisations, which have to publish it on their website. Interested parties are able to submit comments, which have to be taken into account by the TC. After the CEN Enquiry, the TC will work on the final version of the standard. There will then be a weighted vote—a qualified majority of 71% of the votes is required.[96]

[94] By way of example, for the European standardisation project on Aesthetic Surgery Services, NEN (the Dutch standardisation organisation) anticipated that the annual costs would be €21,200. They proposed that the annual costs for participation would be €3,000 for professional associations and government bodies, €2,000 for businesses, €1,000 for non-profit associations and educational institutions and €500 for one-man businesses.

[95] Article 5 of CEN Internal Regulations, Part 2 (2013).

[96] Article 6 of CEN Internal Regulations, Part 2 (2013).

The complete standardisation process usually takes three to four years. Once a European standard has been adopted, it will have to be implemented by the national standardisation organisations as a national standard—very much like with directives. Any inconsistent national standards have to be removed. This obligation to implement European standards does not exist for international standards which have been developed through ISO. The final standard will be published through the national standardisation organisations, which own the copyright in the standard. This is the same both for standards mandated under the New Approach and for non-mandated standards. Standards have to be paid for—the price depends on the number of pages. This is because the national standardisation organisations are dependent on the revenues of the sales of standards. Therefore, standardisation remains quasi-confidential after the adoption of the standard—although the standard is accessible to everyone, it is not freely available. This can cause particular problems if standards are referred to in legislative instruments. It has led to litigation in a number of Member States.[97]

C. Consensus-based Decision-Making and Voting in European Standardisation

Formally, decisions within the TCs are made on the basis of consensus. The precise definition of consensus-based decision-making remains unclear.[98] It would seem to indicate that serious attempts are made to reach decisions by unanimity and that only as a last resort TCs use the possibility of voting. Whilst this sounds convincing in theory, in practice voting plays an important role in the European standardisation process.

There are two formal moments when votes are being taken in the European standardisation process. The first is when a proposal for a European standard has been submitted to CEN. The national standardisation organisations have to vote on whether a proposal should be accepted. The second moment is when the national standardisation organisations have to vote on the final draft of a European standard. On both occasions, significant reliance is placed on the national level. The decision on the votes will be highly dependent on the position of the various stakeholders at the national level. As such, it is easily possible for stakeholders who enjoy a particular dominance at the national level to extend their dominance to the European level. It is somewhat artificial to construe the European standardisation process as based on consensus. A compromise would be a better term to describe the process. Furthermore, it is clear that votes are also taken during

[97] For a detailed discussion of some of the cases, see R van Gestel and H Micklitz, above n 23, 158–61.

[98] Interview with NEN (Delft) on 11 April 2012 and Interview with Chairman of Dutch Mirror Committee for Aesthetic Surgery Services (Goes) on 29 December 2012.

the standardisation process. One of the interviewees described how within his TC votes were needed on every decision whether or not a particular element should be included in the European standard.[99] The result was a painfully slow process, which had very little to do with consensus. The whole standardisation process was dominated by getting a majority in order to get a particular part included in the standard. It is difficult to reconcile this approach with the principle of consensus.

III. EUROPEAN STANDARDISATION AND LEGITIMACY

A. The Distinction Between Mandated and Non-Mandated Standards

When the legitimacy of European standardisation is discussed, it is usually compared with the European legislative process. In the general debate about the legitimacy of decision-making processes in Europe, criteria that are commonly used are representation, transparency and accessibility. These principles are crucial to democratic law-making processes. It is important that these governance criteria are complied with, because the end result will be a binding instrument with which European citizens have to comply. When a European Directive is adopted, this instrument becomes applicable in all Member States. Although it will not directly impose obligations on national citizens, this will be the final result once the Directive has been transposed in national law. As such, citizens are going to be directly bound by the provisions of the Directive. As a consequence, the binding nature of the harmonisation process means that the interests of citizens should be closely safeguarded and taken into account in the law-making procedure.[100]

The situation is different for European standardisation. European standards do not obtain any automatic binding effect in law. However, the effect of European standards adopted under the New Approach is quasi-automatic and quasi-binding. In fact, the impact of these standards is such that their binding effect in law approaches that of European legislation.[101] As a result, it is important to make a distinction between European standards adopted under the New Approach on the one hand, and European standards adopted outside the New Approach on the other hand. Technical standards adopted under the New Approach acquire an immediate legal status after their adoption—or more precisely, after the publication of their reference in the OJEU. The binding nature of the instrument requires sufficient democratic input in the standardisation process—even if this input is likely to be of a very technical nature. Other European standards, such

[99] Interview with Chairman of Dutch Mirror Committee for Aesthetic Surgery Services (Goes) on 29 December 2012.

[100] R Werle and E Iversen, 'Promoting Legitimacy in Technical Standardisation' (2006) 2 *Science, Technology and Innovation Studies* 19, 21.

[101] ibid, 22.

as European services standards, do not obtain an immediate binding status in law. Their subsequent status in the regulation of services is dependent on the application of a standard in a particular sector. This distinction between New Approach standards and standards adopted outside the New Approach has also been recognised by Raymund Werle and Eric Iversen. They have distinguished between 'regulative' standards—which would include standards adopted under the New Approach—and 'coordinative' standards.[102] In their approach, legitimacy is more important for regulative standards, since they will become *de facto* binding in law. A more relaxed approach can be adopted towards coordinative standards, since these standards could be 'indirectly promulgated by governments or courts referencing them in legal regulations or judicial decisions'.[103] However, they have also warned for possible network effects and the possibility of a standard 'locking in'—which would mean that businesses are effectively compelled by market forces to comply with a standard even though it has no formal binding force.[104] This section will now assess European standardisation of services from the perspective of representation, transparency and accessibility.

B. Representation

The standardisation process is open to all parties who are interested and concerned. There are no formal limitations on participation. Everyone willing to participate can do so. When a proposal for a European standard has been submitted to CEN, the national standardisation organisations are obliged to consult all parties who might possibly have something to say about whether or not there should be a European standard, and who might possibly be interested in participating in the making of a European standard.[105] However, the practical limitations are numerous. First of all, a fee has to be paid to be able to participate. Secondly, participation in the standardisation process is time-consuming. The result is that larger businesses are more easily able to participate in standardisation processes. The standardisation process then becomes an easy route for larger companies to dictate their standards on SMEs. Moreover, the fact that there are no formal limitations on participation might create difficulties. Sometimes standardisation processes end up with a very small group of participants who are in no way representative of the various stakeholders in the sector.[106] There is very little national standardisation organisations can do about this. The standardisation process then becomes a way for an unrepresentative minority to impose its ideas on the silent majority.

[102] R Werle and E Iversen, above n 100, 21–22.

[103] ibid, 23.

[104] ibid, 23.

[105] Code of Good Practice for Standardization of the WTO Technical Barriers to Trade agreement, www.wto.org/english/docs_e/legal_e/17-tbt_e.htm.

[106] M Egan, above n 20, 493–94.

The extent to which the silent majority could be blamed for remaining silent depends on their practical and financial ability to participate in European standardisation. Furthermore, it should be noted that standardisation organisations have an interest in European standards being made. The financial sustainability of both the European and national standardisation organisations is dependent on the making of European standards.[107] As a result, although they have to ensure that initiatives for European standards comply with the formal requirements, it cannot be really be expected from the standardisation organisations that they perform an adequate representation test before a European standardisation process is started.[108]

The case studies which are discussed in the next chapters show that concerns about the ability of European standardisation to ensure a sufficiently broad representation of stakeholders are not merely hypothetical. In the healthcare sector, European associations of medical doctors have complained that the European standardisation process for Aesthetic Surgery Services constitutes an attempt by a group of medical professionals, who have been unsuccessful in their standardisation attempts through European associations of doctors, to restrict the market for aesthetic surgery services and to impose their ideas about who should be able to offer aesthetic surgery services on the entire medical profession through CEN.[109] The position of the European associations is that they have complained on numerous occasions to CEN that the parties who are making this standard are not representative of the sector. However, CEN has not taken any action in response to the complaints. In the tourism sector, the standard for Tourist Guide Training has become controversial since it has been made by a group of stakeholders who represent only a part of the sector for tourist guide services, namely local tourist guides.[110] Again, there is a clear view of other parties in the market—primarily tour operators—that the Europeans standard developed through CEN attempts to impose one particular definition of the profession of tourist guide on the entire market.

C. Transparency

From the perspective of transparency, the European standardisation process is not a very open process.[111] Throughout the European standardisation process, the European Technical Committees and the national mirror committees meet

[107] R Werle, 'Institutional aspects of standardization: jurisdictional conflicts and the choice of standardization organizations' (2001) 8 *Journal of European Public Policy* 392.

[108] M Egan, above n 20, 496–98.

[109] Interview with UEMS and CPME (Warsaw) on 19 February 2013.

[110] Interview with the Guild, ITG and APTG (London) on 21 January 2014.

[111] M Egan, *Constructing a European Market: Standards, Regulation and Governance* (Oxford, OUP, 2001), 154–59.

in private. The names of the participants in the standardisation process are confidential—except for the chairman of the European committee and the person responsible for the secretariat. This is normally an employee of the national standardisation organisation that runs the secretariat. The documents which form the basis of their discussion and deliberations are not publicly available. The only exception to the general rule is the publication of the draft standard. The draft is available for a period of a few months. It is published on the websites of the national standardisation organisations. The standardisation organisations will also send out invitations to comment to the same group of people who they had initially identified as interested in participating in the standardisation process.[112] In order to be able to comment on the proposal, parties usually have to register with the national standardisation organisation. As such, there are a few obstacles to overcome before one can comment on the proposal. Moreover, very few people—in particular from those groups that are not sufficiently represented in the standardisation process—find their way to the websites of the national standardisation organisations.

D. Accessibility

From the perspective of accessibility, once a European standard has been formally adopted, it is accessible to everyone. However, it has become a product that has to be bought from one of the national standardisation organisations. The copyright in the European standard is owned by the national standardisation organisations—it is not owned by CEN.[113] The price depends on the number of pages of the standard. It does not always have to be very expensive—the average standard costs between 30 and 50 Euros. However, when a number of standards exist in a particular sector, it might be quite expensive for a business to get access to all standards it has to comply with. Again, larger businesses have significant advantages compared to SMEs. The accessibility problem has given rise to litigation in the Netherlands.[114] However, this was in the context of a standard which had been referred to in a legislative instrument. As such, it is different from the application of a standard in private law. The problem arose because the Dutch legislature had decided to refer to a NEN standard in a public regulation. This had the effect of giving binding status to the standard. However, the standard did not become publicly available in the sector—it remained for the stakeholders in the sector to buy the standard themselves. This legislative practice was challenged in the Dutch courts and it was claimed that the reference in public legislation

[112] Interview with NEN (Delft) on 4 April 2012.
[113] CEN-CENELEC Guide 10, Guidelines for the distribution and sales of CEN-CENELEC publications (Edition 2), January 2010.
[114] Judgment of the Hoge Raad (Supreme Court) of 22 June 2012, LJN: BW0393. For an extensive discussion of this case and its implications, see R van Gestel and H Micklitz, above n 23.

meant that the standards had to be made freely available. Therefore, the issue in the case became whether standards obtained the status of legislation and whether the standards should be free of any copyright. The Dutch Supreme Court finally held that the standard did not obtain the status of legislation as a result of the reference and that, consequently, the standards could remain protected by copyright.

The accessibility problems remain important for standards that do not immediately obtain *de facto* binding status. Services standards will obtain their status through their subsequent application by stakeholders in a sector. If stakeholders have to spend a lot of money on getting access to the standards, they might decide not to buy them and to adopt different standards. Similarly, the fact that the standard is a product might act as an obstacle for stakeholders to get to know a standard and comply with its provisions. From the perspective of service recipients, if they are thinking about going to another Member State to receive services, they might very well want to be able to know what sort of standards are used in that Member State. If a European standard has been adopted, but this standard is not freely available, this effectively prevents service recipients from getting to know an instrument that has attempted to increase convergence in the regulation of a particular service. If service recipients had known about the existence of the standard and its provisions, they could have been more inclined to travel abroad. It is highly unlikely that individual consumers or service recipients will spend money on buying European standards. Moreover, the fact that consumers are unlikely to know about the existence of a European standard will have an impact on the willingness of courts to apply this standard in private law.

IV. THE PERSPECTIVES OF SOME KEY PLAYERS IN EUROPEAN STANDARDISATION OF SERVICES

A. CEN

As one of the main European standardisation organisations, CEN has always been the facilitator of European standardisation projects. It is usually dependent on the Commission or national stakeholders to come forward with proposals for European standardisation. As a result, it is very important for CEN to know the plans of the Commission and national stakeholders. However, CEN is primarily a passive organisation—it has to be approached by other parties with proposals.[115] It will then facilitate the standardisation process at the European level. However, the main part of the work will be undertaken by the national standardisation organisations. CEN's focus on facilitation is clear from its offices in Brussels, which are much smaller than those of some of the national standardisation organisations.

[115] Interview with CEN (Brussels) on 4 April 2012.

Furthermore, most of the rooms are meetings rooms for TCs to work on European standardisation projects.

As an organisation CEN has been very keen to expand its work programme in the field of services. From the 2000s onwards, when it started to increase its focus on services, it has commissioned a number of studies on the benefits of European standardisation of services.[116] It seems that the intention to expand into the services sector has instigated an evolutionary process within CEN. Where it used to wait for people to approach the organisation before, CEN has now taken a more outward-looking approach and has started to actively approach services sectors to offer its standardisation services.[117] This shows that CEN is not purely a facilitator, but that it has its own independent strategy as an organisation. This could have a number of consequences for European standardisation. First of all, there is a possibility that CEN could come in conflict with services sectors in which it would like European standardisation to take place. Secondly, the bottom-up nature of European standardisation could be at risk, if CEN independently decided that there was a need for standardisation in a particular services sector. This would have an impact on the issue of ownership of standardisation in certain sectors—would it still remain a self-regulatory activity or would it actually become much more like a top-down activity imposed from above? Thirdly, it becomes important that CEN investigates to what extent European standardisation as a regulatory tool is compatible with the existing legal regulatory framework for specific services sectors. Although a number of studies have been commissioned on the usefulness of European standardisation of services, these studies have only to a limited extent engaged with the regulatory frameworks in which the European standards would be received. Therefore, there is a risk that the European services standards would not be sufficiently matched to the legal framework in which they are to play a role.[118]

Another important factor in CEN's strategy for European standardisation of services is that it is dependent on services sectors that are capable of bearing the costs of European standardisation.[119] It means that CEN has to look for stakeholders who have sufficient financial means to get involved in European standardisation, and that CEN is operating in a market. For example, CEN has expressed an interest in getting more work in the healthcare sector.[120] However, the healthcare sector is primarily publicly funded and would not seem to have a lot of money available for European standardisation. The result could then be that European standardisation would focus solely on those areas of healthcare services that have already been subjected to privatisation and market forces.

[116] Most recently, see "Study on the implementation of service standards and their impact on service providers and users", Final report submitted by Technopolis Group, 24th January 2012: ftp://ftp.cen.eu/CEN/Sectors/List/Services/Technopolis20120124.pdf.

[117] Interview with CEN (Brussels) on 4 April 2012.

[118] This would confirm the point which was already made in 2006 by H Micklitz, above n 76, 455.

[119] Interview with CEN (Brussels) on 4 April 2012.

[120] ibid.

Finally, focusing specifically on the effects of European standardisation on consumers, it seems that CEN does not intend to make any changes to the confidential nature of the European standardisation process and to the fact that parties have to buy European standards. No changes can be made to the 'business model', as it is called, without putting at risk the basic principles of European standardisation.[121] It has to be accepted that European standards contain a lot of expensive information for which customers have to pay. This approach is difficult to reconcile with CEN's position that European standardisation could be a realistic alternative for legislation,[122] particularly in areas in which the EU has no competence. If standardisation was supposed to supplement or even replace legislation, CEN would also have to work on its transparency and accessibility. Its refusal to consider changes to the model of European standardisation is likely to have a negative impact on the ability to expand to sectors in which European standardisation is not very well known.

B. ANEC

The European Association for the Co-ordination of Consumer Representation in Standardisation ('ANEC') was established as a non-profit organisation under Belgian law in 1995. Its secretariat is based in Brussels. The main aim of ANEC is to represent consumers in the European standardisation process—to provide 'the European consumer voice in standardisation'. Although it is not expressly mentioned, ANEC receives its funding on the basis of the Standardisation Regulation 2012.[123] The Regulation continuously emphasises the need for consumer protection interests to be taken into account in European standardisation. In order to be able to do this, ANEC is funded by the Commission[124] and participates in certain selected European standardisation processes. Furthermore, ANEC will provide comments or input for European standardisation processes in which it is not able to participate. ANEC is a small organisation—much smaller than CEN. Its secretariat only has eight employees. Most of ANEC's work is done through co-ordination and co-operation with national consumer protection organisations. ANEC has created Working Groups for the main areas in which it is operating.[125] These Working Groups consist of national representatives with particular expertise in a certain area. They will often be working for one of the national consumer

[121] ibid.
[122] ibid.
[123] Article 5(1) and Annex III of the Standardisation Regulation 2012.
[124] The Commission provides 95% of its budget. ANEC's total budget in 2014 was around €1.5 million: www.anec.eu/anec.asp?p=about-anec&ref=01-01.
[125] Interview with ANEC (Brussels) on 4 April 2012.

organisations. ANEC will also frequently be represented by national delegates in national mirror committees.

In European standardisation, ANEC's key focus is on the safety of services—quality is of secondary concern.[126] Although ANEC is actively participating in European standardisation of services, it does so 'under protest'. It is lobbying for a horizontal legislative framework for services safety. In fact, its position is that the New Approach should be followed for services. This means that for ANEC the difference between goods and services is not so significant that the approach adopted at the European level for goods cannot be copied for services.[127] Furthermore, it strongly objects to the argument that the diversity of the services sector would be eliminated through European standardisation.[128] This is an argument which has been relied on by the tourism sector to object to European standardisation. According to ANEC, although standardisation should not eliminate diversity, there are certain core safety requirements that have to be complied with regardless of the specificities of particular services sectors.[129]

As an organisation, ANEC is extremely dependent on national input. In fact, it is so dependent on this input that it is not even in a position to impose certain proportionality or minimum requirements on the representation of different Member States in the working groups.[130] Certain Member States are not represented in the working groups. This means that, as an organisation, ANEC is vulnerable and open to abuse by particular national interests which are over-represented in the working groups. The other side of the coin is that ANEC might fail to represent the interests of consumers in the particular Member States which are not participating in the working groups. While this does not have to be fatal to ANEC's effectiveness in representing consumer interests, it also highlights another important problem for ANEC, which is its lack of knowledge and experience. As an organisation representing consumer interests in European standardisation, ANEC has to co-operate with the industry, which has much more technical knowledge and experience.[131] It is not just that ANEC itself is quite a small organisation. This also applies to the national representatives of consumer organisations who represent ANEC in the European committees working on European standards. In terms of knowledge and experience, these representatives cannot really compete with the

[126] ibid.
[127] ibid.
[128] ibid.
[129] ibid.
[130] ibid.
[131] Interview with ANEC (Brussels) on 4 April 2012 and Interview with Chairman of Dutch Mirror Committee for Aesthetic Surgery Services (Goes) on 29 December 2012. See also J Falke, 'Achievements and Unresolved Problems of European Standardization: The Ingenuity of Practice and the Queries of Lawyers', in C Joerges, KH Ladeur and E Vos (eds), *Integrating Scientific Expertise in Regulatory Decision-Making: National Traditions and European Innovations* (Baden-Baden, Nomos, 1997), 187–224, 209 and H Schepel, above n 4, 244–45.

industry. This is likely to have a negative impact on the ability of ANEC to influence European standardisation.

With its lack of expertise, it is interesting to note which aspects ANEC considers important in the European standardisation process. It seems that ANEC focuses on information requirements and protection of vulnerable consumers. For example, in the European standardisation project for Aesthetic Surgery Services, one of ANEC's main targets was to get a provision in the standard which limited the kind of treatments that could be offered to minors.[132] From the perspective of the stakeholders involved in standardisation, these issues might not always seem the most important issues addressed in the standardisation process. From that perspective, ANEC's achievements might occur 'in the margin' of the European standardisation process.[133] However, the strategy of ANEC to focus on a limited number of consumer protection issues could be explained by its lack of (human) resources and by its lack of technical expertise.

C. European Commission

Most of the work on European standardisation within the Commission is done by DG GROWTH (formerly DG Enterprise and Market). It has a special Standardisation Unit, which is responsible for drafting the mandates for standardisation processes. Because most mandates are issued under the New Approach for goods, the Standardisation Unit is not too involved in European standardisation of services. Mandates for services standardisation have previously been issued by DG MARKT, where a number of people within the Business-to-Business team worked on European standardisation of services. Furthermore, for some of the specific services sectors other DGs get involved. For example, DG SANTE (formerly DG Sanco) has done some work in the field of services standardisation.[134] DG GROWTH itself has supervised standardisation activities in the tourism sector.

In January 2013, the Commission issued a new programming mandate to CEN for the development of a number of horizontal services standards.[135] It was the result of a long period of interaction between the Commission and CEN, which was concluded with the CHESSS report in 2008. With the new mandate, which was accepted by CEN in March 2013, it seems that the Commission is attempting to restore the institutional balance between CEN and the Commission. The relationship is turned from horizontal co-operation into more hierarchical supervision. The Commission has changed its position on the desirability of

[132] Interview with ANEC (Brussels) on 4 April 2012.

[133] Interview with Chairman of Dutch Mirror Committee for Aesthetic Surgery Services (Goes) on 29 December 2012.

[134] Interview with DG Enterprise of the European Commission (Brussels) on 29 November 2012.

[135] M/517 Mandate addressed to CEN, CENELEC and ETSI for the Programming and Development of Horizontal Service Standards of 24 January 2013.

one horizontal services standard. Its initial position, encouraged by the CHESSS study, was that it would be desirable to have one big horizontal standard covering all services and all aspects of services.[136] Such a big standard is no longer desirable, since the Commission has discovered, after consultation with the stakeholders, that this is not actually desired by the market.[137] Therefore, the Commission is taking the side of the stakeholders. It does not trust that the views which CEN presents necessarily represent the views of the stakeholders. The implicit claim is that CEN's CHESSS study did not sufficiently take the requirements of stakeholders into account. With the new mandate, the Commission is asking CEN to develop a number of options for horizontal services standards. These options have to focus on aspects of the service provision process. For example, one could think about information requirements on service providers, billing or complaint and redress mechanisms.[138] After these options have been presented, the Commission reserves the right to select, together with the stakeholders, a number of options for further development through CEN.[139] Consequently, the Commission is again keeping control of the process. Although CEN will have to work out in detail how and to what extent the various plans of the Commission can be brought into practice, the scope and boundaries of the programme are clearly within the control of the Commission—the Commission is pulling the strings. The co-operation with CEN takes place on the terms of the Commission. As such, the Commission has given a clear message that CEN should reconsider and reflect on its strategy for services.

The mandate of the Commission foresees an important role for the stakeholders—for the market.[140] Apparently, it is still necessary for the Commission to get an idea of what exactly is required, desired and needed by the market. Again, this is implied criticism of the previous studies of CEN. The new initial assessment would then determine the next stage of the mandate. As such, the Commission is giving a clear message to the market: we are interested in what you want and need, and we are concerned that European services standardisation is compatible with your needs and wishes.[141] Consequently, the mandate would not really be top-down European standardisation, but the mandate itself would be constituted on the basis of the bottom-up wishes of the market. This is an important difference with mandates issued by the Commission where they would like to see European services standardisation as a supplementary tool to EU legislation.

The reason which lies at the heart of the Commission's desire to receive more input from the stakeholders is uncertainty about the benefits of European standardisation of services. This uncertainty is caused by the limited number of services standards,

136 Interview with DG Enterprise of the European Commission (Brussels) on 29 November 2012.
137 ibid.
138 ibid.
139 ibid.
140 ibid.
141 ibid.

and also by the apparent resistance of stakeholders.[142] The Commission strongly feels that this resistance should be thoroughly investigated before further steps are taken in the field of services standardisation. This stakeholder-focused perspective is different from CEN's perspective, which has determined itself—more independently from the stakeholders—that services standardisation through CEN would be a desirable activity. For the Commission, the debate should not just be limited to the 'how' of services standardisation—horizontal or vertical—but it should also focus on the 'why' of services standardisation.

This focus on the 'why' of European services standardisation is also caused by the Commission's role in the internal market. The Commission, as guardian of the Treaties, is concerned that free movement of services, goods and persons should be facilitated in the internal market.[143] This is where the Commission's interests might be different from those of the stakeholders, who might be more concerned about the quality of services. One of its primary concerns is that European standardisation of services could actually act as an obstacle to free movement.[144] The Commission considers it important that these concerns are further investigated before it invests more time and resources in European standardisation of services. There is a concern that without any intervention of the Commission, European services standardisation could develop in the wrong direction. It is clear that the Commission has received concrete signals that European services standards might create barriers to the functioning of the internal market.[145] These signals have made the alarms bells ring and have led to further investigation by the Commission.

What does the Commission think about the possibility of a New Approach to services? This would require the Commission to initiate proposals for directives on the safety of services. These directives would then rely on European services standards to specify the detailed requirements with which services would have to comply. Since the Commission is currently adopting quite a cautious approach towards European standardisation of services, it is not really anticipating any developments towards such a New Approach.[146] First of all, further research is required as well as fundamental reflection on the usefulness of services standardisation for stakeholders and its interaction with the free movement provisions.

V. A PRELIMINARY CONCLUSION

To conclude, this chapter has highlighted three main aspects of European standardisation of services.

[142] ibid.
[143] ibid.
[144] ibid.
[145] Interview with DG Enterprise of the European Commission (Brussels) on 29 November 2012. Specific reference was made to the European standard for Tourist Guide Training (EN15565:2008).
[146] ibid.

First of all, European standardisation of services cannot be considered similar to European standardisation of goods. There are important differences both in terms of substance and in terms of the legal framework in which European standards are made and applied. Standardisation of services has more social dimensions than standardisation of goods. This means the standardisation process becomes less scientific. It raises the question to what extent services should or can realistically be standardised. This is a fundamental question that has not really been discussed by those involved in European standardisation of services. Furthermore, since services standards are adopted outside the New Approach, they remain somewhat isolated in comparison with European product standards adopted under the New Approach. This lack of public law endorsement of European services standards is likely to have an impact on the application of European standards in private law.

Secondly, the European legal framework for services standardisation is fragmented. Although the Standardisation Regulation has been an important step in embedding services standardisation in the European regulatory framework, it does not constitute a development towards a New Approach to services. The simple inclusion of services standardisation in the Standardisation Regulation 2012 seems insufficient for European services standards to start to play a more significant role in the regulation of services at the European level. This is likely to have an impact on the role that these standards will play at the national level. The fragmented approach is visible in the Services Directive, which only contains a soft obligation for the Commission and the Member States to encourage European standardisation of services. The role of Article 26(5) in the overall framework of the Services Directive remains unclear.

Thirdly, the fragmented framework might be explained by the positions of the various actors involved in European standardisation of services. A tension has been identified between CEN and the Commission. While CEN has pro-actively and enthusiastically sought to promote European standardisation of services, the Commission has adopted a more cautious approach. This caution is the result of indications that European standardisation of services might actually be used for market protection purposes rather than for market integration purposes. Moreover, the Commission has discovered that there is uncertainty among stakeholders about the benefits and usefulness of European standardisation of services. A similarly cautious approach is adopted by ANEC, which is generally supportive of services standardisation, but which would like to see it placed in a broader framework of a New Approach to services. The position of ANEC highlights the tension between quality, safety and diversity of services.

Finally, what impact do these three conclusions have on the application of European standardisation of services in private law? It is clear that they pose a challenge. The fact that there is no New Approach in the field of services does not necessarily have a direct impact on the application of standards in private law. However, the lack of European endorsement of services standards, and the EU's ambiguous approach to services standardisation, could have a detrimental impact on the willingness of both stakeholders and the judiciary to apply European services standards at the national level. At the same time, the application of services standards in private law becomes crucial for their effectiveness in law. This leaves private law in something of a limbo, because if these standards are to play a role in the legal regulation of services it is private law that will have to do the main job—although it remains possible that European services standards are applied in public law at the national level. Furthermore, with the recent extension of the application of the free movement provisions to private parties,[147] the application of European services in private law does not mean that they can escape review under the free movement provisions. Therefore, it becomes essential that European standardisation of services takes the requirements imposed by free movement law into account. There are concerns, particularly by the Commission, that this is not currently the case. As a result, closer supervision by the Commission might be necessary.

[147] In particular, in the context of standardisation, see *Fra.bo*, above n 14.

4

European Standardisation of Healthcare Services

AFTER THE ANALYSIS of the legal framework for European standardisation of services, this chapter will focus on European standardisation in the healthcare sector. In order to understand the potential of European standardisation of healthcare services to play a role in private law, the regulatory framework for healthcare services—both at the European and at the national level—has to be set out. The first part analyses the interaction between EU law and healthcare services. This will be done by looking at the impact of primary EU law, secondary EU law and European standardisation. The perspective then shifts to the national level to discuss what the role of private law is in the regulation of healthcare services, and to see what the potential impact of European standardisation could be. Finally, three case studies on European standardisation of services will be introduced. The chapter concludes with an analysis of the interaction between European standardisation and healthcare services.

I. THE INTERACTION BETWEEN EU LAW AND HEALTHCARE SERVICES

A. The Lack of EU Competence to Regulate Healthcare Services

Healthcare is not one of the traditional competences of the EU. The healthcare systems of the various EU Member States are all very different in nature and are based on different cultural perceptions of how healthcare should be delivered and regulated. From a political point of view, it was considered undesirable for the EU to intervene in these national systems. The organisation of the healthcare systems was too closely linked to the national identity of the Member States, which strongly opposed any direct influence of the EU. Furthermore, healthcare services were traditionally local, in that patients would go to the general practitioner or hospital in their neighbourhood. Until relatively recently, the cross-border dimension which could possibly justify regulatory intervention by the EU was missing.

Despite the absence of an express legal basis to regulate healthcare services, there are various areas of EU law which have had an impact on healthcare systems.

For example, the Working Time Directive[1] has had a profound impact on the organisation of healthcare at the national level.[2] As a result, stakeholders in the healthcare sector are well aware of the possible impact of EU regulation on the delivery of healthcare services. Furthermore, various aspects of EU regulation touch on (public) health issues. From the 1970s onwards, several measures had been adopted which could be considered to have improvement of public health as (one of) their main aims. The legal bases of these measures were uncertain or disputed.[3] For that reason and for reasons of transparency, it was decided that the EU should be given a complementary competence in the field of public health. This competence was introduced by the Treaty of Maastricht. It provided that 'the Community shall contribute towards a high level of human health protection by encouraging cooperation between Member States, and, if necessary, lending support to their action'.[4] After the adoption of the Treaty of Lisbon, it is now expressly stated that the protection of a high level of human health is one of the areas in which the EU only has a complementary competence.[5] Harmonisation of legislation is expressly excluded. Wolf Sauter has argued that this express recognition makes it clear that the EU intends to comply with the principle of subsidiarity and that it is recognised that this is an area of national competence.[6] The complementary competence itself is now found in Article 168 TFEU. First of all, it provides that, 'a high level of human health protection shall be ensured in the definition and implementation of all Union policies and activities'.[7] As to the substance of the competence, the provision is now significantly more detailed than before. Article 168(1) provides that, 'Union action, which shall complement national policies, shall be directed towards improving public health, preventing physical and mental illness and diseases, and obviating sources of danger to physical and mental health'. This is then followed by some examples of possible action by the Union. In addition to this, Article 168(2) provides that the EU shall encourage cooperation between the Member States on these issues.

From the late 1990s and early 2000s, various cases have reached the CJEU which dealt with the possibility of reimbursement for patients of the costs of healthcare services which they had received in another Member State.[8] The impact of these

[1] Council Directive 93/104/EC concerning certain aspects of the organization of working time.

[2] Interview with UEMS and CPME (Warsaw) on 19 February 2013.

[3] T Hervey, 'Community and National Competences in Health after Tobacco Advertising' (2001) 38 *CML Rev* 1421, 1422.

[4] Article 129 EC, introduced by the Treaty of Maastricht.

[5] Article 6(a) TFEU, introduced by the Treaty of Lisbon.

[6] W Sauter, 'Harmonisation in healthcare: the EU patients' rights Directive' (2011) *TILEC Research Paper* 6, 3.

[7] Article 168(1) TFEU.

[8] In particular, see Case C-120/95 *Decker v Caisse de maladie des employés privés* ECLI: EU: C:1998:167; Case C-158/96 *Kohll v Union des caisses de maladie* ECLI: EU: C:1998:171; Case C-368/98 *Vanbraekel and others v Alliance nationale des mutualités chrétiennes* ECLI: EU: C:2001:400; Case C-157/99 *Geraets-Smits v Stichting Ziekenfonds* and *Peerbooms v Stichting CZ Groep Zorgverzekeringen*

cases will be discussed below. Most cases were brought on the basis of the right of service recipients to freely receive services in another Member State. The CJEU decided that healthcare services were not excluded from the scope of application of the right to free movement of services. Therefore, in theory, it became possible for the EU to adopt legislation on the basis of its internal market competence. However, the relationship between the internal market competence and the complementary competence in health was uncertain. The extent to which the internal market competence would provide an adequate and correct legal basis for harmonisation of healthcare services was debated.[9] This debate was well illustrated by the opposition to the inclusion of healthcare services in the Services Directive.[10] In the end, it was decided that healthcare services required a special solution. This solution came with the adoption of the Cross-Border Healthcare Directive in 2011.[11] The adoption of the Directive was based both on Article 114 TFEU—the internal market competence—and Article 168 TFEU. The focus of this Directive is on the reimbursement of healthcare services which have been received outside a patient's home Member State. As such, it remains very close to the CJEU's case law and could be regarded as codification of its case law.[12] However, the Directive goes further in that it also includes a number of information rights which are granted to patients who receive healthcare abroad. This means that the EU has chosen to complement the reimbursement rights with a number of traditional consumer rights. The cross-border patient is also considered to be a consumer. This is in line with the arguments of Gareth Davies, who has argued that it would be preferable to realise changes in national healthcare systems through granting individual private law rights to patients rather than through harmonising at the European level aspects of the delivery of healthcare services.[13] Such a consumer-based approach would rely on the individual to challenge obstacles encountered in national healthcare systems and, through individual litigation, to bring about a more outward-looking perspective of national healthcare systems.

Overall, the fact remains that the EU has not intervened in the standards or the quality of healthcare provided to patients at the national level. The Cross-Border

ECLI: EU: C:2001:404; Case C-385/99 *Müller-Fauré v Onderlinge Waarborgmaatschappij ZAO Zorgverzekeringen* and *van Riet v Onderlinge Waarborgmaatschappij ZAO Zorgverzekeringen* ECLI: EU: C:2003:270; Case C-56/01 *Inizan v Caisse primaire d'assurance maladie des Hauts-de-Seine* ECLI: EU: C:2003:578 and Case C-372/04 *The Queen ex parte Watts v Bedford Primary Care Trust and Secretary of State for Health* ECLI: EU: C:2006:325.

[9] D Wyatt, 'Community Competence to Regulate Medical Services' in M Dougan and E Spaventa (eds), *Social Welfare and EU Law* (Oxford, Hart Publishing, 2005) 131–44.

[10] Interview with UEMS and CPME (Warsaw) on 19 February 2013.

[11] Directive 2011/24/EU of the European Parliament and of the Council on the application of patients' rights in cross-border healthcare.

[12] S de la Rosa, 'The Directive on Cross-Border Healthcare or the Art of Codifying Complex Case Law' (2012) 49 *CML Rev* 15.

[13] G Davies, 'The Community's Internal Market-Based Competence to Regulate Healthcare: Scope, Strategies and Consequences' (2007) 14 *Maastricht Journal of European and Comparative Law* 215.

Healthcare Directive provides that high-quality treatment shall be provided, but the meaning of high-quality is not further defined in the Directive. There is also a reference to good quality healthcare in the Directive.[14] It is difficult to interpret these standards as autonomous European standards, since it is expressly provided in the Directive that the standards of care remain national.[15] This is important from the perspective of convergence. While Member States will be required to reimburse healthcare received in another Member State, they have to do so on the basis of the treatment which would have been provided in the home Member State.[16] One could wonder to what extent such reimbursement leads to mutual recognition. This is an interesting question, perhaps more of theoretical than of practical importance, which has not been discussed in the literature. Member States have to compensate patients for treatment in another Member State, but only up to the level which the patient would have received if he had stayed at home. This arrangement does not imply any mutual recognition of the regulatory choices made by the other Member States—the national treatment remains the basis of compensation. It would have been different if the Member States had to reimburse the full rate of treatment—whatever the costs of the treatment in the other Member State. Furthermore, reimbursement does not necessarily imply that the regulatory standards are similar.

The question then remains whether the EU would be able to harmonise standards of healthcare on the basis of its internal market competence. Derrick Wyatt has argued that the EU could circumvent the presumed lack of legal competence through the internal market competence.[17] This would allow the EU to adopt measures which could remove obstacles to free movement or distortions of competition. The various differences in the standards and quality of healthcare services in the 28 Member States could amount to an obstacle to the free movement of healthcare service recipients. Wyatt realistically accepts that 'the proposition that lack of consumer confidence in the minimum guaranteed standards for the supply of goods and services in other Member States should be regarded in itself justifying harmonisation is one of which the present author is sceptical'.[18] However, at the same time, he argues that 'different standards of care resulting from disparities between national rules or administrative action in the various Member States could lead to distortion in the conditions of competition'.[19] This argument appears to be quite formalistic from a legal point of view. Furthermore, it does not face up to the political reality that Member States do not want to limit their own sovereignty in the healthcare sector. Overall, it can be concluded that the EU

[14] Recital 64 and Article 4(1) of the Cross-Border Healthcare Directive (which refers to 'good quality healthcare').

[15] Article 4(1)(b) of the Cross-Border Healthcare Directive.

[16] Article 7(1) of the Cross-Border Healthcare Directive.

[17] D Wyatt, above n 9, 136–38.

[18] ibid, 141.

[19] ibid.

internal market competence is unlikely to be used to harmonise the standards of healthcare provided at the national level. The decision to argue that the internal market competence is sufficient to start harmonising the delivery of healthcare services is highly political and unlikely to be made in the near future. However, this does not mean that internal market law cannot have an indirect impact on the way in which national healthcare systems are regulated.

B. The Impact of the Case Law on Free Movement of Services on the Regulation of Healthcare Services

From *Kohl*[20] and *Decker*,[21] the CJEU has been forced to discuss a number of cases in which patients wanted to move across national borders to receive healthcare services. In general, the distinctive nature of these cases, which distinguished them from cases brought under the Social Security Regulation,[22] was that the sole purpose of the cross-border movement was to receive healthcare services in another Member State. The CJEU included the right to receive healthcare services within the scope of the free movement of services, which is now found in Article 56 TFEU.[23] The CJEU's case law has been extensively discussed elsewhere and it is not necessary to repeat these discussions in this section.[24] However, from the specific perspective of convergence, it is interesting to note the extent to which the case law has had a convergent effect on the national regulation of healthcare services. Therefore, a number of areas will be discussed on which the CJEU's case law has had a particular impact.

i. Procedural Requirements for Prior Authorisation of Healthcare Abroad

On the basis of the case law it is, in principle, possible for Member States to impose a system of prior authorisation for patients who seek hospital treatment in another Member State, if the treatment requires hospitalisation.[25] This could

[20] Case C-158/96 *Kohll v Union des caisses de maladie* ECLI: EU: C:1998:171.

[21] Case C-120/95 *Decker v Caisse de maladie des employés privés* ECLI: EU: C:1998:167.

[22] Regulation (EC) No 883/2004 of the European Parliament and of the Council on the coordination of social security systems.

[23] Article 56 TFEU provides that restrictions to the right to provide services shall be restricted. This includes the right to receive services in another Member State: Joined Cases C-286/82 and C-26/83 *Luisi and Carbone*, ECLI: EU: C:1984:35.

[24] For a recent discussion, see J Baquero-Cruz, 'The Case Law of the European Court of Justice on the Mobility of Patients' in F Benyon (ed), *Services and the EU Citizen* (Oxford, Hart Publishing, 2013), 87–112. See also, in the same volume, R Cisotta, 'Limits to Rights to Health Care and the Extent of Member States' Discretion to Decide on the Parameters of Their Public Health Polices', 113–63.

[25] Case C-157/99 *Geraets-Smits v Stichting Ziekenfonds* and *Peerbooms v Stichting CZ Groep Zorgverzekeringen* ECLI: EU: C:2001:404; Case C-385/99 *Müller-Fauré v Onderlinge Waarborgmaatschappij ZAO Zorgverzekeringen* and *van Riet v Onderlinge Waarborgmaatschappij ZAO Zorgverzekeringen* ECLI: EU: C:2003:270.

have an impact on private law, if patients have to obtain prior authorisation from the health insurer with whom they hold their insurance policy. The exact definition of hospitalisation was never provided by the CJEU, but it was clear that prior authorisation of non-hospital care would never be permissible. Furthermore, the CJEU has made it clear that Member States must have transparent procedures for cases in which authorisation can be required. Decisions of the decision-making body must be open to judicial review or some sort of quasi-judicial review proceedings, and they must be taken within a reasonable time frame.[26]

ii. Substantive Requirements for Prior Authorisation of Healthcare Abroad

As a result of the case law of the CJEU, the substantive criteria which Member States use in deciding whether or not to authorise treatment in another Member State have become more converged. The CJEU held in *Geraets-Smits and Peerbooms* that the Dutch criterion of whether a treatment was 'normal in the professional circles concerned' had to be interpreted from an international perspective—treatment sufficiently tried and tested by international science.[27] Relevant (international) scientific literature had to be taken into account. This means that Member States, in dealing with requests for prior authorisation, must look at treatments from an international point of view. They are not allowed to focus solely on national medical practice if this is unduly restrictive. The consequence is that the pallet of treatment options available to patients becomes broader and has to be interpreted from an international (and possibly European) perspective. This means that for out-going patients Member States are required to look at possible treatments in other Member States.

Secondly, in *Geraets-Smits and Peerbooms*, the criterion that treatment abroad was a medical necessity—which in practice meant that the treatment could not be offered without undue delay in the home Member State—was justified as long as the decision-making body took all the specific circumstances of the case into account.[28] Consequently, Member States are no longer justified in referring to the acceptable lengths of national waiting lists as an outright justification to refuse authorisation to receive healthcare abroad. They must always make an individual assessment based on the current and individual circumstances of the patient.

The result of these substantive criteria for prior authorisation is that Member States are obliged to make an individual assessment of patients who would like to receive medical treatment abroad and that Member States are obliged to take international medical practice into account. This implies that Member States—at least at the level of prior authorisation—can no longer close their eyes to medical practice in other Member States. It also applies to courts when they review decisions

[26] *Geraets-Smits* and *Peerbooms*, above n 25, para 90.
[27] ibid, paras 97–98.
[28] ibid, para 104.

to refuse prior authorisation to patients who would like to receive healthcare services abroad.

iii. Waiting Lists

The individual assessment of the undue delay criterion (or medical necessity) has also had an impact on how Member States manage their waiting lists. It is no longer appropriate to refuse treatment abroad on the basis that the length of the waiting lists is acceptable. Each case requires an individual assessment of the circumstances of the patient.[29] This has obliged Member States to introduce a certain flexibility in their management of waiting lists, and where necessary to pro-actively seek cross-border treatment options. *Watts* is a very clear example of the impact of EU free movement law on the management of waiting lists.[30] The result of that case is that the UK's National Health Service ('NHS') now regularly sends patients to other Member States for treatment.[31]

iv. Transparency of Costs of Treatment

Finally, the fact that non-hospital care has to be reimbursed and that prior authorisation can never be justified for those cases means that healthcare systems such as the NHS have to make the costs of the specific treatments transparent. Otherwise, it would be difficult or impossible to know to what extent treatment abroad will be reimbursed. The result is that Member States must make the costs of treatments accessible to patients. This is the case even if patients normally never see the prices of treatments, since they receive healthcare without having to pay for it.[32]

Overall, the case law has mainly focused on the procedural rules for patients who want to receive healthcare abroad. However, there is one procedural area which might result in substantive convergence. This is the result of the judgment in *Geraets-Smits*. Member States must take international science into account in deciding whether or not to grant prior authorisation. As a result, an obligation is imposed on Member States to analyse international scientific evidence that is available in a particular field and to assess to what extent the national healthcare system is able to provide healthcare services in accordance with this international evidence.[33] It is an implicit recognition that research in medicine has become

[29] Case C-372/04 *The Queen ex parte Watts v Bedford Primary Care Trust and Secretary of State for Health* ECLI: EU: C:2006:325, paras 119–20.

[30] ibid.

[31] J Montgomery, 'Impact of European Union Law on English Healthcare Law', in M Dougan and E Spaventa (eds), *Social Welfare and EU Law* (Oxford, Hart Publishing, 2005) 145–56, 154.

[32] ibid, 154–55.

[33] A den Exter, 'Health Care Access in the Netherlands: a True Story', in C Flood and A Gross (eds), *The Right to Health at the Public/Private Divide* (Cambridge, CUP, 2014) 188–207, 200. See also G Davies, 'Legislating for Patients' Rights' in J. van der Gronden et al. (eds), *Health Care and EU Law* (The Hague, Asser, 2011) 191–210, 204.

significantly internationalised.[34] However, in practice, it has proved difficult for patients to base their claims on international scientific evidence, primarily because Member States retain a degree of discretion in deciding to what extent such international science is evidence-based.[35] Nevertheless, the result of such an evaluation could be that a Member State has to reimburse treatment which is not available in the home Member State, but which could be brought in a broader category of treatments that are compensated by the home Member State. That is what happened in *Elchinov*.[36] In effect, the CJEU imposed a duty of consistent interpretation on national courts—if it is at all possible to bring a foreign treatment within a category of treatments that are reimbursed in the home Member State, the national court should do so.[37] Although no reference was made to fundamental rights, the aim of this approach is to provide substance to the right of patients to have access to healthcare.[38] However, the danger is that it could encourage Member States to restrict the list of treatments at the national level by providing a very clear, but also very restrictive list with treatments available at the national level. This could become a particular problem for patients in the new Member States.[39] If Member States were to adopt such an approach, this could be in breach of the requirement of high-quality or good quality healthcare which is imposed by the Cross-Border Healthcare Directive 2011. In *Stamatelaki*,[40] the CJEU held that private healthcare received in another Member State cannot simply be excluded from reimbursement on the basis of its private nature, when private healthcare is not reimbursed in the home Member State. As a consequence, Member States are required to look at the substance of the treatment—not the status of its provider.

Finally, one can wonder to what extent the case law has had an impact on private law and on the possibility of convergence in private law. Here, it should be noted that this impact is very much dependent on how healthcare services are regulated at the national level. However, in general, the series of free movement cases has had a limited impact on private law relations. Because of the focus on reimbursement and prior authorisation, the cases have intervened in the relationship between patient and the body which is responsible for reimbursing healthcare services. In most Member States, this is a public law relationship. In some Member States, such as the Netherlands, the case law has had an impact on the relationship

[34] N Cortez, 'International Health Care Convergence: The Benefits and Burdens of Market-Driven Standardization' (2008) 26 *Wisconsin International Law Journal* 646.

[35] A den Exter, above n 33, 200–01.

[36] Case C-173/09 *Elchinov* v. *Natsionalna zdravnoosiguritelna kasa* ECLI: EU: C:2010:581.

[37] ibid, paras 68–73.

[38] Expressly recognised in the Bulgarian legislation referred to in the judgment, see para 7.

[39] T Sokol, 'Rindal and Elchinov: A(n) (Impending) Revolution in EU law on Patient Mobility?' (2010) 6 *Croatian Yearbook of European Law and Policy* 167.

[40] Case C-444/05 *Stamatelaki v NPDD Organismos Asfaliseos Eleftheron Epangelmation* ECLI: EU: C:2007:231.

between health insurer and patient, which would in principle be a private law relationship. However, health insurers operate in a regulatory framework which is strictly controlled and regulated by public law. Although the case law has an impact on the contractual relationship between insurer and patient, the content of the contract has to a significant extent been decided by public bodies. Despite this limited effect on the relationship between insurer and patient, it is clear that the case law has not had an impact on the private law relationship between doctor and patient—whether this relationship is considered to be contractual or in tort. All the cases have dealt with the rights of patients vis-à-vis the body that is responsible for paying for healthcare services. The case law under Article 56 TFEU has not had an effect on what patients can claim from their doctor. The next step is then to analyse to what extent the Cross-Border Healthcare Directive 2011 will go beyond the case law on the free movement of services.

C. The Impact of the Cross-Border Healthcare Directive 2011 on the Regulation of Healthcare Services

It is generally agreed that the adoption of the Cross-Border Healthcare Directive was primarily a codification exercise.[41] The Directive codifies the CJEU's case law on the free movement of patients. The articles on reimbursement of healthcare received in another Member State from the one in which the patient is affiliated to the healthcare system, closely follow the rules laid down by the CJEU.[42] The same is true for the rules on prior authorisation. The situations in which cross-border healthcare can be subject to prior authorisation are exhaustively listed.[43] They include hospital treatment. However, an interesting difference—or clarification—with the case law is that the definition of hospital treatment which can be subject to prior authorisation is healthcare which involves overnight accommodation in hospital.[44] As a consequence, it appears that out-patient treatment in hospital can no longer be subject to prior authorisation.

In a number of areas, the Directive goes further than the case law. As such, it attempts to realise convergence of national healthcare regulation through harmonisation in a limited number of areas. The competence on which these harmonisation aspects are based is the same as that of the overall Directive—the competence to regulate the internal market.[45] It should be noted that the Directive was adopted in early 2011 and that the deadline for transposition in national law was

[41] S de la Rosa, above n 12.
[42] ibid, and see also W Sauter, above n 6.
[43] Article 8(2) of the Cross-Border Healthcare Directive.
[44] Article 8(2)(a)(i) of the Cross-Border Healthcare Directive.
[45] Recital 2 of the Cross-Border Healthcare Directive.

25 October 2013. Therefore, the actual effect of the Directive in practice is still difficult to measure. However, it is clear there are significant differences in how and to what extent Member States have implemented the Directive.[46] These difficulties can be explained by some of the new concepts introduced in the Directive and the need for Member States to adapt the requirements of the Directive to their national health systems. There are a number of areas where the Directive adds something to the case law of the CJEU.

i. Quality Standards

The Directive obliges Member States to provide cross-border healthcare in accordance with standards and guidelines laid down by the Member State of treatment.[47] This does not directly encourage any convergence of standards, let alone the creation of European standards, but it does mean that Member States must have standards in place. Member States that have insufficient or no quality standards will be required to adopt such standards for the purpose of cross-border healthcare. If national standards are not available, Member States could decide to adopt international or European standards. It is unlikely that the effect of these standards would be limited to healthcare provided to patients coming from other Member States. Article 4(1) of the Directive also provides that Member States must take the principles of universality, access to good quality care, equity and solidarity into account in providing cross-border healthcare.[48] This could mean that Member States are required to provide healthcare of a certain minimum quality level, and could even be required in certain circumstances to amend their quality standards to provide healthcare of a higher standard.

ii. Accessibility of Quality Standards

In addition to having standards in place, these standards must also be accessible to patients from other Member States.[49] Member States must establish information points which can provide patients in other Member States with relevant information on the standards and guidelines which are in place in the Member State of treatment.

[46] H Nys, 'The Transposition of the Directive on Patients' Rights in Cross-Border Healthcare in National Law by the Member States: Still a Lot of Effort to Be Made and Questions to Be Answered' (2014) 21 *European Journal of Health Law* 1. See also D Goscinska, 'Transposition of the Patients' Rights Directive 2011/24/EU: A Discourse Analysis in Germany, Poland and Austria', *Working Papers in Health Policy and Management*, Volume 8, TU Berlin, February 2014.

[47] Article 4(1)(b) of the Cross-Border Healthcare Directive.

[48] Article 4(1) of the Cross-Border Healthcare Directive.

[49] Article 4(2)(a) of the Cross-Border Healthcare Directive.

iii. Information Requirements

The Directive goes quite far in the information requirements that are imposed on healthcare providers. Article 4(2)(b) obliges healthcare providers to help patients to make an informed choice.[50] This includes information on:

(i) Treatment options;
(ii) Availability of healthcare;
(iii) Quality and safety of healthcare;
(iv) Prices and invoices;
(v) Registration status and insurance of healthcare professionals.

These criteria all go some way towards providing a basis for informed consent. Consequently, the Directive protects patients who are considering cross-border healthcare by granting them a number of information rights. As such, the protection focuses on the service recipient—the patient in this case—and aims as much as possible to make the patient a well-informed consumer.[51] In principle, these requirements are imposed on healthcare providers in the context of cross-border healthcare. However, the practical effect is that domestic patients will also receive this information. It is unlikely that Member States will create different information obligations depending on the origin of the patient. Such a distinction could realistically only be made in respect of language requirements. In this way, the Directive might also improve the provision of information to patients who remain within their home Member State.[52]

iv. Complaints and Insurance

Finally, the 2011 Directive obliges Member States to have transparent complaints mechanisms in place for patients.[53] Furthermore, the Member State is required to have a system of professional liability insurance in place.[54]

Unlike the case law of the CJEU, the Directive seems to have a direct impact on the patient–doctor relationship. This would mainly be through the information requirements. However, it is clear from the wording and the structure of the Directive that the obligations are imposed on the Member States and not directly on healthcare providers. It seems very unlikely that the obligations in Article 4 would

[50] Article 4(2)(b) of the Cross-Border Healthcare Directive.

[51] In line with the arguments of G Davies, above n 13.

[52] D Delnoij and W Sauter, 'Patient information under the EU's patients' rights Directive' (2011) 21 *European Journal of Public Health* 271. See also W Palm and R Baeten, 'The quality and safety paradox in the patients' rights Directive' (2011) 21 *European Journal of Public Health* 272.

[53] Article 4(2)(c) of the Cross-Border Healthcare Directive. The standards for these procedures could be based on Commission Recommendation 98/257/EC on the out-of-court settlement of consumer disputes.

[54] Article 4(2)(d) of the Cross-Border Healthcare Directive.

have direct effect in a dispute between a healthcare provider and a patient. Nevertheless, it is clear that by granting a number of consumer-like rights, the Cross-Border Healthcare Directive has more of an impact on the private law aspects of the patient–doctor relationship. However, its main focus is still procedural rather than substantive. This opens up the possibility for European standardisation to intervene directly in the patient–doctor relationship by regulating substantive aspects of the patient's treatment.

D. The Role of European Standardisation in the Regulation of Healthcare Services

On the basis of the discussion above, it is clear that both the case law on the free movement of patients and the Cross-Border Healthcare Directive have realised some convergence in the regulation of healthcare services in the Member States. The Directive has codified the case law, but has also imposed a number of additional information obligations. This means that the standards of care become more accessible and transparent. However, because of the EU's lack of legal competence to regulate quality of healthcare directly, both the case law and the Directive are still based on the presumption that the standards for healthcare services are defined at the national level. They do not directly interfere with the national definition of quality of care. Member States are merely encouraged to exchange national standards.

In a European internal market for healthcare services, such an exchange could eventually result in a need for a European definition of quality of care. This could be in areas in which there is a significant amount of cross-border movement of patients, or in areas in which the regulation of (private) healthcare services is very different in the various Member States. Member States are allowed under certain conditions to refuse prior authorisation of healthcare abroad.[55] One of them is Article 8(6)(c) of the Cross-Border Healthcare Directive, which provides that concerns about the quality of the healthcare providers are one of the legitimate reasons to refuse prior authorisation.[56] Again therefore, there is an incentive in the Directive for quality to be regulated at the European level.

In this broader framework, standardisation would then become one of the options to regulate quality of care issues at the European level. European standardisation would intervene directly in the patient–doctor relationship by regulating aspects of the treatment. The standards in a European standard could be used directly in contractual disputes between healthcare providers and patients, or as a benchmark to determine the standard of care in contract or tort cases. A European standard would provide substantive rights as a supplement to the procedural rights provided in the Directive.

[55] Article 8(6) of the Cross-Border Healthcare Directive.
[56] Article 8(6)(c) of the Cross-Border Healthcare Directive.

The next step is to see in which areas European standardisation processes have been started and what the underlying reasons for these processes were. However before this can be done, it is necessary to describe in more detail how healthcare services are regulated at the national level, how public law and private law interact in the regulation of healthcare services and how European standardisation would fit in the national regulatory frameworks for healthcare services.

II. THE REGULATION OF HEALTHCARE SERVICES AT THE NATIONAL LEVEL AND THE ROLE OF PRIVATE LAW

A. The Transformation of the Character of Healthcare Services

This section will outline two developments that have taken place in the healthcare sector in the last few decades. The first development has been on the macro level and has affected the way in which Member States have organised the delivery of healthcare services at the national level. The second development, which has partly been caused by the first development, has taken place at the level of the relationship between doctor and patient.

Traditionally, healthcare services have been strictly public and have been organised exclusively by the State. It was considered to be the ultimate responsibility of the State to ensure that its citizens would receive proper healthcare. This position has not really changed, but what we can see in the last decades is that Member States have introduced elements of competition and privatisation in their healthcare systems.[57] The result is that the public law character of the healthcare sector has diminished. One of the contributing factors to this development has been the project of the EU to liberalise services of public interest. Although this project has not had a direct impact on healthcare, it is clear that it has encouraged Member States to transform the healthcare sector in such a way that it also incorporates elements of competition.[58] This creation of a market for healthcare services also means that several provisions of EU law—such as competition law and free movement law—become applicable to the healthcare sector. The extent to which these market elements have been introduced differs among the Member States. What they have in common in a significant number of Member States is that the bodies which—under public legislation—have been given responsibility to ensure the provision of healthcare services to their citizens or customers have to encourage competition among healthcare providers. They have a choice where to buy healthcare services, which means that healthcare providers have to compete for patients.

[57] M Krajewski, 'Healthcare Liberalisation in the EU and the WTO', in C Joerges and J Falke (eds), *Globalisation and the Potential of Law in Transnational Markets* (Oxford, Hart Publishing, 2011) 243. See also T Hervey, 'If Only It Were So Simple: Public Health Services and EU Law' in M Cremona (ed), *Market Integration and Public Services in the European Union* (Oxford, OUP, 2011) 179–250.

[58] T Hervey, above n 57, 209–14.

The tool which is commonly used is a private law tool—contracts are concluded between healthcare 'buyers' and healthcare providers. This has introduced market dynamics in the healthcare sector, in that healthcare providers become more focused on profit-making.[59] Furthermore, public and private healthcare providers will more frequently compete for the provision of healthcare services. It is no longer guaranteed that contracts will go to public hospitals. As such, private healthcare has been given a more significant role in the healthcare system. The scope of private healthcare providers has been broadened. In addition to this, it has become more common for patients to seek private healthcare. The existence of private healthcare providers who provide supplementary services in addition to the public healthcare system means that patient choice is enhanced. Furthermore, for private healthcare which has been sought outside the public healthcare system, the relationship between patient and healthcare provider is contractual. Again, this means that private law will have more of an impact on the regulation of healthcare services. Moreover, the significant increase of private healthcare providers means that it is necessary for supervisory agencies to expand their work to the private sector. Often, it is difficult for them to get a full picture of what is going on in the private sector.[60] In general, both the limited liberalisation and privatisation have had an impact on the regulation of healthcare regulation and have created more of a role for private law, or quasi-private law, in the regulation of healthcare services.

The liberalisation and privatisation of healthcare services have not just had an impact on how the healthcare sector is organised. They have also had an impact on the relationship between doctor and patient. Just like the bodies that are responsible for buying healthcare services have been given more choice, patients have also been given more choice—even within the public healthcare systems of the Member States. Historically, patients go to local hospitals to see a doctor. Healthcare has a strong territorial element. This is not surprising—patients do not want to travel long distances for medical care, they like to build up a relationship with their doctor and they prefer to have quick access to medical care. This local, territorial element of healthcare has not disappeared. However, the various developments in the healthcare sector have resulted in a new 'type' of patient. This process could be described as the 'consumerisation' of the patient.[61] The consumerisation of patients means that patients are becoming more and more like consumers. This

[59] V Hatzopoulos, 'Health Law and Policy: The Impact of the EU', in G de Burca (ed), *EU Law and the Welfare State: In Search of Solidarity* (Oxford, OUP, 2005) 111–68. See also O Odudu, 'Are State-owned healthcare providers subject to competition law?' (2011) 32 *European Competition Law Review* 231 and H Schweitzer, 'Wettbewerb im Gesundheitswesen—rechtliche Grundlagen and rechtspolitische Grundfragen', in U Immenga and T Körber (eds), *Wettbewerb im Gesundheitswesen* (Baden-Baden, Nomos, 2013) 35–72.

[60] Interview with Chairman of Dutch Mirror Committee for Aesthetic Surgery Services (Goes) on 29 December 2012.

[61] See M Hall and C Schneider, 'Patients as Consumers: Courts, Contracts, and the New Medical Marketplace' (2008) 106 *Michigan Law Review* 643.

implies an element of choice, and an element of 'shopping for healthcare'. This choice is granted by the co-existence of public and private healthcare providers and, as has already been said, by the possibility of choice within the public healthcare system. It can no longer be assumed that patients will go to the hospital next door—if there is a hospital a few hours away that offers specialist care of a higher quality, they will often opt for that hospital. This means that healthcare services are, to a certain extent, being removed from their territorial basis. Furthermore, patients have more access to information about the contents, the risks and the consequences of medical treatment. The number of internet fora and patient websites with medical information has increased enormously in the last couple of years—sometimes to the detriment of the accuracy of the information. The result of the increase in information is that patients have become more demanding towards doctors and will not hesitate to ask for a second opinion if they are not pleased with the diagnosis or proposal for treatment. Again, this could mean that patients will travel some distance to obtain a second opinion. Cross-border healthcare becomes a more realistic option. This consumerisation of the patient is also reflected in the Cross-Border Healthcare Directive itself. In addition to the right to reimbursement of cross-border healthcare, the focus of the Directive is very much on ensuring that patients are provided with adequate information.[62]

B. The Interaction Between Public Law and Private Law in the Regulation of Healthcare Services at the National Level

Because of its public nature, it is not surprising that healthcare is heavily regulated by public law at the national level. This section is not intended to provide a detailed overview of the legal regulation of healthcare services and providers at the national level. It will not engage in a detailed discussion of national systems. Rather, it will sketch out the landscape of public law and private law interaction in the healthcare sector in general. Inevitably, this means that certain generalisations are made about national healthcare systems, which are usually highly specific. The same applies to the legal regulation of national healthcare systems. However, this abstract picture of the landscape will provide an idea of the issues that are relevant to the ability of European standardisation to have an impact on the healthcare sector at the national level. The focus is on the interaction between public law and private law in the regulation of healthcare services and providers. Moreover, a distinction will be made between *ex ante* and *ex post* regulation.

Healthcare services would not be provided without medical professionals. Medical professionals need certain qualifications before they are allowed to practise medicine. The training requirements for doctors—as well as a number

[62] W Sauter, above n 6.

of other medical professionals—have been harmonised at the European level.[63] This has enabled the EU to adopt the Professional Qualifications Directive,[64] which provides that doctors who are qualified in one Member State should be allowed to offer their services in another Member States and should be admitted to the profession if they want to practise in another Member State on a permanent basis. It should be noted that this harmonisation has primarily been of a quantitative nature—recognition is based on the number of years of training. This is clear from the Directive itself.[65] The quantitative aspect of the harmonisation is supplemented with a more qualitative description of the substance of the training of medical practitioners. For medical specialists, the Union Européenne de Médicins Spécialists ('UEMS') is responsible for making the syllabi which contain the requirements for training for medical specialists.[66] This involves the bringing together of medical specialists of all Member States to decide on the required standards. As such, UEMS is essentially engaged in a form of standardisation. All of this takes place at the European level. At the national level, access to the medical profession is mainly regulated through public or administrative law. The bodies which are responsible for the registration might be of a quasi-public nature, but there is little direct involvement of private law.

The same applies to healthcare providers. Institutions that wish to provide healthcare services usually have to obtain some sort of licence. Again, this is a public law requirement. The requirements that have to be fulfilled before licenses are awarded are laid down in legislation. Most Member States have supervisory agencies that monitor whether healthcare providers are complying with these requirements. In case of non-compliance, the agencies have powers under public law to (temporarily) close institutions or to order them to restrict their activities. The same applies to medical practitioners, who are also supervised and can be required to stop working in case of non-compliance. Whether the healthcare system is based on insurance or on universal provision of healthcare to all citizens, agreements will have to be made between the healthcare buyers and healthcare providers. In that respect, private law plays a role since, depending on the nature of the healthcare system, these agreements can be of a contractual nature. This is perhaps the sole example of private law fulfilling an *ex ante* regulatory function. In the agreement, it can be agreed under what conditions healthcare services are delivered and with what standards they have to comply. However, the extent to which these agreements actually regulate standards and quality of care is unclear.[67]

[63] Interview with UEMS and CPME (Warsaw) on 19 February 2013.

[64] Directive 2005/36/EC of the European Parliament and of the Council on the recognition of professional qualifications.

[65] Articles 24–30 of the Professional Qualifications Directive.

[66] Interview with UEMS and CPME (Warsaw) on 19 February 2013.

[67] Interview with CZ (Tilburg) on 21 August 2012. For a discussion of the situation in the Netherlands, see R Halbersma, J van Manen en W Sauter, 'Voldoen verzekeraars in hun rol als motor van het zorgstelsel?', *NZA Research Paper* 2012/3, 20–21.

When the doctor and patient meet, in the public healthcare system, they establish a relationship which is essentially of a private law character. In some Member States, this relationship creates both a contractual relationship and a relationship in tort, while in other Member States the private law character is solely expressed through the imposition of a duty of care in tort. However, in practice, this does not make a great difference, as the standard of care is usually similar in contract and in tort. Obviously, in private healthcare, the relationship between doctor and patient is contractual. The contract is then usually concluded with the clinic in which the treatment is provided. This also means that the substance of the contract, which has to be expressly concluded, becomes more important. Despite the private law character of the relationship between doctor and patient, public law still imposes certain duties on medical practitioners. These duties will often evolve around a duty to provide reasonable care—which is not too different from the duty imposed in contract or tort.

In general, it could be said that public law is mostly concerned with *ex ante* regulation of healthcare services. Private law, on the other hand, becomes relevant when something has gone wrong in the relationship between doctor and patient. The patient can then sue the doctor or healthcare provider in contract or in tort. Similarly, disciplinary law—which is difficult to place on the public law-private law spectrum—can also intervene *ex post*. While disciplinary proceedings are often started with a complaint from a patient, the character of the proceedings is less private in that the reputation of the medical profession as a whole is taken into account. Moreover, disciplinary proceedings are usually heavily regulated by public law. Certain Member States, such as Germany, have out-of-court dispute settlement procedures where liability disputes between medical practitioners and patients can be resolved without having to go through the court systems.[68]

What both public law and private law have in common in the healthcare sector is that they usually impose very broad and general obligations and duties on medical professionals and healthcare providers. These duties subsequently have to be defined more precisely. This specification of the duty of care of medical professionals—whether in public law or in private law—can be done *ex post* through judicial or disciplinary proceedings. A court will then be required to define the required standard of care. Alternatively, the required standard of care can be defined *ex ante* through some sort of standardisation. The healthcare sector is full of guidelines, standards and protocols. Some of these standards have been adopted at the international level, while others will be national. It is clear that, especially for scientific standards, there has been a process of internationalisation, which has frequently been encouraged by the United States.[69] This has also been recognised

[68] C Katzenmeier, 'Außergerichtliche Streitbeilegung in Arzthaftungssachen' (2008) 58 *Anwaltsblatt* 819. See also P Weidinger, 'Aus der Praxis der Haftpflichtversicherung für Ärzte und Krankenhäuser—Statistik, neue Risiken und Qualitätsmanagement' (2006) 10 *Medizinrecht* 571.

[69] N Cortez, above n 34, 669.

in the case law of the CJEU discussed above.[70] In many cases, the parties who are making medical standards draw from the same international scientific evidence. However, there is still a broad margin of appreciation in the interpretation of this evidence which can result in the adoption of different standards at the national level.[71] Such standards can apply to hospitals or to individual medical specialists. They will have a different status in medical practice, but in general they are not directly binding in law. They are used to define and specify the requirements imposed on healthcare service providers in public as well as private law.

C. European Standardisation in National Regulation of Healthcare Services

The link from national healthcare standardisation to European standardisation through CEN is then easily made. European standardisation could be one way of specifying the required duty of care of medical professionals in public or private law. However, this is where some caution is required. The way in which the Member States have organised medical standardisation differs significantly. Because of a lack of expertise of the public administration, it is understandable that medical professionals have to be closely involved in the standardisation process. However, the extent to which they are autonomous in the standard-setting process depends on the Member State in question. In some Member States, such as the United Kingdom, medical standardisation is strictly controlled by the State.[72] Although it will always be doctors who define the standards, they are brought to work in a standardisation framework which is strictly publicly supervised. This means that such standardisation is not really private regulation, but more co-regulation under public supervision. The intention behind this is that self-regulation cannot exclusively be relied on to produce outcomes which are beneficial to the public good.[73] There has to be public accountability and control.[74] Therefore, the State is in control of the organisation of the process and of the incorporation and application of the standards in the healthcare sector. Public supervisory agencies act on the basis of these standards, or even on the basis of standards which they have made themselves.[75]

[70] *Geraets-Smits* and *Peerbooms*, above n 25.

[71] N Cortez, above n 34, 656–57. See also R Blank and V Burau, 'Setting Health Priorities Across Nations: More Convergence than Divergence?' (2006) *27 Journal of Public Health Policy* 265 and T Marmor, R Freeman and K Okma, 'Comparative Perspectives and Policy Learning in the World of Health Care' (2005) 7 *Journal of Comparative Policy Analysis* 331.

[72] For a comparative perspective, see D Ngo et al (eds), *Supervising the Quality of Care in Changing Healthcare Systems: An International Comparison*, Department of Healthcare Governance, Erasmus University Rotterdam, August 2008. For the UK perspective, see E Scrivens, *Quality, Risk and Control in Health Care* (Maidenhead, Open University Press, 2004) and G Bevan, 'Changing paradigms of governance and regulation of quality of healthcare in England' (2008) 10 *Health, Risk and Society* 85.

[73] E Scrivens, above n 72, 139–40.

[74] K Syrett, 'Nice Work? Rationing, Review and the 'Legitimacy' Problem in the New NHS' (2002) 10 *Medical Law Review* 1. See also E Scrivens, above n 72, 120–27.

[75] For an example in the UK, see the Care Quality Commission: www.cqc.org.uk.

This public responsibility for medical standardisation cannot be seen in all Member States. For example, in the Netherlands, much more reliance is placed on the medical profession itself, without too much supervision or hierarchy. It is strongly believed that the medical profession itself should be responsible for the making of standards in the healthcare sector.[76] Public supervisory agencies will rely on these standards in their supervisory activities, but they exercise no influence on the making of them. As a consequence, the Dutch system clearly recognises the autonomy of the medical profession in deciding when, how and which standards have to be set. However, it has also become clear that the profession itself cannot be entirely relied on to make sufficient and adequate medical standards. Therefore, the Netherlands has now introduced a Quality Institute for Healthcare.[77] This Institute will not get involved in the actual standard-making process, but it will set out how medical standards should be made and it will provide a public stamp of approval to standards that have complied with their requirements. Moreover, the Institute has been granted the power to force the medical profession to start working on a standard if it considers it necessary that a standard be developed.[78] As such, the Institute could issue a 'top-down' mandate to the profession, which would be similar to Commission mandates in the New Approach. However, the Institute would not get involved in the actual substance for the standard—this would remain within the control of the medical profession.[79] If the Dutch system is compared with the UK system, it is clear that there is a difference in professional autonomy in the two countries. In the UK, the standardisation process is tightly controlled and supervised by public authorities, which are also involved in the standardisation process. As a result, the medical standards that are developed will take more interests into account than just the purely medical scientific issues. This is not necessarily the case in the Netherlands, where medical standardisation remains primarily a scientific evidence-based exercise. The subsequent policy questions which have an inevitable impact on medical practice are not directly dealt with in the standardisation process.

Overall, the lesson which should be learnt from the national systems is that there are significant differences in the extent to which Member States allow private regulation to play a role in the regulation of healthcare services. This is not the same as the scope of private law—private law will always have a role to play through contract law and tort. However, certain Member States have created very public structures of medical standardisation. This might mean that European standardisation of healthcare services, which essentially remains private regulation,

[76] Interview with Quality Institute for Healthcare (Diemen) on 23 August 2012. For the Dutch perspective, see Regieraad Kwaliteit van Zorg, *Een Visie op Richtlijnontwikkeling in Nederland*, The Hague, April 2010. See also J van Everdingen et al (eds), *Evidence-based richtlijnontwikkeling: een leidraad voor de praktijk*, (Houten, Bohn Stafleu, 2004).

[77] Quality Institute for Healthcare: www.zorginstituutnederland.nl/kwaliteit/het+kwaliteitsinstituut.

[78] Interview with Quality Institute for Healthcare (Diemen) on 23 August 2012.

[79] ibid.

might not easily be accepted in these Member States. As a result, one has to look at the scope of private regulation at the national level. If the scope of private regulation is limited, this could result in Member States objecting to European standardisation. This would be likely to have an impact on whether or not they approve European standardisation projects. Consequently, it would be more likely to have an impact on the making of European standards than on their application. However, this would also depend on the question to what extent public authorities get involved in (blocking) European standardisation initiatives in the healthcare sector. This is something that will be discussed in the next section.

III. THREE CASE STUDIES ON EUROPEAN STANDARDISATION OF HEALTHCARE SERVICES

A. Aesthetic Surgery Services

In April 2010, a European standardisation process for Aesthetic Surgery Services was started through CEN. The initiative had been submitted by a number of Austrian plastic surgeons to the Austrian Standards Institute ('ASI'), which was also to act as secretariat to the standardisation process.[80] Two key reasons for the standardisation project can be identified. First of all, aesthetic surgery has become a highly profitable market. This is also clear from the PIP breast implants case, which will be discussed below. Aesthetic surgery is usually provided by private healthcare providers outside the public healthcare system. There is a significant amount of advertisement; treatments are voluntary and easy to obtain. This means that the patient is not really a patient but more of a consumer.[81] This consumer is prepared to travel across borders for treatment. As a result, it is possible to say that aesthetic surgery takes place in a market which is somewhat removed from the traditional public healthcare systems. Furthermore, the market is truly European, or even international. Secondly, the medical professionals which operate on this market have very different qualifications. Various medical specialties perform treatments which could be described as aesthetic surgery. Plastic surgeons are the main specialty that has entered the aesthetic surgery market, but dermatologists, ENT–surgeons and even general practitioners also operate on the market.[82] Moreover, it is possible for doctors with basic training to be involved in aesthetic surgery. In some Member States it is even possible for nurses to perform aesthetic surgery.[83] As a consequence, the market is full of different service providers. Some do not have a fixed location and travel from one Member State to another with their products

[80] Interview with Chairman of Dutch Mirror Committee for Aesthetic Surgery Services (Goes) on 29 December 2012.

[81] ibid.

[82] ibid.

[83] ibid and Interview with ASI (Vienna) on 12 November 2012.

and materials.[84] Some of them have decided to call themselves cosmetic surgeons, which in many Member States is not a protected title.[85] This could create confusion for patients, as the use of the term surgeon would imply specialist training as a surgeon. This is just one example of a lack of regulation of aesthetic surgery services at the national level. The only Member State which has a very clear regulatory framework is France, in which it is provided by law that all aesthetic surgery treatments have to be performed under the supervision of a plastic surgeon.[86] In Denmark, medical professionals who want to get involved in aesthetic surgery first have to receive certification.[87] Following the PIP breast implants scandal, the cosmetic surgery sector has come under the attention of national regulatory agencies which, in co-operation with the EU, are working to fill regulatory gaps and to tighten the regulation of the aesthetic surgery sector.[88] The European standardisation process also seeks to play a role in this regulatory framework. However, one could wonder to what extent the European standardisation initiative has already been overtaken by legislative initiatives at the national level, such as in the UK.[89]

Although the standardisation process covers the complete doctor–patient relationship—including, for example, issues such as consent—its main focus is twofold. Firstly, the European standard intends to regulate which medical professionals can perform which treatments. It introduces a number of competences that medical professionals must have obtained before they can perform certain treatments.[90] The standard has a list with treatments, which have all been given a certain risk factor. Treatments with a higher risk factor can only be performed by medical professionals with more advanced training and experience. Second, the standard sets out what facilities a medical professional must have before certain treatments can be performed.[91] A distinction is made between treatments that can be performed in a treatment room and treatments that require an operating theatre. As such, the standard would prevent doctors from treating consumers at their home. Treatment would have to be provided at a location with a certain minimum of facilities. Overall, the focus of the European standard is on the 'by whom' and 'where' of aesthetic surgery services. The standard does not directly deal with the 'how' of aesthetic surgery.[92] As a result, those who are involved in

[84] ibid.
[85] ibid.
[86] ibid.
[87] ibid.
[88] ibid.
[89] In the UK, a report was published by a Commission chaired by Sir Bruce Keogh: www.gov.uk/government/uploads/system/uploads/attachment_data/file/192028/Review_of_the_Regulation_of_Cosmetic_Interventions.pdf.
[90] Articles 3 and 7 of Draft prEN 16372:2012 'Aesthetic Surgery and aesthetic non-surgical medical services'.
[91] Articles 5 and 7 of Draft prEN 16372:2012 'Aesthetic Surgery and aesthetic non-surgical medical services'.
[92] Interview with Chairman of Dutch Mirror Committee for Aesthetic Surgery Services (Goes) on 29 December 2012 and Interview with ASI (Vienna) on 12 November 2012.

the standardisation process seek to distinguish this standard from evidence-based medical standards, which would set out how specific treatments have to be performed on the basis of scientific evidence.[93] According to them, a distinction should be made between standardising the medical procedure and the medical process.[94] This standard only deals with the process. This does not mean that the standard should not be based on sound medical evidence—however, it is different in nature from evidence–based medical standards. Those who oppose European standardisation argue that the very inclusion of certain aesthetic surgery treatments in the standard already requires scientific evidence and that the standard might appear to justify certain treatments for which there is no legitimate basis in scientific evidence.[95]

Twenty-two Member States are involved in the standardisation process.[96] They all have created national mirror committees to be able to represent the national positions at the European level. In addition, a number of international and European organisations are participating with liaison status. This means they participate in the meetings, but they have no active voting rights. Certain sections of UEMS—committees representing a particular medical specialty—also participated in the meetings. However, they did so without the explicit support of UEMS and, after the draft standard had been published in May 2012, it became clear that UEMS would withdraw any (implicit) support of the standardisation process.[97] It also asked CEN to refrain from referring to UEMS syllabi or other documents in the European standard.[98] This was the first public opposition to the standard. However, there had already been significant tensions in the standardisation process. They were mainly caused by the different positions of the stakeholders in the various Member States—both of the medical profession and the various public bodies involved in the supervision of the healthcare sector. These positions were highly dependent on the national regulatory frameworks. Because France already has legislation in place that provides that only plastic surgeons can provide aesthetic surgery services, the French position in the standardisation process has been to protect the French legislation.[99] This has primarily been done by ensuring a significant amount of a-deviations, which clarify which aspects of the European standard might not comply with the French legislation.[100] This is a fundamentally different position from ensuring that aesthetic surgery services are adequately regulated by creating a good quality standard. A similar position has been taken

[93] ibid.
[94] ibid.
[95] Interview with UEMS and CPME (Warsaw) on 19 February 2013.
[96] Interview with ASI (Vienna) on 12 November 2012.
[97] Interview with ASI (Vienna) on 12 November 2012.
[98] Letter sent by UEMS to CEN on 22 May 2012.
[99] Interview with ASI (Vienna) on 12 November 2012.
[100] Interview with Chairman of Dutch Mirror Committee for Aesthetic Surgery Services (Goes) on 29 December 2012.

by Denmark and Germany.[101] The UK, the Netherlands and Austria have been the main supporters of the standard and have provided most of its input.[102]

A draft standard was published in early 2012.[103] After the various comments had been received, it became clear in September 2012 that the standard would not have sufficient support—the required 71% of the votes—to be adopted.[104] A period of reflection was started. It was decided to make a clearer distinction between aesthetic surgery services and non-surgical aesthetic services. A new draft standard was published in December 2012,[105] which required a new CEN enquiry which took place until May 2013. The new comments were resolved in September 2013. However, it was not until October 2014 when the final vote took place. The standard was formally adopted in December 2014 and is now available through the national standardisation organisations.

From the start, European medical associations have been vehemently opposed to the standardisation process. Their opposition is based on, on the one hand, criticism of the suitability of European standardisation through CEN as a regulatory tool in the healthcare sector and on the other hand, on specific concerns about the standardisation process for aesthetic surgery services.[106] In early 2011, the President of the Comité Permanent de Médicins Européens ('CPME') visited CEN to express the strong view of his organisation that CEN should not enter the healthcare sector.[107] He considered it undesirable for CEN to enter a field which should remain in control of the medical profession. In September 2012, a common position was adopted by a number of European medical associations which rejected the possibility of standardisation through CEN in the healthcare sector.[108] The concerns were threefold.[109] First, the standardisation process of CEN was fundamentally incompatible with traditional methods of medical standardisation based on scientific evidence. It would open up the possibility of non-medical concerns having an impact on the standardisation process, which would not result in optimum medical care. Such standardisation would endanger the autonomy of the medical profession. Secondly, it would not be compatible with the principle of subsidiarity. Thirdly, it would be in breach of the explicit rejection of EU competence to regulate healthcare services in Article 168 TFEU. The latter two objections do not appear to be legally correct, as they are based on a misunderstanding of CEN's role at the European level and the legal status of standardisation. However,

[101] ibid.

[102] ibid.

[103] Draft prEN 16372:2011 Aesthetic Surgery Services.

[104] Interview with Chairman of Dutch Mirror Committee for Aesthetic Surgery Services (Goes) on 29 December 2012.

[105] Draft prEN 16372:2012 Aesthetic Surgery and aesthetic non-surgical medical services.

[106] Interview with UEMS and CPME (Warsaw) on 19 February 2013.

[107] Interview with CEN (Brussels) on 4 April 2012 and Interview with UEMS and CPME (Warsaw) on 19 February 2013.

[108] Joint Resolution Standards in Medical Practice (14 September 2012).

[109] ibid.

the medical associations argued that there is a strong top-down element to the standardisation process and that it would be likely that the European standard would be made legally binding in one way or another.

These general concerns were supplemented by specific concerns about the standardisation process for Aesthetic Surgery Services. The first concern was that the standardisation process had insufficient procedural safeguards to ensure that the standards that would be set would be based on sound scientific evidence.[110] The European standardisation process could be abused to provide a sense of medical legitimacy to aesthetic surgery treatments that were not, in fact, evidence-based.[111] Furthermore, the standardisation process and its revision process were too slow to ensure that the standard would always be based on up–to–date medical evidence. The second concern was that the standardisation process would be used to establish aesthetic surgery as a separate medical specialty.[112] This had previously been tried through UEMS, but UEMS had resisted and refused to recognise aesthetic surgery as a separate specialty.[113] The result of this could be that European standardisation would now be used to achieve the same result and essentially to engage in some sort of market protection and restriction of the market by reserving treatments to this new quasi-specialty. It would provide a route to a small group of medical doctors to restrict the aesthetic surgery market to a limited group of doctors.[114]

B. Cleft Lip Surgery Services

In December 2010, BDS, the Bulgarian standardisation organisation, submitted a proposal to CEN for a European standard on Cleft Lip Surgery.[115] The initiative was submitted to BDS by the European Cleft Organisation ('ECO'), a European patient organisation which seeks to promote high-quality medical care for babies born with cleft lips throughout Europe. It had specifically chosen BDS as the standardisation organisation to administer the process, since this would help to raise awareness for the standardisation process in the new Member States.[116]

ECO is a European organisation for cleft patients throughout Europe. The organisation is run by a group of cleft patients and medical doctors. Its main aim is to ensure that there are minimum standards for cleft lip treatment in all EU Member States. It recognises that standards of care are widely divergent in the EU, but it argues that all EU citizens should be entitled to a minimum level of care.[117]

[110] Interview with UEMS and CPME (Warsaw) on 19 February 2013.
[111] ibid.
[112] ibid.
[113] ibid.
[114] ibid.
[115] BT N 8561- (Draft Resolution BT C4/2011), Issue date: 2011-01-13.
[116] Interview with ECO (Skype) on 14 March 2012.
[117] ibid.

Its position is that this minimum level of care is not provided in all EU Member States.[118] It is dissatisfied with the quality of care provided in certain Member States, in particular Bulgaria and Romania. To remedy this, ECO is involved in the training of medical specialists and nursing personnel in a number of new Member States.[119] It has developed and co-ordinated training programmes. There are very few standards on cleft lip treatment in these Member States and the level of research is much less advanced than in some of the older Member States. For these reasons, ECO believed that it would be good to have a European standard that would set out the minimum level of care required for patients with cleft lips.[120] Cross-border movement of patients is not a realistic possibility for babies born with clefts. Because of a lack of financial resources, patients in the new Members are not able to travel to the old Member States for treatment.[121] In addition, babies born with clefts need a series of treatments, which would make cross-border movement for treatment difficult—if not impossible. For that reason, the Cross-Border Healthcare Directive 2011 is not of much practical help. A European standard could help to raise the overall level of care throughout the EU. Furthermore, it would empower patients to require a certain level of care from the doctors in their home Member State.

The aims of the standardisation initiative were clearly put in the proposal submitted to CEN in December 2010:

> The benefits of standardisation in this field will be the establishment of a clear and accurate specification of the healthcare management process for infants born with clefts. A European Standard will help to reduce the health inequalities in the EU countries and support patients' safety.[122]

For some time, ECO had thought about which route could best be taken to develop such a standard. As a patient organisation, it was in a more difficult position than associations of medical doctors, which have traditionally been involved in the making of their own evidence–based standards for medical treatment. The route a patient organisation had to take if it wanted to initiate a standard on cleft lip treatment was not immediately clear. One of the members of ECO's board was a surgeon in the United Kingdom who had previously been involved in the creation of standards for medical devices through CEN.[123] As a result, the attention of ECO was drawn to CEN. In the end, ECO decided that a standardisation process through CEN would be a suitable means to achieve its aim of realising a minimum level of care in all EU Member States.[124]

[118] ibid.
[119] ibid.
[120] ibid.
[121] ibid.
[122] BT N 8561–(Draft Resolution BT C4/2011), Issue date: 2011-01-13.
[123] Interview with ECO (Skype) on 14 March 2012.
[124] ibid.

ECO was very much aware that this was an experimental process, but for three reasons it considered a standardisation process through CEN to be particularly worthwhile. Firstly, the standardisation process would bring together at the European level various stakeholders involved in cleft care. The standard would derive a sense of authority from this consensus-based process.[125] At the time of the initiative there were too many standards throughout Europe, none of which had particular authority over other standards. CEN would provide a mechanism to develop a standard that would potentially be authoritative in all Member States. Secondly, the standard would help to create a degree of consistency. Although ECO would never claim that there should be one uniform treatment process provided to all cleft patients in the EU, there should at least be consensus about the minimum level of care which has to be provided to all patients.[126] Thirdly, and finally, ECO recognised that a CEN standard would not override national legislation. As such, the fact that national legislation would be very different in the various Member States would not cause any direct difficulties.[127]

The care of babies born with cleft lips is not a market. Unlike aesthetic surgery, cleft lip care is still very much provided by public hospitals as part of public healthcare systems. Therefore, it could be expected that cleft care can more easily be exclusively regulated by the medical profession through traditional methods of medical standardisation based on scientific medical evidence. However, it is apparent from this initiative that, from the perspective of a European patient organisation, there are significant differences in knowledge and expertise within the Member States. The proposal for a European standard involved the linking of national structures of medical standardisation through opening up national medical standardisation to a European market. CEN would be used as a catalyst for this process.

After the submission of the proposal to CEN, the national standardisation organisations had to consult with their stakeholders. These meetings took place in early 2011 and in April 2011 all national standardisation organisations voted on the proposal.[128] Five Member States voted against the proposal, while fifteen Member States voted in favour. Eleven Member States abstained. Because of CEN's weighted voting procedures the proposal was rejected. The Member States that voted against the proposal were Finland, France, Germany, the Netherlands and Spain.[129] Broadly speaking, three categories of objections can be identified: (i) healthcare services provided in public healthcare systems should be regulated by the State without interference of private regulation; (ii) European standards would lower the level of care provided in some of the old Member States; (iii) European

[125] ibid.
[126] ibid.
[127] ibid.
[128] Voting Results: "*Creation of a new CEN Project Committee on 'Healthcare services for cleft lip and/or palate*'", CENBT/8561, Brussels, April 2011.
[129] ibid.

standardisation would not be the right mechanism to create standards for healthcare services.

After the negative vote, ECO organised a number of meetings in France and Spain to increase the support for a European standardisation process in late 2011 and early 2012.[130] In May 2012 it became clear that, after some additional meetings with national stakeholders, there would still not be sufficient support to start a European standardisation process.[131] ECO then considered the possibility of creating a Workshop Agreement through CEN. This would not have the same status as a European standard, but could potentially be a first step towards a European standard. However, even the possibility of a Workshop Agreement was (informally) rejected by a number of standardisation organisations.[132] As an alternative, ECO decided to develop a Technical Report through CEN, using ASI as the secretariat.[133] The first meeting was held in Vienna in September 2013. A Technical Report does not have the same status as a European standard—it is even softer than a European standard—but it can still be used to lay down standards for services. In May 2015, the Technical Report was finally adopted.[134]

C. PIP Breast Implants[135]

The third case study in this chapter is the PIP breast implants scandal. It is not directly concerned with European standardisation of healthcare services. Breast implants are considered medical devices and come within the scope of the New Approach. However, because they are closely linked to aesthetic surgery services and form an important part of the next chapters, an introduction to the role of European standardisation in the PIP breast implants scandal will be provided in this chapter.

In recent decades, breast implants have become a very popular product for women throughout the world. The PIP factory, located in France, was one of the main producers of breast implants in Europe, and possibly even in the World. It started producing breast implants in the early 1990s. At some point in the early 2000s, PIP started having financial difficulties and decided to develop an ingenious strategy to cut costs. Instead of filling the breast implants with the required medical silicone gel, PIP started to use industrial sub-standard industrial silicone

[130] Interview with ECO (Skype) on 14 March 2012.

[131] Interview with ECO (Skype) on 2 May 2012.

[132] E-mail correspondence with ECO on 14 March 2013.

[133] E-mail correspondence with ECO on 8 April 2013.

[134] Technical Report on care services for babies born with cleft lip and/or palate (CEN/TR 16824:2015).

[135] This case study is based on an article that has been published in the European Journal of Risk Regulation: B van Leeuwen, 'PIP Breast Implants, the EU's New Approach for Goods and Market Surveillance by Notified Bodies' (2014) 3 *European Journal of Risk Regulation* 338.

gel in the production process. This was obviously significantly cheaper. Unfortunately, it is still unclear how systematic the use of sub-standard industrial silicone gel was—it seems that certain badges of PIP implants contained only the required medical gel, while others contained a mix or only industrial gel. The randomness of the production process has made it much more difficult to identify risks and has led to significant delay in taking action against PIP.

In any event, sub-standard PIP breast implants were distributed throughout the EU for a significant period of time. In 2009, the first concerns that the breast implants might be defective were raised in France.[136] However, it was not until 2011 that the French public supervisory agency responsible for medical devices, AFSSAPS,[137] issued a warning and PIP breast implants were taken off the market. By that time, many thousands of women had already received PIP breast implants. They were faced with great uncertainty—there was no way for them to find out whether the breast implants that they had received were sub-standard. Sometimes it was not even possible for them to be sure whether or not their implants had been produced by PIP.[138] Furthermore, a medical report that had been written at the request of the European Commission stated that although the PIP breast implants might have a higher risk of rupture, it could not be proved that there were any particular health risks associated with the higher risk of rupture (such as a higher risk of cancer).[139] Faced with this uncertainty, many women decided to have their breast implants removed. In some situations, the removal of the breast implants was covered by their health insurance. However, most of the time, health insurers—whether public or private—refused to pay the removal costs if the original decision to have breast implants was based purely on aesthetic reasons and not on a medical indication.[140] Some cosmetic surgery clinics offered to remove the breast implants at cost price or even for free. However, they would still require women to pay for the costs of new breast implants. As a consequence, many women had to pay a significant amount of money as a result of having received—or possibly having received—defective breast implants. Moreover, there was a possibility of psychological harm. For all of these reasons, it is understandable that women wanted to seek legal redress.

To be able to understand the various litigation strategies that have been pursued since the PIP breast implants scandal, it is important to understand the regulatory

[136] Judgment of Tribunal de Commerce in Toulon of 14 November 2013 (N° de rôle: 2011F00517).

[137] Agence française de sécurité sanitaire des produits de santé, which is now called the Agence Nationale de Sécurité du Médicament et des Produits de Santé.

[138] Interview with VKI (Vienna) on 5 November 2013.

[139] European Commission, Scientific Committee on Emerging and Newly Identified Health Risks, 'Preliminary Opinion on the safety of Poly Implant Prothèse (PIP) Silicone Breast Implants (2013 update)', September 2013, http://ec.europa.eu/health/scientific_committees/emerging/docs/scenihr_o_038.pdf.

[140] Interview with VKI (Vienna) on 5 November 2013.

framework in which the breast implants were marketed and distributed. The regulatory framework of the New Approach has been introduced in chapter three. Breast implants are considered medical devices and as such, come within the New Approach.[141] The Medical Devices Directive[142] lays down the essential requirements which breast implants have to fulfil,[143] while the specific technical requirements have been laid down in a European standard adopted through CEN.[144] Before medical devices can be placed on the market, the manufacturer must attach the CE marking to goods and issue a declaration of conformity, declaring that the goods comply with the provisions of the Directive—and necessarily, of the European standard.[145] A notified body then has to inspect the manufacturer's quality system and design dossier.[146] Each Member State has to notify to the European Commission which bodies can fulfil this role in their country—hence the term 'notified body'. Once a notified body has approved the quality system and design dossier the product can be placed on the market. The notified body will then continue to undertake regular surveillance of the quality system.[147] In the case of PIP, the notified body was TÜV Rheinland, a large German certification body. It is not necessary for a manufacturer to obtain the approval of a notified body in their own Member State—it is possible to choose a notified body in another Member State. The conformity assessment by the notified body focuses solely on the quality system and the design of the product. Therefore, there is no direct control of whether the medical devices actually comply with the specific provisions of the European standard. The assessment focuses exclusively on the quality system and the design dossier in place. In addition to the role of notified bodies, an important function is performed by national supervisory agencies, which are responsible for surveillance of the market.[148]

In a case like the PIP case, there are a number of parties a case could be brought against to claim damages. The most probable defendant would be the PIP factory or its management. However, rather unsurprisingly, the PIP factory had gone into liquidation in 2010. Furthermore, the owners of the factory did not have any traceable assets and criminal proceedings were brought against the management of the factory before the Tribunal de Grand Instance in Marseille. In December 2013, the main owner of the factory, Jean Claude Mas, was sentenced to four years'

[141] Commission Directive 2003/12/EC on the reclassification of breast implants in the framework of Directive 93/42/EEC on medical devices.

[142] Council Directive 93/42/EEC concerning medical devices ('the Medical Devices Directive').

[143] Articles 3 and 5 and Annex I of the Medical Devices Directive.

[144] In this case, EN ISO 14630:2009 Non-active surgical implants—General requirements and EN ISO 14607:2009 Non-active surgical implants—Mammary implants—Particular requirements.

[145] Article 17 of the Medical Devices Directive.

[146] Article 11 and Annex XI of the Medical Devices Directive.

[147] Article 5.1 of Annex II of the Medical Devices Directive.

[148] Article 10 of the Medical Devices Directive.

imprisonment.[149] Therefore, bringing a case against the management also had little chance of success. Many victims joined the criminal proceedings as victims, which meant that they were able to claim compensation from a criminal compensation scheme developed by the French State.[150] Although compensation by this scheme is limited to 3000 Euros, it meant that the victims would obtain at least some redress.

In light of the difficulties in suing PIP or its management, different litigation strategies have been pursued in various Member States. The Austrian consumer organisation VKI has brought proceedings against Allianz, a German insurer with which PIP had obtained insurance.[151] As the insurance contract was concluded with the French subsidiary of Allianz, the proceedings have been brought in Paris by a French lawyer who is instructed by VKI. The claim has been brought on behalf of around 70 Austrian victims. A number of legal issues have to be decided first by the French court.[152] First of all, it is uncertain whether a valid insurance contract has been concluded between Allianz and PIP. Allianz submits that it had been deceived by PIP as to the nature of the product and the production process.[153] As a consequence, the insurance contract would be void. Secondly, Allianz claims that there is a clause in the contract which excludes residents outside France from the scope of the insurance contract. This would mean that the damage incurred by the Austrian victims would not be covered by the insurance contract.[154] The Paris court still has to decide these preliminary issues. In a separate judgment in 2012, the Tribunal de Commerce in Toulon held that the deceit by PIP did not invalidate the insurance contract between Allianz and PIP and that there was a valid insurance contract in place. However, it is clear that the case against Allianz remains complicated. An alternative strategy has been to sue TÜV Rheinland, the German certification company. A group of victims have brought proceedings against TÜV for its alleged failure to carry out the required surveillance and inspections at the PIP factory. The case has been brought in tort—it is claimed that TÜV has breached the duty of care which it owed to the women who received PIP breast implants. In the UK, claimants have started group litigation against a number of clinics and individual surgeons who had provided PIP breast implants to them. The litigation is based on the contract between the patients and the clinics in which they received the breast implants. It is claimed that the breast implants were not of satisfactory quality. Overall, different strategies have been pursued in various Member States. These strategies will be analysed in chapter six.

[149] Judgment of the Tribunal correctionel in Marseille of 10 December 2013, (N° minute: 7206/13), (N° parquet: 12048000148).

[150] Interview with VKI (Vienna) on 5 November 2013.

[151] ibid.

[152] ibid.

[153] ibid.

[154] ibid.

IV. THE INTERACTION BETWEEN EUROPEAN STANDARDISATION AND HEALTHCARE SERVICES

A. Traditional Evidence-Based Medical Standardisation and European Standardisation Through CEN

Medicine and standardisation is not a natural combination. Medical doctors are one of the traditional professions.[155] As a result, there is a very strong emphasis on the autonomy and integrity of the profession. Medical knowledge is made, maintained and developed within the medical profession, which has created its own structures to communicate and protect this knowledge.[156] External interference with these structures of knowledge is deemed to be an attack on the integrity of the profession. In addition, doctors place strong reliance on the individual nature of the relationship between doctor and patient. They have sworn the Hippocratic Oath, which means they must always act in the best interests of the individual patient. This is one of the founding pillars of medical practice. The primary 'standard' among medical doctors is that the interests of the individual patient should always prevail over existing standards or guidelines.

These two principles—professional autonomy and individualism—could appear to be fundamentally inconsistent with any kind of attempt to standardise medical practice. At the same time, doctors also recognise that it is in the interests of patients to share medical knowledge and to create medical standards with guidelines on best practice.[157] However, these standardisation activities are a special kind of standardisation and are based on two fundamental pillars.[158] Firstly, the development of medical standards should be in the exclusive control of the medical profession itself. The creation of medical standards is an evidence-based medical science for which only the medical profession has the necessary knowledge and experience. The inclusion of other, non-medical interests in the setting of medical standards would not be in the best interests of patients and would not result in the provision of optimum medical care.[159] Secondly, the standards developed by the medical profession should not obtain strict binding force. This is because they are always inferior to the primary standard among doctors—that the individual patient should be treated as an individual case and in their best interests. A doctor must always be able to reject a standard and to depart from a standard in the best interests of the individual patient.[160] The medical profession

155 E Freidson, *Profession of Medicine: A Study of the Sociology of Applied Knowledge* (Chicago, UCP, 1988).

156 Interview with UEMS and CPME (Warsaw) on 19 February 2013. See also E. Freidson, above n 155, 137–57.

157 ibid.

158 ibid. See also E Freidson, above n 155, 137–57.

159 ibid and interview with NEN (Delft) on 12 April 2012.

160 Interview with UEMS and CPME (Warsaw) on 19 February 2013. See J van Everdingen et al (eds), *Evidence-based richtlijnontwikkeling: een leidraad voor de praktijk* (Houten, Bohn Stafleu, 2004), 75–76.

has developed a principle for this: the 'comply or explain' principle. In principle, doctors are expected to comply with existing medical standards. There is a presumption of compliance. At the same time, it must always be possible for doctors to refuse to follow a particular standard in an individual case. However, there is a professional burden on the doctor to explain why the standard was not followed in the circumstances of the case.[161]

In the Cleft Lip Surgery example, the key problem is that there are many medical standards that deal with aspects of the treatment of babies born with cleft lips. There are both international, European and national standards for cleft lip treatment. This is the direct result of the fact that there is very little consensus about how babies with cleft lips should be treated. In Member States with less medical expertise, such as in Eastern Europe, this could lead to uncertainty about which guidelines should be applied and a preference for minimum standards that would reduce costs. Therefore, the European standardisation process through CEN is used as a facilitator to bring some order in the existing medical standards and to assist the new Member States with adopting a coherent and good quality guideline. CEN could help to provide substance to the concept of international scientific evidence developed by the CJEU.[162] However, at the same time, the process has shown that if there is insufficient agreement about the status of international science, it is unlikely that European standardisation will be successful. Although Bulgaria and Romania would benefit from more international input in medical standardisation, there are insufficient incentives for medical professionals in other Member States to export their international science to the new Member States. Furthermore, they do not believe that European standardisation through CEN would be the right way to do this, since the standardisation process through CEN does not have sufficient safeguards to guarantee that the standards which are produced are evidence-based.

The situation is different for Aesthetic Surgery Services. The problem there is that aesthetic surgery has emerged as a new field of medicine. Practitioners in this new sector do not feel bound by existing medical standards, because they do not cover their new specialty. The medical professional associations deny that there is a lacuna because they do not consider aesthetic surgery as a separate specialty—the sector is already sufficiently covered by medical standards for plastic surgery, ENT surgery and dermatology. From that perspective, European standardisation through CEN would be unnecessary and a threat to existing medical standards. At the same time, those in favour of the standardisation process argue that market forces have resulted in dangerous practices in the aesthetic surgery sector and that, with the traditional medical standardisation routes being blocked by the professional associations, European standardisation through CEN has become the

[161] See A Samanta, J Samanta and M Gunn, 'Legal Considerations of Clinical Guidelines' (2003) 96 *Journal of the Royal Society of Medicine* 133, 137.

[162] See A den Exter, above n 33.

only realistic alternative to impose some regulation on a sector which has *de facto* become self–standing.

With respect to methodology, most Member States or associations of medical professionals have developed methods to ensure that any medical standards are based on sound medical evidence.[163] This methodology has been adopted from institutes in the United States, which were frontrunners in the field of evidence–based medicine.[164] The medical standardisation process starts with a thorough search of the available medical literature on the topic of the standardisation. After this search, the participants in the standardisation process have to make a qualitative analysis of the literature. They have to decide, on the basis of their professional judgment, which studies are relevant and which studies are not relevant, and they have to decide which studies provide sufficient medical and scientific basis to serve as inspiration for the standardisation process.[165] It is expected that throughout the standard, references are made to the relevant literature. Furthermore, the standard has to explain how the literature supports the guidance, or why a particular study or strand of the literature has not been followed in the standard.[166] All of this means that scientific evidence plays a key role in medical standardisation. The parties that are involved in medical standardisation still need to reach consensus on the basis of the literature. They are also expected to use their professional judgment to decide on the weight of the literature. However, in the end, the consensus has to be based on scientific evidence. No such requirements exist for European standardisation through CEN. Although medical literature will play a role in the process, the process is inherently less scientific. The safeguards that exist in traditional medical standardisation do not exist in European standardisation.

This is readily acknowledged by participants in European standardisation processes in the healthcare sector—the evidence-based nature of the European standard for Aesthetic Surgery Services is rather slim.[167] Their response to any criticism is that European standardisation through CEN is a different kind of medical standardisation that does not focus on the medical procedure, but more on the entire process of the doctor–patient relationship.[168] The standards would not be about how the doctor should treat the patient, but more about the entire relationship between patient and doctor. This relationship involves many issues which are not scientific and which do not have to be evidence-based. The question of what information should be provided to patients and what facilities should be offered to patients does not (always) have to be evidence-based. Such European

[163] P Shekelle et al., 'Clinical Guidelines: Developing Guidelines' (1999) 318 *British Medical Journal* 593.

[164] J van Everdingen et al. (eds), above n 160, 14–15.

[165] P Shekelle, above n 163. See also J van Everdingen et al. (eds), above n 160, 145–157.

[166] J van Everdingen et al. (eds), above n 160, 158–171.

[167] Interview with Chairman of Dutch Mirror Committee for Aesthetic Surgery Services (Goes) on 29 December 2012 and Interview with ASI (Vienna) on 12 November 2012.

[168] ibid.

standards would then be supplementary, or additional, to evidence–based medical standards. However, the medical profession claims that it is never entirely possible to distinguish between procedure and process. Furthermore, such process–based standards have a direct impact on the medical procedure. There is a real risk that European standardisation could be used to circumvent traditional medical standardisation and to impose standards which could not realistically be made through traditional medical standardisation.[169] This is confirmed by some other recent European standardisation initiatives in the healthcare sector. The chiropractors were the first profession to make a healthcare services standard through CEN and the osteopaths quickly followed in their footsteps.[170] For these professions, European standardisation constitutes an attractive mechanism to provide a sense of professional legitimacy to healthcare services that are not evidence-based.[171] While this should not be a direct problem for the medical profession, it becomes more of a problem when the medical profession itself directly engages in European standardisation, such as in the Aesthetic Surgery Services project.

Another element of traditional medical standardisation that cannot easily be accommodated in the European standardisation process is authorisation. For evidence-based medical standards, authorisation, or verification, by the appropriate medical associations is a key requirement to the standard obtaining a status as the relevant professional standard.[172] This is both from the professional as well as from the legal point of view.[173] The standard must have been accepted by the profession as the appropriate standard before it comes into force in the sector. There is no such requirement for European standardisation. In fact, in the examples discussed above, the interaction between the European standardisation and the relevant medical associations was extremely tense. It is highly unlikely that authorisation would take place after the strong objections from within the medical profession. Therefore, it is less likely that the European standard will be applied in the regulation of healthcare services at the national level.

B. European Standardisation and De-Professionalisation of the Medical Profession

Closely linked to the discussion of the non-evidence-based nature of European standardisation is the argument that European standardisation would lead to

[169] Interview with UEMS and CPME (Warsaw) on 19 February 2013.

[170] EN 16224: 2012 Healthcare Provision by Chiropractors, and EN 16686: 2016 Osteopathic service provision.

[171] See H Willensky, 'The Professionalization of Everyone' (1964) 70 *American Journal of Sociology* 137.

[172] J van Everdingen et al. (eds.), above n 160, 210–19.

[173] See A Samanta et al., 'The Role of Clinical Guidelines in Medical Negligence Litigation: A Shift from the Bolam Standard?' (2006) 14 *Medical Law Review* 321.

de-professionalisation of the medical profession. This has become evident in the standardisation process for Aesthetic Surgery Services. There is a real fear among the medical profession that European standardisation would be used as a tool for anti-competitive protectionism. This is particularly caused by the fact that aesthetic surgery services are provided in a market. Such protectionism would reduce medicine to all other services that are exposed to market forces. It would place medicine on the same level as those services regulated by the Services Directive 2006.[174] However for parties like UEMS and CPME, this is no justification to allow aesthetic surgery to escape the traditional methods of medical standardisation. This is because treatments will still be provided by medical doctors who should be bound by professional and ethical obligations.[175] Professionalisation requires that doctors operating on a market should not abandon their professional hat and simply change it for a business hat. The fact that treatments might be subject to market forces is not sufficient to allow them to use European standardisation.

The nature of the European standardisation process facilitates de-professionalisation—not only because of the lack of scientific evidence, but also because all interested parties can freely participate. This has resulted in a difficult paradox in the European standardisation process for Aesthetic Surgery Services. The process has been started to regulate the competence of medical professionals on the market and to increase transparency in a market where many providers with different qualifications are operating. The Chairman of the Dutch mirror committee for Aesthetic Surgery Services described this situation as a market with 'good guys and bad guys'.[176] Traditional medical standardisation has been unable to deal with this situation.[177] As a consequence, it is legitimate to escape these structures of medical standardisation to attempt to find a solution through external mechanisms such as CEN. This has to be done in order to protect the integrity of the medical profession itself. In order to do this, they have to surrender part of their professionalisation by sitting around the table with practitioners who are acting as pure market players and who are also able to participate in the European standardisation process. Sometimes these practitioners are not even medical professionals—they often do not have the necessary qualifications to do what they are doing and they do not feel bound by professional or ethical obligations. In order to reach agreement with these practitioners, the more traditional medical professionals have to abandon some of their own professionalisation. At the same time, the dialogue with the market players is used to attempt to impose a process

[174] Interview with UEMS and CPME (Warsaw) on 19 February 2013. See also H Willensky, above n 171.

[175] Interview with UEMS and CPME (Warsaw) on 19 February 2013. See also E Freidson, above n 155, 305–08.

[176] Interview with Chairman of Dutch Mirror Committee for Aesthetic Surgery Services (Goes) on 29 December 2012.

[177] ibid.

of professionalisation on them. That could again be considered as an ultimate indication of professionalism. It would mean that 'the bad guys' would no longer be able to perform certain treatments, or at least that the standard would reject the possibility of these treatments being performed by them. This professional starting point will always result in a compromise, but at least the underlying intention has been to approach professionalisation as closely as possible.

C. The Role of Public Authorities and the Protection of National Legislation in European Standardisation

Another important aspect of European standardisation in the healthcare sector is to what extent public authorities play a role in it, and to what extent European standardisation is regarded as a threat to national regulatory frameworks for medical standardisation, which are under strict public control in a number of Member States. It has already been noted that these national regulatory frameworks are starting to open up to the market, which also means that European standardisation through CEN could become a more realistic possibility. Public authorities have to respond to this. The role of public authorities in the standardisation process for Aesthetic Surgery Services is important. In particular, the French position was very much based on the protection of national legislation.[178] The position of national public authorities was even more obvious in the Cleft Lip Surgery process. Here, the French Ministry of Health directly intervened to object to the standardisation process.[179] This position has been made more explicit in some of the comments that were made when the national standardisation organisations voted on the proposal for a Cleft Lip Surgery standard. In particular, the French position should be noted:

> Such a topic is considered as a very sensitive one linked to the patient safety. This is why in France the management of cleft lip and palate falls within the remit of the public authorities in charge of the health system, organised by dedicated regulations. Moreover, the production of recommendations for good practices that contribute to the continuous improvement of quality and safety of care is in the competence of an administrative and independent scientific authority (the Haute Autorité de Santé).[180]

This comment illustrates a 'competence justification' used by Member States to refuse to engage with European standardisation. There is no engagement with the substantive provisions of the proposed European standard. The simple existence of national regulatory competence is sufficient to reject the possibility of European

[178] ibid.
[179] Interview with ECO (Skype) on 14 March 2012.
[180] Voting Results: "*Creation of a new CEN Project Committee on 'Healthcare services for cleft lip and/or palate*'", CENBT/8561, Brussels, April 2011.

standardisation. In this particular example, the invoked clash is also framed as a clash between private regulation and public legislation. In that respect, it is important that France has in a way 'publicised' traditional medical standardisation by creating an authority and a public regulatory framework through which medical standards are made.

In France, the Haute Autorité de Santé ('HAS') is responsible for the supervision of the quality of healthcare services.[181] Although it is not strictly speaking a Government body, it is a public body on which the French State exercises significant influence. The French State appoints delegates to the Board of HAS. The majority of the budget of HAS comes from licence fees for the advertising of medication, grants from health insurers and from the French State. HAS is responsible for the supervision and certification of hospitals, individual doctors and for the development of scientific healthcare standards. These standards are developed within the organisational structure of HAS. The initiative for a standard can be taken by the Ministry of Health, scientific organisations or HAS itself. HAS can decide to outsource the making of a particular standard, but it will always remain fully responsible for the final instrument. Medical doctors are brought within the organisation to work in committees within HAS to develop standards. They will usually be joined by public officials and health economists. As a result, it can reasonably be concluded that the medical profession has surrendered at least some of its autonomy. At the same time, it should be noted that the medical profession has never been completely autonomous vis-à-vis the State and that the medical aspects of the standardisation process are likely to remain within the exclusive control of the medical profession.

The French comments provide evidence that the French State is able to impose its views on AFNOR, the French standardisation organisation. In an indirect way, this has an impact at the European level. It shows that an initiative for European regulation of a private nature does not take away the competence of the State to control regulation in the healthcare sector. If the co-operation between public and private parties in medical standardisation at the national level is hierarchical, this hierarchy will effectively be transplanted to the European level. This might be specific for the regulation of healthcare services, for which the State is still assuming the main responsibility at the national level. However, the French and Spanish reactions clearly show that if the regulation of a particular service is still vertically, or hierarchically, controlled by the State at the national level, this position can also be enforced at the European level. Essentially, what this means is that the CEN standardisation process is not sufficiently transnational to take matters out of the control of the State. The State is able to 'infiltrate' in the standardisation process and protect the hierarchical nature of national regulation. This is not the same for all Member States. For example, in the UK and in the Netherlands, the State,

[181] Haute Autorité de Sante: www.has-sante.fr/portail/jcms/c_1002212/fr/missions-de-la-has.

public bodies or agencies do not have the same influence on the national standardisation organisations.[182]

D. European Healthcare Standards Vis-à-Vis National Healthcare Standards

Finally, a common objection to European standardisation in the healthcare sector is the argument that European standards would be unnecessary or undesirable because there are already sufficient and adequate national standards. With the Cleft Lip Surgery proposal, some Member States took the position that there was no need for a European standard, since they already had national standards that were perfectly capable of guaranteeing good quality healthcare.[183] The creation of European standards would be a risk to these national standards, as it could result in the lowest common denominator. If there are Member States which feel a need for higher medical standards, these Member States would be happy to share their national standards with them. This position has been taken by Germany and the Netherlands.

The comments of the Netherlands were very clear:

> European standardization of healthcare services across Europe is unrealistic. Healthcare services for cleft lip and or palate in the Netherlands is aiming for optimal healthcare. Optimal healthcare might not be realistic (financially) for all individual countries. European standardization would most likely aim for an average level of healthcare. It is not of the interest of the Netherlands neither to develop nor to contribute to such a standard.[184]

This statement clearly expresses the fear that European standards would result in a lowering of national standards. A response to this objection could be that a European minimum standard would not mean that a higher national standard could no longer be used. The European standard would only provide the required minimum level of care. However, it would then be useless for Dutch stakeholders to participate and to contribute financially to the standardisation process. Moreover, the objection was based on a fear that public authorities, or health insurers, would use European standards to make them legally binding in their contact with healthcare providers.[185] A lower European standard would mean a reduction in costs. The use of European standards would then result in a lower level of care than the level of care provided on the basis of national standards. This would not be in the best interests of patients. An additional complication

[182] Interview with NEN (Delft) on 12 April 2012 and Interview with Chairman of Dutch Mirror Committee for Aesthetic Surgery Services (Goes) on 29 December 2012.

[183] Voting Results: '*Creation of a new CEN Project Committee on "Healthcare services for cleft lip and/or palate*"', CENBT/8561, Brussels, April 2011.

[184] ibid.

[185] Interview with NEN (Delft) on 12 April 2012.

is that in many Member States there are not even national medical standards for certain treatments. For example, although the Netherlands has managed to adopt a national standard for certain aspects of cleft care, most care is still provided on the basis of regional protocols.[186] Europeanisation of such standards would be in conflict with the principle of subsidiarity in healthcare and would threaten the individual or local nature of healthcare provision.

V. A PRELIMINARY CONCLUSION

The first section of this chapter showed that the European regulatory framework for healthcare services provides scope for European standardisation. In particular, the emphasis on information requirements in the Cross-Border Healthcare Directive means that European standardisation could regulate aspects of the doctor–patient relationship at the national level. However, this European regulatory framework does not necessarily match with national regulatory frameworks. It defers to national standards for medical treatment. With the various national differences in how these standards are made, it is unlikely that a European standard would play a uniform role in the regulation of healthcare services at the national level. This is primarily because the extent to which private regulation is allowed to play a role in the regulation of healthcare services is widely divergent across the EU. This is not something European standardisation could necessarily have an impact on. On the contrary, national cultures of standardisation could act as obstacles to European standardisation. This would be purely on the level of the standard-making, and not necessarily on the level of their application. It would not necessarily mean that European healthcare standards would not be applied in private law. However, the public law dominance in the making of healthcare standards is also likely to have a negative impact on the use of the standards in private law, because it limits their scope of application. Finally, the fact that there is limited scope for private regulation of healthcare services at the national level will result in very few private European standards being adopted. This is because Member States are likely to defend and reinforce their public dominance in medical standardisation at the European level.

Overall, two main problems with European standardisation of healthcare services can be identified. First of all, the European standardisation process is incompatible with evidence-based medical standardisation. Although it might be possible to incorporate elements of evidence-based standardisation in the process, the standardisation process through CEN is significantly more political than traditional medical standardisation. Decisions are taken on the basis of consensus among the various European participants. There is no guarantee in the process that this consensus reflects medical scientific evidence. Participants in European

[186] ibid.

standardisation would argue that they are working on a different, and additional, type of healthcare standards. However, this argument is not accepted by a majority of the medical profession. Moreover, there is a fear that European standardisation is used by outsiders—or even medical professionals themselves—as a justification to cut funding, or as a tool to protect and restrict the market for certain treatments. In addition, European standardisation could become an escape route to doctors or to pseudo-medical professions to provide a sense of public legitimacy to what they are doing. Whether or not this strong criticism of European standardisation by the medical profession is justified does not really matter. What matters is that it is a genuine concern which means that the medical profession is strongly opposed to European standardisation. Without the support of the medical profession and the various European medical associations, it is unlikely that European standardisation will become more prominent in the healthcare sector.

Secondly, European standardisation faces strong opposition from public authorities in the Member States. This is particularly true for those Member States in which public authorities are in strict control of medical standardisation. This hierarchical relationship between public and private regulation is subsequently protected at the European level. The result is that these Member States are likely to vote against European standardisation projects in the healthcare sector. Moreover, if a project is started, they will send representatives of the public authorities whose primary purpose is to protect national legislation. As a result, the participation of these Member States is not constructive. Moreover, there is a serious concern in the old Member States that any standards which are adopted through European standardisation will be lower than existing national standards. This is again a reason to refuse to engage with European standardisation of healthcare services. Although the European standard would not obtain binding force after its adoption, it would be useless for Member States and for stakeholders to participate in the creation of a standard that would be lower than their existing standard. The Cleft Lip Surgery proposal shows that European standardisation is not accepted as a tool for development aid for the new Member States. One of the reasons is that the funding of European standardisation has to come from the stakeholders themselves.

In conclusion, there are a number of serious obstacles to European standardisation of healthcare services. They are also reflected in today's reality—very few standards have been adopted, those standards that are in the process of being made face strong opposition both at the national and at the European level, and there are no indications that European standardisation is likely to become more prominent in the healthcare sector in the future. On that basis, it can be concluded that European standardisation of healthcare services remains both controversial and marginal.

5

European Standardisation of Tourism Services

THIS CHAPTER WILL focus on the tourism sector. While the regulatory framework for healthcare services at both European and national level is highly complicated and technical, the tourism sector is less strictly regulated. Moreover, in the tourism sector, private law has always played a more prominent role. The chapter has the same structure as chapter four. It starts with an analysis of the interaction between EU law and tourism services. Secondly, the national regulation of tourism services and the role of private law will be discussed. The chapter continues with two case studies: the European standard for Tourist Guide Training and the interaction between European standardisation and classification. It concludes with an analysis of the interaction between European standardisation and tourism services.

I. THE INTERACTION BETWEEN EU LAW AND TOURISM SERVICES

A. EU Competences in Tourism and EU Tourism Policy

The focus of this chapter is on tourists once they have arrived at their holiday destination. Since tourists normally have to travel some distance to their holiday destination, transport is an important element of tourism services. Since the EU is well aware of the implications of these activities for free movement, it has created an elaborated legal framework for transport services,[1] in particular for air transport.[2] This framework has been based on the specific competences of the EU in transport.[3] The standards of care expected from transport providers and the level of protection provided to travellers have been almost exhaustively laid down

[1] J Karsten, 'Travel and Tourism' in F Benyon (ed), *Services and the EU Citizen* (Oxford, Hart Publishing, 2013) 25–46.

[2] M Huttunen, 'The Development of the Air Transport Policy of the European Union from the Point of View of the Consumer: From the Creation of the Internal Market to the Regulation of Consumer Rights Proper' in F Benyon (ed), above n 1, 9–24. See also J Balfour, 'Air Transport: A Community Success Story?' (1994) 31 *CML Rev* 1025.

[3] Now found in Title VI of the TFEU: Articles 90–100 TFEU.

in European legislation. Because the legal framework is so well-developed at the European level, there is very limited scope and need for European standardisation. This is not the case for other core services related to tourism, such as hotel services or restaurant services. Here, the EU has for a long time not enjoyed any specific competence and most of the legal regulation of tourism services has been introduced at the national level by the Member States.

However, it should immediately be emphasised that, unlike patients in chapter four, tourists have always been likely to get involved in cross-border activity. This is simply based on the nature of tourism services. Although many tourists will travel to destinations within their own Member States, other tourists will travel across borders to their destinations. Therefore, tourism services are likely to engage issues of free movement of services between the EU Member States.[4] As a consequence, the EU's competence to improve and regulate the internal market becomes applicable. This also makes it possible for the Commission to issue mandates for European standardisation projects on tourism services. Although there has not been any specific EU competence in tourism until the adoption of the Treaty of Lisbon, its internal market competence has been used to regulate aspects of tourism services. The main example is the Package Travel Directive,[5] which will be discussed in detail below. Furthermore, if a comparison with healthcare services is made, the national regulation of tourism services is not so different and complicated that regulatory intervention by the EU is deemed undesirable. However, at the same time, tourism services are very context-specific and very diverse. In fact, diversity is one of the very reasons why tourists move across borders. As a result, it is important for the EU to respect subsidiarity and proportionality in the adoption of legislative or policy instruments. Although subsidiarity concerns would seem to be of minor importance to the transport sector, hotels and restaurants strive to distinguish themselves on the basis of national or even regional characteristics.[6] Cross-border movement in tourism takes place not because tourists expect to find similar standards or characteristics at their holiday destination—on the contrary, the attraction of tourism services is the difference between the various holiday destinations. Furthermore, the internet has made the tourism sector a much more transparent market in which customers are able to make informed choices.[7] From that perspective, regulatory intervention at the European level becomes less desirable. At the same time, it should be emphasised that diversity should not serve as an excuse to refuse to regulate safety aspects of tourism services. Consumer protection organisations claim that there should be a minimum safety level across the

[4] M McDonald (ed), *European Community Tourism Law and Policy* (Dublin, Blackhall Publishing, 2003) 135.

[5] Council Directive 90/314/EEC on package travel, package holidays and package tours.

[6] Interview with HOTREC (Brussels) on 29 November 2012.

[7] ibid.

EU which all service providers should respect.[8] The tension between harmonisation, diversity and safety is one with which the EU and stakeholders in the tourism sector have been struggling.

In addition to the inherent cross-border dimension of tourism services, it is also clear that the tourist is a consumer. Again, this is a fundamental difference with patients, who for a long time were not considered consumers. Tourists will pay for services at the destination of their holiday, or they might have bought a holiday package in their home Member State. In addition to the Package Travel Directive, which is very much an instrument to improve consumer protection, the Unfair Contract Terms Directive[9] and the Unfair Commercial Practices Directive[10] might also be applicable to tourism services. The tourist as a consumer is quite well-protected in the EU. However, it should be noted that this protection is primarily focused on information requirements and remedies in case of non-compliance. The primary focus is on the pre-contractual and post-contractual stage. The EU instruments do not really deal with the standards of care applicable at the destination of the holiday. As will be discussed below, the Package Travel Directive, for example, only provides that the organiser or retailer should be liable to customers for the proper performance of the contract.[11] The standards of care which are expected with respect to performance are not defined.[12] Here, European standardisation could play a role.

Finally, the Lisbon Treaty has introduced a specific complementary competence in the field of tourism. In the same article as the one where we find the EU competence in the field of public health, the EU is granted a competence to 'carry out actions to support, coordinate or supplement the actions of the Member States'.[13] Article 195 TFEU then provides that 'the Union shall complement the action in the tourism sector, in particular by promoting the competitiveness of Union undertakings in that sector'.[14] This will be done by 'encouraging the creation of a favourable environment for the development of undertakings in this sector'[15] and by 'promoting cooperation between the Member States, particularly by the exchange of good practice'.[16] As a result, Article 195 TFEU encourages the adoption of soft law in the tourism sector which increases the convergence in the regulation

[8] Interview with ANEC (Brussels) on 4 April 2012.

[9] Council Directive 93/11/EEC on unfair terms in consumer contracts.

[10] Directive 2005/29/EC of the European Parliament and of the Council concerning unfair business-to-consumer commercial practices in the internal market.

[11] Article 5(1) of the Package Travel Directive.

[12] European Parliament Policy Department, 'Study on Safety and Liability Issues Regarding Package Travel', IP/A/IMCO/ST/2007-14: www.europarl.europa.eu/meetdocs/2004_2009/documents/dv/999/999000/999000en.pdf. See also K Tonner, *Münchener Kommentar zum Bürgerlicher Gesetzbuch, Band 4: Schuldracht—Besondere Teil II* (München, CH Beck, 2012), §651f.

[13] Article 6(d) TFEU.

[14] Article 195(1) TFEU.

[15] Article 195(1)(a) TFEU.

[16] Article 195(1)(b) TFEU.

of tourism services at the national level.[17] The last part of Article 195 TFEU could be linked to the obligation imposed on the Commission in Article 26(5) of the Services Directive to improve the quality and compatibility of services through European standardisation. European standardisation could be one way to promote co-operation between Member States and to decide on good practice.

The specific EU competence in the field of tourism focuses primarily on tourism services from a macro-perspective. The emphasis is put on competitiveness, which is a rather general term. There is no indication that, through this specific competence, the EU will intervene in the private law relationship between tourism service providers and customers. Such private law intervention will be realised through its internal market or consumer law competences. As a result, the impact of the competence in Article 6 TFEU on private law would seem to be limited. This is confirmed by the Commission's Communication in 2010, in which it outlined the role of the EU in tourism policy.[18] Its aim is to ensure that Europe will remain 'the world's No. 1 tourist destination'.[19] To this end, it focuses on the development of a European heritage label, on more innovation in the field of ICT, on more co-ordination of information and on introducing mechanisms to measure consumer satisfaction.[20] Moreover, significant emphasis is placed on making European tourism more sustainable and ecologically friendly.[21] With the exception of consumer satisfaction mechanisms, these measures do not appear to be focused on the private law dimension of tourism services.

B. The Impact of the Case Law on Free Movement of Services on the Regulation of Tourism Services

As regards the impact of primary EU law on the regulation of tourism services, a distinction should be made between the impact on tourists and the impact on tourism services providers.

In the early years of the European Community, it was not clear whether tourists came within the scope of the free movement provisions. This was because it was uncertain whether tourists could be considered as economically active, which was a necessary requirement to benefit from the free movement rights.[22] After all,

[17] P Craig and G de Burca, *EU Law: Text, Cases and Materials* (Oxford, OUP, 2011) 86. See also E Grabitz, M Hilf and M Nettersheim (eds), *Das Recht der Europäischen Union*, (München, Beck, 2014) Titel XXII.

[18] Commission Communication, 'Europe, the world's No 1 tourist destination—a new political framework for tourism in Europe', COM(2010) 352 final.

[19] ibid, 2.

[20] ibid, 8–10.

[21] ibid, 10–12.

[22] M van der Woude and P Mead, 'Free Movement of the Tourist in Community Law' (1988) 25 *CML Rev* 117, 118.

moving to another Member State as a tourist is quite a different matter from moving to another Member State to take up employment there. The CJEU ruled on this question in *Luisi and Carbone*.[23] It held that tourists were recipients of services and came within the scope of the free movement provisions. In this case, Italian legislation provided for a cap on the amount of foreign currency that could be exported by individuals from Italy. The CJEU held that this constituted a restriction on the right of Italian tourists to enjoy tourism services abroad.[24] In both cases, the amounts of money which had been taken would have been used for travel purposes. Being able to take cash while abroad was considered as a necessary pre-condition for exercising the right to freely receive services in another Member State.

After tourists had been brought within the scope of the free movement provisions, the next question was exactly what rights they would enjoy. It is clear tourists should be allowed to enter another Member State—and, by analogy, to leave their own Member State—to receive tourism services there (right of entry) and that they should not be discriminated against on the ground of their nationality (right to non-discrimination).[25] The right to entry is now almost exhaustively regulated by the Citizen Rights Directive 2004,[26] which provides that EU citizens have an unqualified right to enter and to stay in another Member State for up to three months. Tourists will usually be covered by that provision. Therefore, the convergent effect of the Citizens Rights Directive is on the conditions for EU citizens to enter and to reside in another Member State. The provisions are primarily—if not exclusively—directed at the public authorities of the Member States that are responsible for immigration matters and border controls. As a result, they are unlikely to have an impact on convergence in private law.

With respect to the right to non-discrimination, it is clear that tourists are protected against discrimination on the grounds of nationality by public authorities.[27] However, it is another matter whether they are also protected against discrimination by tourism service providers. This would depend on the extent to which the actions of private parties are caught by the free movement provisions. If their actions were caught, this would have an impact on the contractual relationship between tourism service providers and tourists. On the basis of the CJEU's case law following *Walrave and Koch*,[28] it is likely that decisions or campaigns of associations or federations of tourism service providers come within the scope of the free movement provisions. From the perspective of convergence, it is important

[23] Joined Cases C-286/82 and C-26/83 *Luisi and Carbone* ECLI: EU: C:1984:35.

[24] ibid, para 37.

[25] M McDonald, above n 4, 144–45.

[26] Directive 2004/38/EC on the rights of citizens of the Union and their family members to move and reside freely in the territory of the Member States.

[27] M McDonald, above n 4, 135.

[28] Case C-36/74 *Walrave and Koch v Association Union cycliste internationale and others* [1974] ECR 1405.

to note that the convergent effect of regulation through a right to non-discrimination is minimal. It is mainly concerned with negative integration through the prohibition of discriminatory conduct or discriminatory legislative prohibitions. However, it does not make a positive case for the standards of care which tourists can expect—the only guarantee is that they can expect to be treated equally to other EU citizens.

The case law on the right to free movement of services has also had an impact on the qualifications of tourism service providers. The main example is a series of cases which were brought by the Commission against some Member States in the late 1980s.[29] In these cases, the Commission challenged the legality of national legislation that provided for specific requirements with which tourist guides had to comply if they wanted to offer their services to tourists in a particular Member State. In most of the cases, Member States required tourist guides to have passed a national exam or to have obtained a national licence. Tourist guides regularly travelled with a group of tourists from their own Member State to another Member State to provide guided tours at the holiday destination. A requirement to take a national exam or to obtain a national licence in the Member State of destination was a clear obstacle to the right of tourist guides to provide services in that Member State. The Member States attempted to justify this restriction to free movement by the need to ensure 'the proper appreciation of places and things of historical interest and the widest possible dissemination of knowledge of the artistic and cultural heritage of a country'.[30] While the CJEU accepted that this was a legitimate reason to restrict free movement, it was found to be disproportionate in all cases. The disproportionality was based on the fact that the requirements were much more likely to be fulfilled by local tourist guides, who enjoyed a competitive disadvantage.[31] As such, a licence or an exam would not be a suitable means to achieve the legitimate aim. Moreover, the CJEU held that, since the tourism market was highly competitive, the pressure from the competition in the market would be sufficient incentive for tour operators to ensure that tourist guides were adequately qualified to provide their services.[32] On that basis, strict legal requirements for qualifications were not necessary.

This series of cases essentially resulted in a liberalisation of the tourist guide profession. It provoked a counter-reaction from associations of tourist guides.[33] They decided to create a European standard for Tourist Guide Training through CEN. The standardisation project could be seen as a response to the negative integration

[29] Case C-154/89 *Commission v France (tourist guides)* ECLI: EU: C:1991:76; Case C-180/89 *Commission v Italy (tourist guides)* ECLI: EU: C:1991:78; Case C-198/89 *Commission v Greece (tourist guides)* ECLI: EU: C:1991:79; Case C-375/92 *Commission v Spain (tourist guides)* ECLI: EU: C:1994:109.

[30] *Commission v France (tourist guides)*, above n 29, para 17.

[31] ibid, para 19.

[32] ibid, para 20.

[33] Interview with the Guild, ITG and APTG (London) on 21 January 2014.

through the CJEU's law. The case law of the CJEU has now to a significant extent been superseded by the adoption of the Professional Qualifications Directive 2005.[34] Tourist guides are covered by the Directive. It provides that if a profession is regulated in the host Member State—where the tourist guide is offering their services—but not in the home Member State, the host Member State may not prevent professionals from offering their services if they have at least two years of prior experience in the previous ten years.[35] This prior experience cannot be tested by the host Member State—the only thing it can do is to ask the service provider to submit a declaration to that effect.[36] The tourist guide profession is regulated in 13 Member States and most of these Member States have adopted such a requirement.[37] The interaction between the Professional Qualifications Directive, the right to freely provide services in another Member State and the European standard adopted through standardisation will be discussed in detail in the case study below. For now, it should be noted that the case law of the CJEU resulted in negative integration, which was followed up by an approach based on mutual recognition in the Professional Qualifications Directive. Any possible European standardisation would interact with and would come within the scope of that regulatory framework.

C. The Impact of the Package Travel Directive 1990 on the Regulation of Tourism Services

Up to about 10 years ago, most tourists would make their travel arrangements through a travel agency. The travel agency would organise a combined package of travel and accommodation, sometimes even combined with specific services at the holiday destination (such as excursions). National legislation on package travel was widely divergent. As this was a truly European market, the regulatory divergence led to distortions of competition as well as to obstacles to the right of tourists to enjoy services in other Member States. This was detrimental to consumers, who were insufficiently protected. Therefore, already in the late 1980s, the Commission took the initiative for a Package Travel Directive, which would provide adequate protection to consumers who bought package holidays.[38] Since the regulatory diversity at the national level was considered to distort competition across the EU, the Package Travel Directive was eventually adopted on the basis

[34] Directive 2005/36/EC of the European Parliament and of the Council on the recognition of professional qualifications.

[35] Article 5(1)(b) of the Professional Qualifications Directive.

[36] Article 7(1) of the Professional Qualifications Directive.

[37] Commission, 'Performance Checks: State of Play in the Internal Market in the Tourism Sector', 1 9th December 2011: http://ec.europa.eu/internal_market/services/docs/services-dir/performance-check/tourism_en.pdf.

[38] Commission, 'Proposal for a Council Directive on Package Travel', COM(1988) final.

of the EU's internal market competence.[39] It covered a broad range of aspects related to the buying and enjoying of package holidays. It was clearly an instrument of positive integration, which provided in detail for a number of rights consumers enjoyed vis-à-vis the retailer of the package holidays or the organiser. As such, it intervened directly in the private law relationship between consumer and retailer or organiser. At the same time, the Package Travel Directive only constituted minimum harmonisation.[40] It was still possible for Member States to go over and beyond the minimum rights that had to be guaranteed under the Directive. Research by the Commission has shown that this is in fact what most Member States have done.[41]

The Package Travel Directive was one of the first instruments to improve consumer protection adopted by the EU. It was later followed by the Unfair Contract Terms Directive and the Unfair Commercial Practices Directive. Both these Directives are also applicable to tourism services, but the Package Travel Directive is sector-specific. However, as it was adopted in 1990, it does not really reflect the reality of the tourism market anymore. With the rise of the internet, tourists are no longer using travel agencies as frequently as they used to do.[42] Furthermore, various new types of packages have been created which do not come within the scope of the current Package Travel Directive.[43] For example, a number of airlines offer the possibility of adding accommodation or car hire to a flight ticket. Such customised holidays, also called combined travel arrangements, are not covered by the Package Travel Directive.[44] Many tourists mistakenly believe that they are covered by the protection of the Directive. Moreover, there is a significant amount of legal uncertainty as to which combinations are covered by the Directive and which are not. For that reason, the Commission issued a proposal for a new Package Travel Directive, which would also cover combined travel arrangements, in July 2013.[45] In addition to including the new customised holidays, the proposed Directive abolishes the requirement of a printed brochure.[46] Moreover, it provides that in cases of non-performance, it is only the organiser which is liable.[47] This should be easier for the tourist. If the organiser is located outside the EU, it is still

[39] Council Directive 90/314/EEC on package travel, package holidays and package tours.

[40] M Dougan, "Minimum Harmonisation and the Internal Market' (2000) 37 *CML Rev* 853, 856. See also H Unberath and A Johnston, 'The Double-Headed Approach of the ECJ Concerning Consumer Protection' (2007) *CML Rev* 1237, 1276.

[41] European Commission, 'Report on the Implementation of Directive 90/314/EEC on Package Travel and Holiday Tours in the Domestic Legislation of EC Member States', SEC (1999) final 1800, 5.

[42] European Commission, 'Proposal for a Directive of the European Parliament and of the Council on package travel and assisted travel arrangements, amending Regulation (EC) No 2006/2004, Directive 2011/83/EU and repealing Council Directive 90/314/EEC', COM(2013) 512 final.

[43] ibid.

[44] ibid.

[45] ibid.

[46] ibid.

[47] ibid.

possible for tourists to hold the retailer liable. The new Package Travel Directive was adopted in November 2015.[48]

In comparison with the discussion of the relationship between the case law under Article 56 TFEU and the Cross-Border Healthcare Directive, the Package Travel Directive is much more of a self-standing directive.[49] It did not constitute codification of case law. It directly provides for a set of rights that can be enforced by consumers in their private law relationship with tourism service providers. Therefore, the Directive has resulted in convergence in private law for a number of aspects.

i. Information Requirements

The Directive provides in detail what information has to be provided in a holiday brochure, if one is made available to the consumer.[50] The precise characteristics of the organised transport, the prices, the type of accommodation and any visa or passport requirements have to be set out.[51] The information provided is binding on the organiser and/or retailer. In addition to the general information, once a consumer has booked a package holiday, he is entitled to receive the same information—but then specifically for his own holiday—in writing or by other appropriate means. The terms of the contract have to be comprehensible and accessible.

ii. Amendments and Cancellation

The consumer is given the right to transfer his booking to another person on giving reasonable notice to the retailer.[52] Prices shall not be changed before departure unless the contract expressly provides for this possibility. And even if this is the case, variations are only possible for a number of elements of the package holiday. If the organiser is aware before the departure that he will have to make significant changes to any of the essential terms of the contract, he is under an obligation to inform the consumer, who is given the possibility to withdraw from the contract. In the case of withdrawal, except in certain unforeseen circumstances, the organiser shall provide the consumer with adequate compensation or reasonable alternatives.[53]

[48] Directive (EU) 2015/2302 of the European Parliament and of the Council on package travel and linked travel arrangements.

[49] The initiative was based on a Commission survey of the degree of consumer satisfaction with package travel and on an assessment of the differences in national legislation on package travel. See European Commission, 'Proposal for a Council Directive on Package Travel', COM(1988) 41 final.

[50] Article 3 of the Package Travel Directive.

[51] See Case C-122/10 *Konsumentsombudsmannen v Ving Sverige AB* ECLI: EU: C:2011:299.

[52] Article 4(3) of the Package Travel Directive.

[53] Article 4(5) of the Package Travel Directive.

iii. Emergency Assistance

If, during the performance of the contract, a significant amount of the services that have been provided for in the contract cannot be performed, the organiser is obliged to make suitable alternative arrangements or to reimburse the consumer.[54] If, after the departure, it is impossible to make such arrangements, the organiser shall be responsible to provide transport back to the place of departure. The organiser does not have to offer compensation or alternative arrangements if the number of persons who have bought the package holiday has not reached a certain number of which consumers have been informed in advance, or if the non-performance was due to force majeure.[55] In *Blödel-Pawlik*, the CJEU held that the insolvency of a tour operator due to its own fraudulent conduct did not constitute a legitimate ground for a travel insurer to refuse to compensate tourists who had been victims of the fraud.[56]

iv. Liability

The Directive provides that the organiser shall be liable to the consumer for non-performance of the contract.[57] This means that the organiser is also liable for the acts of suppliers of services which are part of the package. As such, the Directive has a convergent effect on the scope of liability of organisers. The possibility of contractual liability on the part of the organiser must be provided for. Furthermore, the extent of the liability has to some extent been harmonised, in that the Directive provides that no damages are due if the fault is attributable to the consumer, to a third party unconnected with the contract (provided the failure was unforeseeable and unavoidable), or to force majeure (again, which was unforeseeable and could not have been avoided).[58] With these three exceptions the Directive provides a limited number of defences. If a case does not come within any of these defences, there would appear to be a presumption that the organiser is liable.

v. Damages

The Directive prohibits unreasonable limitation or exclusion of damages.[59] Personal injury and damage to property were always likely to be covered as they were mentioned in the Directive. However, it was unclear whether non-material damage was also covered by the Directive. This question was resolved by the CJEU in

[54] Article 4(7) of the Package Travel Directive.
[55] Article 4(6) of the Package Travel Directive.
[56] Case C-134/11 *Jurgen Blödel-Pawlik v HanseMerkur Reiseversicherung* ECLI: EU: C:2012:98.
[57] Article 5(1) of the Package Travel Directive.
[58] Article 5(2) of the Package Travel Directive.
[59] Article 5(3) of the Package Travel Directive.

Leitner.[60] In that case, a family had booked a package holiday. Their daughter fell ill due to food poisoning at the holiday destination. As a result, she was unable to enjoy a significant part of the holiday. The Austrian legislation which implemented the Package Travel Directive did not allow for compensation for non-material damages. The CJEU held that this constituted an incorrect transposition of the Directive, and that Member States had to provide for the possibility of compensation for non-material damages.[61] As a consequence, the scope of damages available under the Directive has also been harmonised.

Overall, it can be said that the Directive focuses on the pre-contractual and post-contractual stages of package travel. Its focus is on making sure that consumers make a choice on the basis of sufficient and accurate information, and that they are adequately protected in case of non-compliance with the promised performance of the contract. However, it says nothing about what that performance should be like. From the perspective of quality and consumer expectations, this is not surprising at all. The expectations of tourists depend on the price they have paid and the destination of their holiday. For example, it might depend on what they have been promised in the brochure of their choice. If these aspects were harmonised at the European level, there would be no more need for tourism as the expectations of tourists would be similar in all Member States. Tourism would become a unified concept and there would hardly be any need to travel. As a result, it is understandable that the EU does not wish to get involved in the harmonisation of quality of tourism. Quality is to be left to the market. This is also related to the transparency of the market, which has been increased not only by the Package Travel Directive, but also by new technologies that have made it possible to share experiences and reviews of tourism services very quickly and easily at the European, or even the international level.[62]

At the same time and in addition to quality issues, there is also the safety aspect of package travel. Article 5(1) of the Package Travel Directive provides a very broad obligation on organisers and retailers, which makes them responsible for the conduct of all service providers involved in the package travel.[63] However, two important problems have arisen. First of all, it is not clear whether liability for non-performance of the contract is strict or fault-based.[64] Although certain defences

[60] Case C-168/00 *Simone Leitner v TUI Deutschland* ECLI: EU: C:2002:163. See also W Roth, 'Case C-168/00, Simone Leitner v. TUI Deutschland GmbH & Co. KG, Judgment of 12 March 2002 (Sixth Chamber)' (2003) 40 *CML Rev* 937.

[61] *Leitner*, above n 60, paras 19–24.

[62] European Commission, 'Proposal for a Directive of the European Parliament and of the Council on package travel and assisted travel arrangements, amending Regulation (EC) No 2006/2004, Directive 2011/83/EU and repealing Council Directive 90/314/EEC', COM(2013) 512 final.

[63] See K Tonner, 'Article 5: Haftung', in E Grabitz, M Hilf and M Nettersheim (eds), *Das Recht der Europäischen Union*, (München, Beck, 2014).

[64] European Parliament Policy Department, 'Study on Safety and Liability Issues Regarding Package Travel', IP/A/IMCO/ST/2007-14: www.europarl.europa.eu/meetdocs/2004_2009/documents/dv/999/999000/999000en.pdf.

are provided for in Article 5(2) of the Package Travel Directive, the Directive could be interpreted as imposing strict liability on organisers and retailers.[65] For example, if a tour operator has been cautious in the selection of service providers connected to package travel, would that be sufficient to be protected from liability? What level of control is required from organisers of package travel? National courts have struggled with these questions. Secondly, national courts have struggled with the question of what safety standards a consumer can expect.[66] Should organisers be expected to comply with safety standards of the Member State in which they are based and have bought the package holiday, or those of the Member State of destination in which the services are delivered? Here, most Member States have held that local safety standards are applicable, which means that an English tourist in Greece can only expect that service providers comply with Greek safety standards.[67] For tour operators and other organisers of package travel which operate at the European level, ensuring compliance with national standards is a burdensome exercise. As a consequence, there is scope for European harmonisation or standardisation. To illustrate the problems, some of the most important cases in Germany and in the UK will be discussed.

In Germany, the most famous case is the *Balcony Fall* case, decided by the Bundesgerichtshof ('BGH') in 1988.[68] A tourist had fallen of the balcony of his hotel because the bars of the balcony had not been properly fixed. The question was whether the tour operator was liable for safety defects in the hotel. The BGH held that a tour operator was under an obligation to regularly check the safety of the hotels with which it had contracted. In the case in question, there had been no such checks and the tour operator was held liable. The judgment left the precise standard of care relatively open, which resulted in a significant amount of case law. Clarifications were necessary.[69] For example, tour operators cannot be expected to export national safety standards to holiday destinations through their duty of care—local standards are applicable. The BGH itself provided clarity in the *Water Chutes* case.[70] It held that tour operators owed a duty of care to their customers to check the safety of all the facilities of a hotel, even if the hotel charged for admission to these facilities. The extent of the obligation imposed on tour operators was broadened. As a result of this series of cases, the Deutsche ReiseVerband

[65] M McDonald, 'Revisiting Organiser Liability under the Package Travel Directive. Part 2' (2003) *International Travel Law Journal* 211. See also H Schulte-Nölke, C Twigg-Flesner and M Ebers, *EC Consumer Law Compendium* (Munich, Sellier, 2008) 181.

[66] K Tonner, 'Liability According to the EU Package Tours Directive and National Implementation' (2005) *International Travel Law Journal* 203.

[67] S Mason, 'Evans v Kosmar: Where Are We Now on Health & Safety' (2007) *International Travel Law Journal* 193.

[68] BGHZ 103, 298 = NJW 1988, 1380.

[69] K Tonner, *Münchener Kommentar zum Bürgerlicher Gesetzbuch, Band 4: Schuldrecht—Besondere Teil II*, (München, CH Beck, 2012), §651f, paras. 18–19.

[70] BGH NJW 2006, 3268 = RRa 2006, 206.

decided to create a checklist for tour operators to enable them to show that they have complied with the duty of care imposed on them after the *Balcony Fall* and *Water Chutes* cases.[71] The EU has also adopted a non-binding instrument on fire safety in hotels.[72] However, the impact of this standard in practice has been minimal.[73] In 2012, the Commission proposed an update that should be developed by HOTREC, the European association of hotel owners. Fire safety in hotels has also been one of focus points of ANEC, which claims there is a need for European legislation on hotel fire safety.[74]

In the UK, courts have struggled in a similar way. In *Hone v Going Places Leisure Travel Ltd*,[75] the Court of Appeal agreed with the trial judge that a tour operator's duty did not go further than to exercise reasonable care and skill in the selection of the service providers with which it would contract.[76] This duty had been well established in *Wilson v Best Travel*,[77] in which Phillips J held that tour operators were under an obligation 'to exercise reasonable care to exclude from the accommodation offered any hotel the characteristics of which were such that guests could not spend a holiday there in reasonable safety'.[78] More specifically, he held that '[t]he duty of care of a tour operator is likely to extend to checking that local safety regulations are complied with'.[79] Furthermore, *Wilson* is considered as authority for the fact that tour operators have to ensure compliance with local safety standards—not with higher standards that might be applicable in the UK.[80] More recently, in *Evans v Kosmar*,[81] a drunken tourist had dived into the shallow end of a swimming pool whilst on a holiday in Crete. The Court of Appeal held that a tour operator was under no duty to protect tourists against obvious risks.[82] However, in *Griffin v My Travel UK Ltd*,[83] a case from Northern Ireland, a tour operator was held liable on the basis that it, or its suppliers, should have inspected the fastening mechanisms of a bed which had collapsed on the foot of a tourist who was about to go to bed. The bed had not been checked for three years. On that basis, it found that the tour operator had breached its duty of care.

[71] Interview with Professor K Tonner (Rostock) on 13 August 2013.

[72] Council Recommendation 86/666/EEC on fire safety in existing hotels.

[73] European Parliament Policy Department, 'Study on Safety and Liability Issues Regarding Package Travel', IP/A/IMCO/ST/2007-14: www.europarl.europa.eu/meetdocs/2004_2009/documents/dv/999/999000/999000en.pdf.

[74] ANEC, 'Preliminary position paper on Accommodation services safety', February 2013: www.anec.eu/attachments/ANEC%20preliminary%20position%20paper%20on%20accommodation%20safety.pdf.

[75] *Hone v Going Places Leisure Travel Ltd* [2001] EWCA Civ 947.

[76] M McDonald, above n 66, and K Tonner, above n 67, 206–08.

[77] *Wilson v Best Travel* [1993] 1 All ER 353.

[78] ibid.

[79] ibid.

[80] M Chapman, 'The Local Safety Standards Defence: Another Wrong Turn?' (2006) *International Travel Law Journal* 136.

[81] *Evans v Kosmar Villa Holidays* [2007] EWCA Civ 1003.

[82] See also M Harvey, (2008) 2 *Journal of Personal Injury Law* C71.

[83] *Griffin v My Travel UK Ltd* [2009] NIQB 98.

To conclude, it has proved difficult for national courts to define the exact scope of the duty of care for which a breach might give rise to liability under Article 5(1) of the Package Travel Directive. Without specific standards, cases will be decided on a case-by-case basis. This will be a very time-consuming process. Moreover, it means that there is a significant amount of uncertainty for both tour operators and consumers.

D. The Role of European Standardisation in the Regulation of Tourism Services

The discussion above has shown that the impact of Article 56 TFEU on the regulation of tourism services has been quite different from the impact of the Package Travel Directive.

With regards to Article 56 TFEU, the harmonising impact of the case law has been limited. While the right of entry and non-discrimination have now been well established and to a significant extent been harmonised, these rights are unlikely to have an impact on the private law relationship between tourism service providers and tourists. The most important impact of the case law has been on qualifications of tourism service providers, in particular of tourist guides. Here, Article 56 TFEU has been employed by the Commission to facilitate free movement of tourist guides through de-regulation of the profession. The level of control which can be exercised by Member States in regulating incoming tourist guides from other Member States has been decreased. The result has been a significant liberalisation of the tourist guide profession. European standardisation could then be initiated by way of reaction to such a process of liberalisation to re-regulate qualification requirements through self-regulation. The European standard would fill a gap which was left after the judgments of the CJEU. As will be discussed below, this is exactly what happened with the European standard for Tourist Guide Training.[84] It aims to regulate the duration and contents of the training which tourist guides should have had before they can offer tourist guide services. Moreover, it provides guidance on the required language skills for tourist guides. Since this standard was a counter-reaction to the case law under Article 56 TFEU, it is not surprising that its compatibility with Article 56 TFEU will have to be closely scrutinised.[85] Moreover, the standard interacts with the Professional Qualifications Directive 2005, which came into force around the same time as the European standard. This Directive provides a clear framework for the recognition of qualifications in which the European standard could play a role. However, it does not exclude the possibility of Article 56 TFEU being invoked as a means of reviewing qualification requirements that are outside the scope of the Professional Qualifications Directive.

[84] Interview with DG Enterprise of the European Commission (Brussels) on 29 November 2012.
[85] ibid.

The relationship between European standardisation and the Package Travel Directive would be different. Although there are at the moment no European standards that are specifically linked to the Package Travel Directive, European standardisation could be used to specify and supplement the duties of care imposed by the Directive. It would be more of a supplementary function to existing secondary EU law. Such supplementary standards would necessarily also have to comply with Article 56 TFEU. Their focus would be on safety aspects related to package travel. From the analysis of cases in Germany and in the UK, it is clear that courts have struggled to clarify the precise standards of care and of liability in package travel cases. This has resulted in uncertainty both for tour operators and tourists, which could be taken away by a common European standard.[86] This standard could set out the supervision requirements expected from tour operators, in particular the intensity and frequency of such safety checks. Such standardisation would not take away the need for local safety standards, but would help to clarify to what extent tour operators, which most of the time operate in a cross-border context, would be required to check and inspect facilities of their contractors in other Member States.

II. THE REGULATION OF TOURISM SERVICES AT THE NATIONAL LEVEL AND THE ROLE OF PRIVATE LAW

A. The Interaction Between Public Law and Private Law in the Regulation of Tourism Services at the National Level

It is likely that the relationship between tourist and tourism service provider is of a contractual nature. Unlike in the healthcare sector, contracts have an important role to play in the tourism sector. From the moment tourists buy a package holiday to the moment they open the door of their home again on their return, they enter into a number of different contractual relationships. The importance of contracts in tourism is also emphasised by the adoption of the Package Travel Directive. Here, the distinction between ex ante and ex post regulation is relevant. In combination with the Unfair Terms Directive and the Unfair Commercial Practices Directive, the importance of contracts in the tourism sector allows a significant emphasis on ex ante regulation. It provides for a means to enforce certain standards in the process leading towards the conclusion of the contract. As a consequence, unlike in the relationship between doctor and patient, private law has more of an ex ante regulatory function in the relationship between tourist and tourism service provider.

Furthermore, the Package Travel Directive provides for the possibility of ex post regulation with its Article 5 on liability. However, that provision is significantly

[86] Such as the recommendation on hotel fire safety referred to above.

less detailed in comparison with its ex ante provisions. The role of tort in tourism is less prominent, since the relationship between tourist and tourism service provider is often of a contractual nature. In such cases, there is no need to bring a case in tort. Many national cases brought on the basis of the Package Travel Directive do not actually make it clear whether they were brought in contract or in tort. Often, this is not relevant, because the determination of the appropriate standard of care is similar.[87] With its ex post focus, tort is perhaps less suitable to adequately regulate tourism services.[88] Moreover, disputes about tourism services are often about relatively small amounts of money. This could make legal action, whether in contract or tort, quite a burdensome activity. As a result, it is not surprising that in a number of Member States mediation or arbitration–like mechanisms have been introduced to deal with complaints of tourists. It is in these fora that claims about the alleged non-performance can be dealt with.

As has already been emphasised above, the tourism sector is a real market. While performance on the market is primarily regulated through private law, public law has a role to play in the regulation of the entry to the market. The importance of administrative law regulation in the tourism sector differs across the EU. As a result, the role of the State in the regulation of tourism services is more important in some Member States than in others.[89] By way of illustration, most Member States impose some specific licence requirements on tourism providers, for example on hotels. Through such licencing requirements, public authorities are able to enforce health and safety standards and other legal requirements. They do not really have an impact on the private law relationship between tourist and tourism service provider. Similarly, some Member States have licencing requirements for certain professions in the tourism sector, such as tourist guides or ski instructors.

Another important area in which some Member States have adopted private regulation—while other Member States rely on public regulation—is the classification of hotels. To enable tourists to distinguish between the quality of hotels, many Member States have introduced classification systems for hotels.[90] Usually, such classification systems award stars to hotels. If a hotel has five stars tourists can expect luxurious accommodation, while a hotel with one star can only be expected to provide a very basic level of comfort. Traditionally, classification systems have been created at the national level. The arrangements are quite different across the EU. In some Member States, such as in France, public authorities are responsible for the classification.[91] Classification can take place at the national or even at

[87] U Magnus and H Mickliz, *Liability for the Safety of Services* (Baden-Baden, Nomos, 2006) 551–52.

[88] See S Shavell, *Economic Analysis of Accident Law* (Cambridge (MA), Harvard University Press, 2007). See also D Wittman, 'Prior Regulation versus Post Liability: The Choice between Input and Output Monitoring' (1977) 6 *Journal of Legal Studies* 193, and U Magnus and H Mickliz, above n 87, 553.

[89] This is also clear from the tourist guide cases, which were all infringement proceedings brought against Member States by the Commission on the basis of national legislation or administrative law practices.

[90] Interview with HOTREC (Brussels) on 29 November 2012.

[91] ibid.

the regional level. In these Member Standards, the standards for classification are likely to have been laid down in administrative acts, ie in public law. The making of the standards might have been delegated to a private body. In other Member States classification is organised by private associations. Regardless of the public or private nature of the classification scheme, certain schemes are voluntary, while other schemes require all hotels to be classified.

The extent to which private regulation might play a role in classification depends on the public or private nature of the scheme. HOTREC, the European association for hotels, restaurants and cafés, has initiated a European-wide classification system, the Hotel Stars Union.[92] This scheme provides for the possibility of classification on the basis of a common, European, set of principles. The implications of the scheme for European standardisation will be discussed in the case study below. So far, 15 Member States have signed up and have harmonised their classification criteria.[93] This includes Member States with both public and private classification schemes. Apparently, the fact that classification schemes were administered through public law did not necessarily form an obstacle to the use of private regulation in the standard–setting process. However, it should be noted that none of the southern Member States—with the exception of Greece—have signed up to the Hotel Stars Union. Most of the Member States which have signed up to the scheme are Nordic or Central European.

B. European Standardisation in National Regulation of Tourism Services

In the national regulatory frameworks for tourism services, what role could there be for European standards? Tourism is not only a market—it is also a truly European market. The density of the national regulatory frameworks is not such that it leaves no scope for private regulation. Furthermore, public law and private law have relatively different roles to play in the regulation of tourism services. While public law focuses on the entrance of tourism service providers to the market, their actual performance is mainly regulated through private law—primarily through contract law, although tort also has a role to play. The broad scope of application of private law and private regulation—in combination with the European nature of the tourism sector—means that there is definitely scope for European standardisation.

This is reinforced by the fact that a significant amount of the national regulation of tourism services is based on a European legal instrument, namely the Package Travel Directive. As has been discussed above, these legal standards could be supplemented by European standards adopted through European standardisation.

[92] See www.hotelstars.eu.

[93] Interview with HOTREC (Brussels) on 29 November 2012.

There are existing European legal standards which could be supplemented by European standardisation. However, a recurrent theme throughout this chapter is that stakeholders in the tourism sector are afraid of too much standardisation, since it would threaten national and regional diversity of tourism services. Diversity at the national or regional level acts as an obstacle to European standardisation.[94] Diversity has to be linked to quality. In the tourism sector, it is claimed that there is sufficient transparency for tourists to make judgments about quality without a need for European standardisation. However, quality is closely linked to safety. The Package Travel Directive leaves scope for standardisation of safety aspects of tourism services. While the European (and international) standards on scuba diving do deal with safety aspects of scuba diving,[95] there is much more scope for European standardisation of the safety of services. In the next section, two case studies of European standardisation of tourism services will be discussed.

III. TWO CASE STUDIES ON EUROPEAN STANDARDISATION OF TOURISM SERVICES

A. Tourist Guide Training

A tourist guide is a professional who guides tourists around a certain location. When groups of tourists arrive on a coach in London, tourist guides will pick them up from the coach and show them the main sights of London. They might have a particular area or sight of specialisation, such as Westminster Abbey or the Tower of London. As such, tourist guides consider themselves as representatives of their country in welcoming and informing tourists from abroad.[96] Tourist guides are locally established guides who want to share their local knowledge and experience with tourists. By definition, this means that someone who is a tourist guide in London cannot also be a tourist guide in Paris. Being a tourist guide is considered to be an area-specific profession. As a result, tourist guides are extremely cautious to distinguish their profession from tour managers.[97] Tour managers travel with a group of tourists to a particular destination. They do not necessarily possess any special knowledge of the area of destination. Their main function is to supervise the group and to make sure that the programme is carried out according to plan. When the tourists get off the bus to visit St Paul's Cathedral in London, the tour manager will hand over the group to a tourist guide who will guide them through the cathedral.

[94] Interview with HOTREC (Brussels) on 29 November 2012.

[95] See http://standards.cen.eu/dyn/www/f?p=204:32:0::::FSP_ORG_ID,FSP_LANG_ID:6310,25&cs=155D293280BEDE1B5E32BB51F9C418EA2.

[96] Interview with the Guild, ITG and APTG (London) on 21 January 2014.

[97] ibid.

The tourist guide profession is a regulated profession in 13 Member States.[98] In these Member States, the State exercises control over entry to the profession and over professional standards. The series of cases brought by the Commission against Member States in which the tourist guide profession was regulated showed that the profession was too restrictively regulated in a number of Member States. Requirements imposed by Member States could include license requirements or the requirement to sit a local examination. In other Member States, in which the tourist guide profession is not a regulated profession, the State does not have any involvement in the regulation of the profession. Here, the regulatory function will usually be performed by professional associations. In the UK, for example, tourist guides can join the Association of Professional Tourist Guides ('APTG') or the Guild of Registered Tourist Guides ('the Guild').[99] Both associations require their members to have passed certain examinations and to have obtained particular qualifications. The syllabi for the examinations and the accreditation of course providers are the responsibility of the Institute of Tourist Guiding ('ITG').[100] Like the two professional associations, ITG is a purely private institute with no State support. Its primary functions are to set the standards for examinations and to accredit institutions which want to offer courses in tourist guiding. In the UK, tourist guides who have passed the highest examination level are awarded the Blue Badge qualification. Sights like Westminster Abbey and the Tower of London require tourist guides to have a Blue Badge qualification.

Tourist guides operate in a tourism market which is highly competitive and very much focused on free movement of service recipients and service providers. However, due to its local nature, the tourist guide profession by definition poses certain problems to free movement. This does not necessarily have to cause problems in the case of tourist guides who want to establish themselves in another Member State. However, tourist guides who want to offer their services in another Member State on a temporary basis might encounter certain problems. This could be because of a licence or examination requirement imposed in Member States in which the profession is regulated, or because of a Blue Badge-like requirement imposed by sites or professional associations. This is essentially the private law equivalent of a State-imposed licence requirement.

The series of infringement cases effectively resulted in a wave of liberalisation in the tourist guide profession. This was further enhanced by the adoption of the Professional Qualifications Directive 2005. The Directive regulates how Member States have to deal with professional qualifications in the case of establishment in another Member State or in the case of temporary service provision in another Member State.[101] Because there are no special provisions for tourist guides—such

98 ibid.

99 Interview with the Guild, ITG and APTG (London) on 21 January 2014.

100 ibid.

101 ibid.

as, for doctors or lawyers—tourist guides are governed by the general provisions of the Directive. They would very much have liked to have been exempted from the Directive on the basis of the local nature of their profession.[102] However, the Commission did not accept that tourist guides could be exempted. The Directive is primarily relevant for Member States in which the tourist guide profession is regulated. How do they deal with incoming tourist guides from other Member States in which the profession is not regulated? Because this is not a profession in which health and safety concerns play a direct role, the only requirement Member States with a regulated profession can impose is that incoming tourist guides sign a declaration, in which they provide a number of personal details and declare that they have at least two years of professional experience in their home Member State.[103] Therefore, a guide who has guided tourists through the Notre Dame in Paris for two years should equally be able to provide tours of St Paul's Cathedral in London. From the perspective of tourist guides as a local profession, built on local knowledge and experience, this is obviously an undesirable situation. It would encourage a confusion of the duties of tourist guide and tour manager—a distinction which the tourist guide profession has sought to uphold for a long period of time.[104]

As a result, it is not surprising that national associations of tourist guides felt it necessary to take action at the European level. Most national membership organisations are members of the European Federation of Tourist Guide Associations ('FEG').[105] Initially, after the adoption of the Directive, FEG started working on a common platform, where information about tourist guide qualifications could be shared. However, in 2005, stakeholders in Germany and Austria decided to take the initiative for a European standardisation process through CEN.[106] The standardisation process would lay down the required training and examination requirements for tourist guides. It would also seek to re-establish tourist guides as a local profession which should be distinguished from tour managers. The initiative was strongly supported by DIN and ASI and by various other commercial parties in the tourism sector—not just tourist guides.[107] FEG decided to support the initiative and the document that had been used for the common platform was used as one of the basic documents for the European standard. The secretariat was run by DIN.

The European standard on Tourist Guide Training was adopted in January 2008. A tourist guide was defined as someone with an area-specific qualification. Its key provisions were that the minimum training for tourist guides was 600 hours, and

[102] ibid.
[103] Interview with the Guild, ITG and APTG (London) on 21 January 2014. See Articles 5 and 7 of the Professional Qualifications Directive.
[104] ibid.
[105] ibid. See www.feg-touristguides.com.
[106] Interview with the Guild, ITG and APTG (London) on 21 January 2014.
[107] ibid.

that 40% of the training had to consist of practical training at the location where tourist guides wanted to offer their services.[108] Furthermore, the standard contained provisions on the assessment and examination of tourist guides.[109] Another significant part of the standard was the imposition of certain language requirements on tourist guides.[110]

From the moment of its adoption, the European standard has been controversial. The initial opposition to the standard came from tour operators, who were worried that they would no longer be able to bring their own guides to guide groups at the destination of their holiday. Tour operators were against the very strict separation of duties between tourist guides and tour managers. If the European standard was applied in practice, it would mean a loss of flexibility for tour operators in deciding and planning tours for groups of tourists. The criticism of the European standard did not only come from tour operators. In December 2010, at a seminar on standardisation in the tourism sector organised by CEN, the Chairman of CEN's Technical Committee on tourism services, who had not been the Chairman of the committee that had adopted the standard, stated that the standard was 'no solution for the problems concerning the access to the profession'.[111] Its implementation had been hindered by the fact that it focused only on a part of the guiding profession, namely local guides. The presentation provoked strong reactions from FEG, which wrote to CEN in support of the standard after the seminar.[112]

Similarly, the Commission now regards the Tourist Guide Training standard as an example of European standardisation that does not actually facilitate free movement of services.[113] The standard constitutes one of the reasons why the Commission believes that it is necessary to review the purposes and usefulness of European standardisation of services. The standard constitutes an obstacle to free movement of services, because it provides that tourist guides have to be trained in the area where they want to offer their services. The tourist guide associations claim that the Commission has changed its position on the standard.[114] While it initially accepted the distinction between tourist guides and tour managers, it no longer supports this distinction. The tourist guides do not regard the European standard as a means to restrict entry to the market. They recognise that the legislation of some Member States, which was attacked by the Commission in the early 1990s, constituted a restriction, but they argue that the current European standard

[108] ibid.

[109] Interview with the Guild, ITG and APTG (London) on 21 January 2014.

[110] ibid.

[111] Presentation by R Jansen, 'Benefits from Established European Tourism Standards?', CEN Seminar on Standardisation in the Tourism Sector, 8 December 2010.

[112] Letter by C Ortega, Chairman of FEG Tourist Guides, to CEN after the Workshop in December 2010.

[113] Interview with DG Enterprise of the European Commission (Brussels) on 29 November 2012.

[114] Interview with the Guild, ITG and APTG (London) on 21 January 2014.

does not go quite that far.[115] The standard should be seen as a means to distinguish themselves from tour managers. As such, it provides a mechanism to make the quality of their services more transparent. Such increased transparency is necessary in a market in which price concerns are very important for tour operators and in which tourists are not always properly informed.[116]

B. HOTREC's Opposition to European Standardisation and the Alternative of European Classification

At the European level, hotels, restaurants and cafés are represented by HOTREC. From very early on, HOTREC has been one of the main opponents of European standardisation in the tourism sector. It adopted a position paper on the development of standards at the European and international level in November 2009.[117] This position paper still expresses the current position of HOTREC on European standardisation—little has changed in the past five years. The main objections of HOTREC to European standardisation are twofold. Firstly, tourism services are custom-made and heterogeneity is a key component of tourism services.[118] As a result, tourism services should not be open to any kind of standardisation similar to standardisation of goods. This is made very clear in HOTREC's position paper.

> Heterogeneity is the main competitive feature for the hospitality industry. In relation to our services, diversity reflects different cultures, approaches as well as geographical situations, and constitutes one of the major attractions for customers. Most of them do not expect nor wish to find standardised conditions everywhere they travel. On the contrary, their expectations vary according to their destinations, their ages, their budgets as well as the purpose of their trips, be it a business trip or a trip for leisure.[119]

Second, the European standardisation process through CEN does not sufficiently facilitate the wishes of stakeholders in the tourism sector.[120] As a result, HOTREC requires that a substantial number of changes are made to the European standardisation process. HOTREC is not against standardisation *per se*, but the current procedure through CEN is not suitable to facilitate the needs and wishes of HOTREC's members. In reality, this means that HOTREC is against European standardisation, because it is unlikely that all required changes would be made to the European standardisation process.[121]

[115] ibid.

[116] Interview with the Guild, ITG and APTG (London) on 21 January 2014.

[117] See www.hotrec.eu/Documents/Document/20110913111252-D-0909-374-MV-Standards_position_paper-FINAL-5-11-09.pdf.

[118] ibid.

[119] ibid.

[120] ibid.

[121] Interview with HOTREC (Brussels) on 29 November 2012.

In a way, this objection to standardisation is not too different from the objections raised by the medical profession that were discussed in chapter four. Although the medical profession invokes professional autonomy and evidence-based science as a justification to refuse to get involved in European standardisation, the starting point in both sectors is the same: our wishes are not sufficiently taken into account in the European standardisation process. A further argument made by the tourism sector is that the market is regulating itself very well.[122] Standardisation would normally address a need to impose some kind of external regulation on the market. This is very clear in the initiative for the European standard on Aesthetic Surgery Services. The lack of national regulation, which enables doctors to use certain titles without being supervised, means that the market has become non-transparent. Patients suffer from that lack of transparency. European standardisation would then attempt to address these market failures. However, according to HOTREC, tourism services are not suffering from a lack of transparency.[123] On the contrary, because information is spreading fast on the internet through the various review and opinion sites, consumers have easy access to information about the quality of services. These sites impose some kind of regulation on the market. Sites like Expedia and Booking.com provide a mechanism for consumers to give their opinion about service providers in the tourism sectors. Moreover, consumers who are considering certain tourism services can read these websites in order to make an informed choice. This review mechanism takes place outside of the control of tourism service providers themselves. There is an obvious risk that they will submit their own reviews on the websites, or that they will encourage consumers to write a review. However, in general, review websites provide informative and reliable assessments of the quality of service providers in the hotel sector.[124] The result is that the market is sufficiently transparent to regulate itself—no intervention through standardisation is necessary.

The opposition of HOTREC to European standardisation does not mean that it has not been involved in attempts to make quality of hotels more visible at the European level. HOTREC has been very involved in the creation of a European hotel stars system, the 'Hotel Stars Union'.[125] This system has harmonised the criteria for classification of hotels. At the moment, 15 Member States have harmonised their criteria on the basis of the criteria developed by the Hotel Stars Union. According to HOTREC, classification should be clearly distinguished from standardisation.[126] Although they accept that classification involves elements of standardisation, the system has a degree of flexibility which cannot be introduced through the adoption of a European standard. Classification is not as strict as standardisation. It is a system

[122] ibid.
[123] ibid.
[124] ibid.
[125] www.hotelstars.eu.
[126] Interview with HOTREC (Brussels) on 29 November 2012.

which has both mandatory and voluntary criteria. Hotels are given points, which determine the number of stars which a hotel is awarded. For each category—one star, two stars etc—there are certain mandatory requirements. In addition, there are voluntary criteria that allow hotels to specialise. As a result, it is possible for hotels to specialise in different services and to distinguish themselves in the market.[127] The hotel stars just have a guidance function for tourists. They do not have a direct impact on the contractual relationship between tourist and hotel.[128] The fact that a hotel with five stars does not provide mini bars in the hotel rooms does not automatically entitle guests to bring a claim for breach of contract. However, the non-compliance with the requirements of a certain star category could be used as evidence to establish a breach of contract on the part of the hotel.[129]

As such, classification offers a degree of flexibility that can accommodate the heterogeneity of tourism services and the variation in customer expectations. At the same time, it provides some certainty to customers about what they can expect from a particular hotel. Quality is made more transparent. Standardisation would be more inflexible.[130] Furthermore, classification allows for specialisation within its own framework. Overall, this raises the question of whether the European system of classification itself could be standardised through CEN. HOTREC is very sceptical about this. This is primarily again because of their concern that stakeholders would not be able to get involved in the standardisation process.[131]

According to HOTREC, the European standardisation process cannot accommodate the needs and wishes of stakeholders in the tourism industry.[132] It is concerned about the ability to participate effectively in European standardisation both at the European level and at the national level. At the European level, organisations like HOTREC would only be able to obtain a liaison status, which means they would not be much more than an observer. They would not have voting rights. There are insufficient guarantees that European standardisation would always be based on market demand. Moreover, national associations are experiencing difficulties with getting involved in European standardisation at the national level through the national mirror committees.[133] They have to be very cautious about their expenditure. As a result, they do not want to get involved in standardisation which is not really desired by the sector. Associations would be required to spend thousands of Euros just to be able to have a look at the documents of European standardisation processes. Classification is significantly less expensive. Another advantage of classification is that the associations themselves pay for the development

[127] ibid.

[128] Interview with Prof. K Tonner (Rostock) on 13 August 2013 and Interview with HOTREC (Brussels) on 29 November 2012.

[129] ibid.

[130] Interview with HOTREC (Brussels) on 29 November 2012.

[131] ibid.

[132] ibid.

[133] ibid.

of the classification schemes. Small enterprises do not directly have to contribute to the costs of the development of the scheme.

All of this criticism is based on the argument that European standardisation of tourism services would not really be a market–driven activity. Rather, from the perspective of the tourism sector, European standardisation would be abused to impose external regulation on the sector. This position is not shared by ANEC, which has lobbied actively for more standardisation in the tourism sector—in particular, to improve the safety of hotel accommodation.[134] This is where a parallel can be drawn with the healthcare sector, in which medical associations have expressed fear that European standardisation would be used by external parties, such as public authorities or insurers, to cut costs. In the tourism sector HOTREC is more concerned about certification organisations, which would rely on European standardisation in support of their certification activities. Certification would be much more expensive than classification, and it would again mean that external parties would seek to exercise influence on the tourism sector.

IV. THE INTERACTION BETWEEN EUROPEAN STANDARDISATION AND TOURISM SERVICES

A. SMEs and Stakeholder Participation in European Standardisation of Tourism Services

The tourism sector consists of 92% SMEs. For such small businesses to participate in European standardisation, the benefits have to be clear to them. After all, SMEs would be required to pay the costs of participation in European standardisation. From the discussions with HOTREC, it is clear that many stakeholders do not believe that their voices will be adequately heard in European standardisation.[135] The potential benefits of European standardisation do not outweigh the costs that would be incurred. The administrative burden imposed on SMEs who want to participate in European standardisation is significant. SMEs would possibly have to employ specific persons to take responsibility for European standardisation processes. All of this means that participation in European standardisation is an expensive and burdensome activity. A possible solution would then be for professional associations to participate in European standardisation. However, such associations would often only be granted an observer status. They would have to pay more if they wanted to have access to particular documents which are relied on in the standardisation process. For that reason, professional associations do

[134] Interview with ANEC (Brussels) on 4 April 2012. See ANEC, 'Preliminary position paper on Accommodation services safety', February 2013: www.anec.eu/attachments/ANEC%20preliminary%20position%20paper%20on%20accommodation%20safety.pdf.

[135] ibid.

not feel that they could adequately participate in and contribute to European standardisation.[136]

Overall, it would seem that the European standardisation process does not sufficiently facilitate the possibility for SMEs to participate. Attempts have been made to improve this in the Standardisation Regulation 2012. However, Articles 5 and 6 of the Standardisation Regulation do not change the current situation in any significant way.[137] Article 6 on access to standards for SMEs contains no real obligations for standardisation organisations—it only provides some examples of how they could encourage and facilitate the participation of SMEs in European standardisation.[138] No 'hard' or enforceable obligations are included and more importantly, the Article does not really give SMEs something they do not already have. The obligation is imposed on national standardisation organisations themselves, not on the Member States.[139] No particular role for the Commission is envisaged. A fundamental problem for European standardisation is that the standardisation process is vulnerable to abuse by stakeholders who are not representative of a particular sector. European standardisation could facilitate the attempts of outsiders to impose regulation on a particular sector. This is primarily because CEN does not impose strict requirements as to which stakeholders in a particular sector should definitely be represented in a European standardisation process.[140] CEN is open to any initiative for which there is sufficient support of the national standardisation organisations. Consequently, if SMEs cannot or do not want to participate, it might be possible for other parties to use European standardisation as a means of imposing regulation on the sector.

In conclusion, the self-regulatory nature of European standardisation is questioned by stakeholders. In fact, European standardisation can become a tool for external parties to seek to exercise influence in a particular sector. In the tourism sector, there are serious concerns that European standardisation will be used by private certification organisations or companies. Such companies have an interest in the adoption of standards that they can use for their certification activities.[141] They would like to make their business out of certifying SMEs against such European standards. Obviously, they need standards for their certification

[136] Interview with HOTREC (Brussels) on 29 November 2012 and Interview with UEMS and CPME (Warsaw) on 19 February 2013.

[137] Articles 5 and 6 of the Standardisation Regulation 2012. For the discussion, see Chapter II, section i (c).

[138] ibid.

[139] ibid.

[140] CEN is bound by the Code of Good Practice for Standardization of the WTO Technical Barriers to Trade agreement, which means that it is obliged to consult all parties concerned. However, this applies only to consultation—there are no fixed rules about who should be represented in the standardisation process itself.

[141] Interview with HOTREC (Brussels) on 29 November 2012 and Interview with UEMS and CPME (Warsaw) on 19 February 2013.

activities and European standards would broaden the market. The fear of SMEs in the tourism sector for certification bodies would suggest that, while certification would normally be a voluntary activity, once European standards were adopted there would be market pressure on stakeholders in the tourism sector to obtain certification.

Finally and independently from the fear of stakeholders of external regulation being imposed on them through European standardisation, European standardisation can also be used by fragments of a particular sector to impose regulation on the complete sector. This is the criticism which is made of the Tourist Guide standard. Here, a particular group of tourist guides—namely guides with an area–specific qualification—has used European standardisation to attempt to impose a particular definition of the tourist guide profession on the entire tourism sector. The fact that this definition is not always accepted by another segment of the tourism sector—mainly tour operators—means that the Tourist Guide standard is not considered to be a genuine instrument of self-regulation.[142] A parallel can be made with the Aesthetic Surgery Services standard, where some of the associations of medical professions have accused those involved in the making of the standard of attempting to restrict the market and to escape supervision of the entire profession.[143] In both cases, a segment of the profession is accused of restricting the market to themselves. Their justification for doing this is that quality, and patient safety is made more transparent by the standardisation process. The standardisation process should contribute to consumer protection. The interaction between quality, safety and European standardisation will be discussed below.

B. European Standardisation of Services and Free Movement

With the inclusion of Article 26(5) in the Services Directive, European standardisation of services is supposed to facilitate free movement of service recipients and free movement of service providers. Therefore, the emphasis of Article 26 is on improving the compatibility of services. This should result in a minimum level playing field for services in the EU. Such a minimum level playing field should in turn result in more cross-border movement. The general presumption is that European standardisation should be a tool to strengthen the internal market for services.[144] This is exactly what happened with products in the New Approach—European standards contributed to the creation of a genuine and well-functioning European market for products. On that basis, it could be presumed that European standardisation of services would contribute to free movement in a similar way.

[142] A Ogus, 'Rethinking Self-Regulation' (1995) 15 *Oxford Journal of Legal Studies* 97, 98.
[143] Interview with UEMS and CPME (Warsaw) on 19 February 2013.
[144] Interview with DG Enterprise of the European Commission (Brussels) on 29 November 2012.

However, the reality has proven otherwise. So far, European standardisation in the tourism sector has not had the improvement of the internal market as its primary objective. On the contrary, some of the projects seem to have created obstacles to the functioning of the internal market. As a consequence, European standardisation is not naturally a market-facilitative exercise. It has to be put in a broader regulatory framework in order to be able to contribute to free movement of services. The Commission is now well aware of this. Recent standardisation projects, like the European standard for Tourist Guide Training, have alerted the Commission to the potential negative impact of European standardisation on the internal market. It could be argued that the Commission itself should take control of the situation by ensuring that European standardisation of services becomes more internal market-friendly. The most radical way of doing this would be through the creation of a New Approach to services. However, as it currently stands, the Commission is hesitant to go quite as far as that.[145] This hesitation has to be explained by the fact that services are very different in nature from goods and that they are much more difficult to put in a unified legislative framework. An alternative approach would then be for the Commission to start issuing more mandates in the field of services to support or supplement legislative projects. This would potentially make stakeholders aware of the role and function of European standardisation in the internal market for services. The final possibility would be for the Commission to much more closely supervise standardisation projects in the services sector which have been initiated by stakeholders.[146] Formally, the Commission takes part in every standardisation process. On that basis, it could take up a more pro-active supervisory role. It certainly seems necessary to make parties involved in the making of European standards for services aware of the role of these standards in the internal market. Closer supervision by the Commission could ensure that standardisation projects would not develop in the wrong direction. However, this would require quite an investment on the part of the Commission. Alternatively, the Commission could also encourage CEN, as the organisation which facilitates the making of these standards, to take a more pro-active role in verifying whether or not a desired European standardisation project would really contribute to the improvement of the internal market. The problem with placing too much reliance on CEN to perform a filtering function is that CEN has an interest in as many standards as possible being made.[147] As a result, it cannot really be relied on to perform a gatekeeper's role. It might even be argued that this is not what it should do—as it mainly facilitates the wishes of the national standardisation

[145] ibid.

[146] B van Leeuwen, 'Free movement of services, European standardisation and private law', in H Micklitz, Y Svetiev and G Comparato (eds), 'European Regulatory Private Law: The Paradigms Tested', *EUI Working Papers Law* 2014/04, 27-40, 40.

[147] Interview with DG Enterprise of the European Commission (Brussels) on 29 November 2012 and Interview with CEN (Brussels) on 4 April 2012.

organisations. From that perspective, the Commission should certainly take a more active supervisory role.

In general, the case study on the Tourist Guide Training standard shows that stakeholders cannot be relied on to adopt regulation which improves—or even is compatible with—the EU internal market. It was primarily a counter-reaction to protect the interests of local tourist guides after the series of judgments of the CJEU. The tourist guides wished to protect their position in that market. It was based on a very one-dimensional perception of the wishes of tourists—the idea that local tourist guides will indeed be best placed to inform tourists about local guides and attractions. However, as had already been emphasised by the CJEU in *Commission v France*, relying exclusively on local tourist guides 'may have the drawback that tourists who are the recipients of the services in question do not have a guide who is familiar with their language, their interests and their specific expectations'.[148]

Despite the criticism of the standard, its legality under EU law has not been tested in court so far. Although the standard appears to have been broadly implemented and applied by associations of tourist guides throughout the EU, its implementation has not yet led to the provisions of the standard being challenged on the ground that they constituted a restriction on the right of tourist guides to freely provide services in another Member State. This suggests that the application of the European standard might have been more flexible than the legislation of some Member States that was challenged before the CJEU in the late 1980s. As a consequence, it could be argued that a European standard does not constitute as much of an obstacle to free movement as the legislation that was challenged before the CJEU.[149] The application of a European standard would be more flexible. This is supported by an example of the application of the Tourist Guide Training standard in the UK. Although the standard formally requires tourist guides to have spent 40% of their training at the location where they want to offer their services, the ITG has implemented the standard in such a way that it is possible for external candidates to take the exams without necessarily having spent 40% of the training at the location where the services would be offered.[150] The assessment requirements would still be similar, but external candidates—candidates who are living abroad—are given the chance to take the exam without the amount of training formally required by the European standard.

Another and possibly more likely, explanation for the fact that the Tourist Guide Training standard has not been challenged in law could simply be that the impact of the standard on the dynamic market for tourism services has been minimal.[151]

[148] *Commission v France (tourist guides)*, above n 29, para 19.

[149] Interview with the Guild, ITG and APTG (London) on 21 January 2014.

[150] ibid.

[151] Presentation by R Jansen, 'Benefits from Established European Tourism Standards?', CEN Seminar on Standardisation in the Tourism Sector, 8 December 2010.

The market has ignored the standard and does not feel bound by it. There are some indications that this is in fact what has happened—it would suggest that the forces of the market are in the end able to overcome the regulatory power of a European standard. As tourist guides who support the European standard readily admit,[152] this would mean that they would have to distinguish themselves solely on the basis of quality. The determination of what the required quality level should be would then be entirely left to the market rather than to European standardisation.

C. European Standardisation of Services and Quality, Safety and Diversity

The tourism sector provides a very good example of the interaction between quality, safety and diversity in European standardisation of services. It should be emphasised that the quality of services is normally left to the market. This is particularly true for tourism services, for which the perception of what constitutes good quality tourism services might be widely divergent across the EU. If quality is normally not regulated, what impact would European standardisation have on quality? And what is the interaction between safety, quality and European standardisation?

It would seem that, from the perspective of quality, European standardisation is not necessary in the tourism market. The market is sufficiently transparent for tourists to make informed choices about the quality of services they want to receive. European standardisation is not sufficiently flexible to allow for diversity in the market. On the contrary, the standardisation process would eliminate diversity. The result would be that the market would be more limited. The regulation of quality would result in a decrease of consumer choice. In the tourism sector, classification provides a more flexible means to make quality even more transparent without eliminating the diversity of tourism services and tourism service providers. However, even classification seems hardly necessary anymore with a highly transparent and visible market in which reviews can easily be shared on the internet. Regulation through European standardisation has no role to play in this market. When it does attempt to play a role, such as in the Tourist Guide Training example, it in fact eliminates diversity through the emphasis on one definition of what constitutes good quality. The Tourist Guide Training standard does not just represent an attempt to make quality more transparent. It equally represents an attempt to restrict the market to a certain *type* of quality. From a consumer choice perspective, this is undesirable. Overall, it can be concluded that if the market is sufficiently transparent and if consumers are sufficiently informed, European standardisation is not necessary from a quality point of view and would only eliminate the diversity of the market.

[152] ibid.

The relationship between quality and safety is different. Safety constitutes a pre-requisite for quality. Services must satisfy a certain minimum level of safety before they can compete on quality. Therefore, there might be more scope for European standardisation of the safety aspects of services. This is supported by the analysis of the Package Travel Directive, which leaves scope for European standardisation of safety obligations of tour operators. However, it should be noted that while there is scope for such standardisation, very few standards have in fact been adopted.[153] As a result, it could be argued that stakeholders cannot sufficiently be relied on to adequately regulate safety aspects of their services. It could be said that such regulation only really takes place in respect of product standards, where the regulatory framework has been created with the New Approach and is closely controlled by the European Commission. While diversity can be an excuse to refuse to regulate quality, it does not provide an excuse to refuse to regulate safety.[154] Therefore, it would seem that the scope for safety regulation at the European level is then primarily left to public regulation—for example, to courts in tort or contractual cases against tour operators. An alternative solution would be for Member States to adopt legislation on the safety aspects of services. The only positive example of European standardisation of the safety aspects of services is the series of European standards on scuba diving. These standards are very similar to product standards.[155] Although some of the standards regulate the training of scuba diving instructors, most standards are mainly related to the safety of the equipment. As a consequence, they are almost identical to product standards. As such, they provide an example of the possibility of European standardisation of products that are closely linked to the provision of services.

V. A PRELIMINARY CONCLUSION

In this chapter it has been argued that, in the tourism sector, there is scope for standardisation to supplement European legislative instruments, such as the Package Travel Directive. Consequently, there is a potential need for European standards. In principle, both the European and the national regulatory frameworks would allow for European standardisation to play a role in private law. Although a limited number of standards have been made, it seems that the tourism sector is generally not very interested in European standardisation. Service providers and service recipients are content to rely on competition in the market without the need to impose regulation through European standardisation. The market for tourism services is highly transparent and competitive.

153 Interview with DG Enterprise of the European Commission (Brussels) on 29 November 2012.

154 Interview with ANEC (Brussels) on 4 April 2012.

155 Telephone interview with NOB (not recorded) on 29 January 2013 and Interview with HOTREC (Brussels) on 29th November 2012.

One of the important reasons for the lack of interest of stakeholders in standardisation is that European standardisation is unable to accommodate their wishes and needs. In a market which consists of more than 90% SMEs, it is difficult to raise sufficient financial and administrative support for European standardisation. This is reinforced by the fact that professional associations feel that they are not really able to exercise influence on standardisation at the European level. In light of this scepticism, and given the fact that they are doubtful about the necessity and benefits of European standardisation of tourism services, it is not surprising that stakeholders have not been enthusiastic about European standardisation. However, what is even more worrying is that there appears to be a genuine fear that European standardisation might be used by external parties or by parts of the sector to impose regulation on the entire sector. The procedure adopted by CEN and the national standardisation organisations is not able to guarantee complete and adequate stakeholder representation. As a result, one can question the extent to which European standardisation constitutes genuine self-regulation.

On the substance of European standardisation, it has become clear that the motives for stakeholders to get involved in European standardisation initiatives often have little to do with the facilitation of free movement in the internal market for tourism services. Although there is a presumption at the European policy level that standardisation should be facilitative of free movement, the reality has proved that European services standards could in fact create obstacles to free movement. One of the reasons for this is that European standardisation of services does not take place in a regulatory framework that is controlled by the Commission. Purely private initiatives for European standardisation might not contribute to the improvement of the internal market for services. The Commission considers it necessary to do further research on the purposes and usefulness of European standardisation for services sectors.[156] However, it should also intensify its supervision of European standardisation of services and take its role as guardian of the Treaties more seriously.

Finally, the interaction between standardisation, quality and safety has been analysed. An important argument in the tourism sector is that diversity should be protected, because it is one of the very foundations of tourism services. European standardisation is not sufficiently flexible to allow for diversity. From that perspective, classification provides a more reasonable alternative for the tourism sector. However, the case law on Article 5 of the Package Travel Directive shows that more regulation of the safety aspects of tourism services is desirable. This regulation is necessary to provide a level playing field on which service providers can compete on quality. With the exception of the European standards for scuba diving, there has not been European standardisation of the safety aspects of tourism services. This is left by the market to public regulation, for example to courts, and the regulation is usually ex post.

[156] Interview with DG Enterprise of the European Commission (Brussels) on 29 November 2012.

6

The Application of European Standards in Contract Law and Tort Law and the Role of the Unfair Contract Terms Directive

CHAPTERS FOUR AND five have focused on the making of European services standards in the healthcare and tourism sectors. However, the European standardisation process is just a first step towards convergence. The starting point explained in chapter one was whether a link can be made between European standardisation and the application of European standards in private law. The convergence takes place through their application in private law. This chapter will focus on the application of European standards to find out to what extent the link between European standardisation and private law can successfully be made. Two areas of private law are discussed: contract law and tort. In both areas of law European standards could be applied and could increase convergence in private law. Furthermore, the role of the Unfair Contract Terms Directive as a review mechanism for the application of European standards will be discussed.

I. FROM THE MAKING OF EUROPEAN SERVICES STANDARDS TO THEIR APPLICATION IN PRIVATE LAW

European standardisation of services is a relatively new phenomenon and most services standards have only been developed in the last decade or so. As a result, it is difficult to trace the application of European services standards in private law. For that reason, this chapter will also discuss cases in which European product standards were applied in private law. There is no European regulatory framework which provides for a role for European services standards in the ex ante regulation of services. There is no New Approach to services which provides that compliance with European services standards is necessary before services can be offered in the internal market. Similarly, there is no European regulatory framework which links European services standards to liability for defective services. The impact of European services standards on the determination of liability in private law is not regulated by the EU. This is an important difference with European product standards. First of all, European product standards have an important role to play in the New Approach to goods, in which they provide a way of establishing compliance with the essential requirements of a directive. Secondly, the EU has created a regulatory framework which links European standardisation to liability for defective products. Although European standards do not have a direct impact on liability under the Product Liability Directive,[1] the EU has created a framework in which these standards could play a role. Compliance with a European standard becomes a way to prove that a product was not defective under the Directive.[2]

The main argument of this chapter is that convergence in private law through European standardisation of services becomes more difficult because of the absence of a European regulatory framework which links European standardisation to liability in private law. The fact that there is no European control of the application of European services standards means that the application is entirely dependent on national private law.[3] This is not helpful from the perspective of convergence, which requires a more uniform approach to the application of European standards in private law. As a consequence, it becomes more difficult for the EU to provide a direction to the process of convergence.

II. EUROPEAN STANDARDS IN CONTRACT LAW

A. Framing Convergence in Contract Law

Contract law provides one of the main tools for European services standards to be applied in private law. If stakeholders are asked what they intend to do with a European services standard once it has been adopted, they usually point to contract law as a strategy for applying the standard. Although the contract law terminology in the various Member States is different,[4] there are essentially three functions that European services standards can have in contract law. These functions provide three different routes towards convergence.

First of all, a European standard can become applicable by agreement between the service provider and service recipient. The provisions of a European standard would be incorporated in the contract and would become directly applicable to the contractual relationship. They would obtain binding force in law through

[1] F Cafaggi, 'Product safety, private standard-setting and information networks' in F Cafaggi and H Muir Watt (eds), *The Regulatory Function of Private Law* (Cheltenham, Edward Elgar, 2009) 207–42, 217–20.

[2] H Schepel and J Falke, *Legal Aspects of Standardisation of the EC and EFTA, Volume 1: Comparative Report* (Luxembourg, Office for Official Publications of the European Communities, 2000) 199–202 and 235–37.

[3] F Cafaggi, 'Private Regulation in European Private Law' in A Hartkamp et al (eds), *Towards a European Civil Code* (Alphen aan de Rijn, Kluwer, 2011) 91–126, 110–12.

[4] See C Valcke, 'Convergence and Divergence of the English, French and German Conceptions of Contract' (2008) 16 *European Review of Private Law* 29.

their incorporation in the contract.[5] The role of the European standard would be very much like that of standard terms.[6] For example, a contract between a private clinic for plastic surgery and a patient could expressly provide that the clinic and its employees would comply with the provisions of the European standard for Aesthetic Surgery Services. The result would be that if the surgeon who operated on the patient did not have the level of training required by the European standard, the clinic would be in breach of contract. There would be an automatic link between compliance with the European standard and a breach of the contractual standard of care. In other words, the service would be defective because the clinic did not comply with the European standard.

Secondly, a European standard could become the objective standard with which service providers have to comply in contract law. Although the contract itself would be silent about the European standard, the court would apply the European standard as the contractual standard of care with which the service provider has to comply. Consider the following scenario: a tour operator hires a local tourist guide in London to guide a group of Spanish tourists through the Westminster Abbey. The guide does not appear to know very much about recent renovation work that has been undertaken in the chapel. It turns out he has not taken any courses for the last five years. Therefore, he has not complied with the continuing professional development requirements imposed by the European standard for Tourist Guide Training. If the tour operator brought a claim for breach of contract against the tourist guide, a court could find that the European standard represented the required contractual standard of care and that the tourist guide was in breach of contract on the basis of his failure to comply with its provisions. In effect, compliance with the European standard would be implied in the contract. Again, the result would again be that non-compliance with the standard would automatically result in the service provider being in breach of contract.

The third function would essentially fall within the objective standard category, but there would be an important difference. A European standard could also be used to specify a different objective contractual standard of care. While the standard would not become a direct source of contractual obligations, it would be used to shape an objective standard of care. For example, if a patient attends a private clinic in London for plastic surgery, there would be an implied term in the contract that the doctors would use reasonable skill and care in the provision of aesthetic surgery services to them. The European standard for Aesthetic Surgery Services could then be used to define what reasonable skill and care means in the context of a particular case. Non-compliance with the European standard could be used as evidence to establish that the service provider was not using reasonable care and, as a result, was in breach of contract. The difference with the second category is that the European standard would not become a direct source of

[5] H Schepel and J Falke, above n 2, 215–16.

[6] See H Micklitz, 'Regulatory Strategies on Services Contracts' in F Cafaggi and H Muir Watt (eds), *The Regulatory Function of European Private Law* (Cheltenham, Edward Elgar, 2009) 16–61.

contractual obligations, but would only be used as a 'building stone' to establish a breach of a different objective contractual standard of care. There would not be an automatic link between non-compliance with the European standard and a breach of contract.

With each of the functions, the application of European standards would increase convergence in contract law. The contractual standards that would be expected from service providers would become converged through the application of a common European standard in private law. At the same time, each of the three functions would provide a slightly different route towards convergence and would be dependent on different factors. Before these factors are analysed in more detail below, we will discuss a case study based on the PIP breast implants scandal, which was introduced in chapter four.

B. Case Study: PIP Breast Implant Group Litigation in the UK[7]

Patients who would like to receive plastic surgery for cosmetic reasons usually seek medical treatment outside the public health systems. The result is that plastic surgery services are normally offered in private clinics. Patients conclude a contract either with the clinic or with individual surgeons who offer their services in the clinic. For women who would like to receive breast implants, the contract contains both the provision of services and goods. After all, the surgeon offers medical treatment that involves the implementation of breast implants in the patient's body. The result is a mixed contract in which both goods and services play an essential role.[8] The provision of goods—in this case, the breast implants—is intrinsically linked to the provision of services. If the product that is supplied in the process of providing the service is defective, from the perspective of the patient, the service itself would be defective as well. As a result, both European product and services standards could become applicable to the contractual relationship between service provider and service recipient. The European standard for breast implants adopted under the New Approach could have a direct impact on the relationship between doctor and patient.

It is clear that, with the New Approach, the regulatory framework for placing breast implants on the EU's market is complicated. Various public and private actors are involved. The aftermath of the PIP scandal provides evidence of the difficulties which claimants might encounter in their attempts to hold parties liable for the (possible) defects in the breast implants which they received. Various litigation strategies have been pursued in different Member States—both in contract law and in tort. In this section, a contractual case will be discussed, while the

[7] This case study is based on an article which has been published in the European Journal of Risk Regulation: B van Leeuwen, 'PIP Breast Implants, the EU's New Approach for Goods and Market Surveillance by Notified Bodies' (2014) 3 *European Journal of Risk Regulation* 338.

[8] See E Hondius et al. (eds), *Principles of European Law: Sales* (München, Sellier, 2008) 118–20.

various cases brought in tort against the certification body TÜV Rheinland will be discussed in the next section.

In 2016, the English High Court will hear a group action which has been brought on behalf of 1000 to 2000 victims. All of the victims received PIP breast implants in private clinics in the UK. The cases have been brought against the private clinics where they had their operations. In some cases in which it is uncertain whether victims had concluded a contract with the clinic or with the individual surgeon who provided services in the clinic, claims are also brought against a number of individual surgeons.[9] Furthermore, in certain cases where the victims paid for the breast implants with a credit card, claims are also brought against the credit card companies.[10] Originally, the hearing was scheduled for October 2014. However, the judge decided to adjourn the hearing—with the consent of all parties—after it was discovered that one of the main defendants, a private clinic which provided plastic surgery services in the UK, had a dispute with its insurer about the existence of a valid insurance contract.[11]

The cases are based on the contracts between the victims and the clinics or surgeons. The judge will decide two preliminary issues after the hearing in 2016. First of all, the main issue is whether the breast implants were of satisfactory quality. Under the Sale of Goods and Services Act 1982, there is an implied term in the contract between doctor and patient that the goods which were supplied by the doctor were of satisfactory quality.[12] This immediately shows the link between goods and services in this case. The claimants are arguing that the goods were not of satisfactory quality. The Act provides that the quality of the goods includes their state and condition and a number of other aspects, such as their appearance and finish, their safety and their durability.[13] On the basis of these criteria, the judge will have to decide whether the PIP breast implants were of satisfactory quality.[14] This will be done in a sample of four cases which are considered to be representative of the issues and which have been selected for the hearing.[15] All four victims had their operation in the same clinic. The second preliminary issue is to establish which remedies the claimants would be entitled to if the breast implants were found not to be of satisfactory quality. The issue here is whether the victims have a right to require the clinics to replace the breast implants under the Act—based on what English lawyers call the Euro-remedies[16] provided by the Sale of Consumer

[9] Interview with UK barrister (London) on 28 January 2014.

[10] ibid.

[11] E-mail correspondence with UK barrister (London) on 5 October 2014.

[12] Supply of Goods and Services Act 1982, s 4(2). The Sale of Goods Act 1979 has now been replaced by the Consumer Rights Act 2015. The implied term of satisfactory quality can now be found in s 9 of this Act.

[13] Supply of Goods and Services Act 1982, s 18(3).

[14] See G Brüggemeier, 'Schadensatz für Implantierte fehlerhafte Medizinprodukte—Zwei Vorlagebeschlüsse des Bundesgerichtshofs' (2014) 32 *Medizinrecht* 537.

[15] Interview with UK barrister (London) on 28 January 2014.

[16] Supply of Goods and Services Act 1982, s 11M(2). This right can now be found in section the Consumer Rights Act 2015, s 23.

Goods Directive.[17] The question is whether the replacement of the breast implants would be proportionate.[18] The alternative would be damages under common law. One of the key questions for the English court will be to decide whether or not the potential risk that PIP breast implants might rupture is sufficient for them to be of insufficient quality. That highlights one of the important issues from the broader EU law perspective: are PIP breast implants potentially risky products or simply of inferior quality?[19] If we are dealing with products of inferior quality, they could come within the scope of the Sale of Consumer Goods Directive, which is what the action in the UK is based on.[20] However, products which only carry potential risks might fall outside the scope of the Directive. The traditional distinction that quality is regulated by the market through contract, while safety remains the responsibility of the State through monitoring remains important.[21] It should be noted that in *Berger* the ECJ has more or less equated inferior quality with potential risks in the field of food safety.[22]

European standardisation plays a role in the group litigation in the UK. The claimants are aware of the existence of the European standard for breast implants and are using it as a basis to establish the contractual liability of the clinics. They are employing two different strategies to apply the European standard, which can be directly linked to the different functions of European standards discussed above. Their first strategy is to claim that that the European standard represented the objective contractual standard of care with which the breast implants had to comply—the second category set out above. The claimants submit that there was an implied term in the contract between the victims and the clinics that the breast implants supplied by the clinics did not only have the CE mark on them, but that they also de facto complied with the provisions of the European standard.[23] As such, the European standard for breast implants would directly set the objective standard with which the breast implants had to comply. Compliance with the European standard would become an implied term of the contract between the clinics and the victims. A breach of the European standard would automatically result in a breach of contract on the part of the clinics. It is unclear to what remedies the claimants would be entitled in case of a breach of this term. This is a new approach in English law, and there is no authority to support the arguments of the claimants.[24]

[17] Directive 1999/44/EC on certain aspects of the sale of consumer goods and associated guarantees.

[18] See Joined Cases C-65/09 and C/87-09 *Gebr. Weber GmbH v Jürgen Wittmer and Ingrid Putz v Medianes Electronics GmbH* ECLI: EU: C:2011:396.

[19] G Brüggemeier, above n 14, 540–41.

[20] ibid.

[21] P Rott and C Glinski, 'Ramsch-Implantate: Ein Lehrstück europäischer Produktsicherheit' in C Joerges, T Pinkel and U Uetzmann (eds), 'Josef Falke zum 65. Geburtstag', *ZERP-Diskussionspapier* 1/2014 137–52, 149.

[22] Case C-636/11 *Karl Berger v Freistaat Bayern* ECLI: EU: C:2013:227. See K Purnhagen, 'Beyond Threats to Health: May Consumers' Interests in Safety Trump Fundamental Freedoms in Information on Foodstuffs? Reflections on Berger v Freistaat Bayern' (2013) 38 *EL Rev* 711–19.

[23] Interview with UK barrister (London) on 28 January 2014.

[24] ibid.

The second strategy of the claimants is to use the European standard to specify the concept of satisfactory quality in the Supply of Goods and Services Act 1982.[25] This links directly to the third function of European standards described above. Evidence of a breach of the provisions of the European standard would be used in support of the argument that the breast implants were not of satisfactory quality. The European standard would not be the only factor taken into account, but would be added to the various factors set out in the Act, such as fitness for purpose, appearance and safety. In order to use the European standard in this way, the claimants have to rely on expert evidence to be able to decide to what extent it can be argued that the PIP implants did not comply with the European standard for breast implants.[26] The difference with their first strategy is that with this second strategy, compliance with the European standard is only used as evidence in support of the argument that the clinics had breached the contractual standard of care. A breach of the provisions of the European standard would not in itself establish a breach of contract, but it would be used to establish a breach of the implied term that the breast implants would be of satisfactory quality.

C. Convergence in Contract Law

The UK group litigation provides a good example of the potential application of European standards in contract law. This case will now be linked again to the three different functions of European standards in contract law that have been set out in the first section. This will make it possible to draw conclusions about the potential for European standardisation of services to realise convergence in contract law.[27]

First of all, European services standards could become applicable to services contracts by an agreement between service provider and service recipient. In that respect, the character of services contracts in the healthcare and tourism sectors is important. The contracts in these sectors are usually between service provider and service recipient—in other words, between business and consumer. It is unusual for direct references to standards to be made in such contracts.[28] This has no doubt to do with the fact that standardisation of services is a relatively new development. But there is a more fundamental reason, which is that service providers are hesitant to make the compliance with standards contractually binding. The contract is just the starting point of the relationship between service provider and customer which does not require a precise definition of the contractual standards of care.[29] The delivery of services requires a certain

[25] ibid.

[26] ibid.

[27] See also F Cafaggi, 'Self-Regulation in European Contract Law' (2007) 1 *European Journal of Legal Studies* 1.

[28] Interview with HOTREC (Brussels) on 29 November 2012 and Interview with Chairman of Dutch Mirror Committee for Aesthetic Surgery Services (Goes) on 29 December 2012.

[29] U Magnus and H Mickliz, *Liability for the Safety of Services* (Baden-Baden, Nomos, 2006) 573–74.

amount of flexibility that enables the service provider to tailor the service to the customer and to the particular circumstances of a case.[30] While standards can always be used as guidelines, in particular for safety aspects, service providers do not consider it desirable for standards to be made contractually binding. This is an important difference with European standards for goods. It is more common for contracts in a supply chain to contain direct references to (European) standards.[31] Such contracts are usually contracts between businesses—'B2B contracts'. A good example of this is *James Elliott*,[32] the recent preliminary reference made by the Irish Supreme Court. The result is that all parties in the supply chain know precisely what criteria goods have to comply with.[33] Such standardised performance is unusual for services, which are more tailored and individualised. It is possible that services contracts refer to compliance with the relevant guidelines or standards in a particular sector, but this is not the same as the express incorporation of a particular standard. It leaves discretion to the parties and to the courts to make a decision about the relevance and applicability of a certain standard.[34] This would not be possible if the provisions of a European standard were made an express term of the contract.

Secondly, compliance with a European services standard could become an objective contractual standard with which the service provider would have to comply. In such cases, although the contract itself would be silent on the European standard, it would be implied in the contract that the service provider complied with its provisions. This is the first strategy employed by the claimants in the UK group litigation. The problem with such an approach is that the determination of the objective standard of care is normally based on custom or business practice in the sector.[35] It has already been emphasised that there is no European legislation which imposes compliance with a European services standard as an objective contractual standard. The upgrading of European standards made through self–regulation to a binding status in contract law would occur only if courts found that the European services standard adequately represented the custom in a particular sector.[36] At the moment, there is no empirical evidence to suggest that European services standards are regularly applied in contractual relations. There is no consensus among service providers to apply European services standards in

[30] Interview with HOTREC (Brussels) on 29 November 2012 and Interview with Chairman of Dutch Mirror Committee for Aesthetic Surgery Services (Goes) on 29 December 2012.

[31] F Cafaggi, above n 27, 16–20. See, for an interesting example of the use of European and national standards in a B2B contract, the judgment of the Rotterdam District Court of 15 October 2008, 295401, HA ZA 07-2802.

[32] Case C-613/14 *James Elliott Construction Limited v Irish Asphalt Limited*, preliminary reference made by the Irish Supreme Court on 30 December 2014.

[33] For an example of a UK case where a European standard was an express term of the contract, see *Messer UK v Britvic* [2002] EWCA Civ 548.

[34] U Magnus and H Micklitz, above n 29, 575.

[35] H Schepel and J Falke, above n 2, 215. See also F Cafaggi, above n 3, 108.

[36] H Schepel and J Falke, above n 2, 216–17. For the impact of mass-production and standardisation on the development towards an objective contractual standard of care in Germany, see R Knieper, *Zwang, Vernunft, Freiheit* (Frankfurt, Europäische Verlagsanstalt, 1981) 144–56.

practice. As a result, it is unlikely that courts would be willing to imply a term to this effect in contracts between service provider and service recipients and would set the European standard as the objective standard of care. This is also one of the difficulties for the claimants in the group litigation in the UK. With their first strategy, they argue that the European standard is the objective standard of care with which the breast implants have to comply. However, there is no European or national legislation which provides for this impact on contract law and the claimants are unable to point to a custom on the basis of which such a term could be implied.

The claimants could argue that compliance with the European standard should be implied in the contract as a matter of EU law. The argument could be made that the effectiveness of the New Approach to goods requires that service providers who transfer goods to service recipients should provide goods which are compatible with the relevant European standard. The New Approach has been created to improve the effective and safe free movement of goods within the EU. While it has primarily been created to facilitate free movement of goods, it also attempts to protect the recipients' goods. On that basis, one could argue that the effectiveness of EU law, in this case the Medical Devices Directive,[37] would require courts in contractual disputes to impose an obligation on service providers to provide goods which comply with the relevant European standards. A contractual requirement of compliance with the European standard would raise the level of protection for recipients of goods. This would be particularly important if an action under the Product Liability Directive was impossible, for example because the manufacturer had gone bankrupt. This is something which will be discussed in the next section on tort. From the perspective of convergence, it would be desirable if the European standard was set as the objective contractual standard of care because it would result in a uniform standard across the EU. Furthermore, convergence would be required as a matter of EU law—to guarantee the effective application of EU law—which would mean that national courts would only have a limited margin of discretion.

Thirdly and finally, it is possible for a European standard to have an evidential role in a contractual case. For this third category, the European standard does not directly become the contractual standard of care, but can be used to provide substance to a different objective standard of care.[38] This is the second strategy of the claimants in the group litigation in the UK. The claimants are using the European standard to argue that the PIP breast implants did not comply with he term that they would be of satisfactory quality. The possible non-compliance with the European standard is used to support the argument that the breast implants were not of satisfactory quality. Such an evidential application of a European standard relies significantly on parties and courts to refer to European

[37] Council Directive 93/42/EEC concerning medical devices.

[38] H Schepel and J Falke, above n 2, 218. See also *Medivance Instruments Ltd v Gaslane Pipework Services Limited* [2002] EWCA Civ 500.

standards. They will only do so if they believe that European standards adequately reflect the standard of care which can be expected from service providers. This also links back to the question whether or not European services standards are applied by the sector in practice. In the context of the New Approach, it can certainly be argued that European product standards adequately represent the safety standard with which goods should comply. They derive a sense of professional legitimacy from the fact that they have been adopted in a European regulatory framework. This is different for European services standards, which have not been adopted in a European regulatory framework. It is by no means certain that parties and courts will choose to rely on European services standards to determine the contractual standard of care. The impact of European services standards as professional standards will be discussed in more detail in the section on tort. Overall, the evidential application of European standards leaves a significant amount of discretion to national courts to determine what role the standard could play in the determination of contractual disputes. Moreover, the extent to which the European standards are applied would be determined entirely by national private law.

To conclude, convergence in private law through European standardisation of services is a two-stage process. The initial European standardisation process has to be followed by the application of European standards in private law. Contract law is obviously one of the prime candidates for the application of European standards. However, the reality is that service providers are hesitant to make standards contractually binding. The ex ante regulation of the provision of services through the contractual inclusion of European standards is unusual in the two services sectors that have been investigated in this book. This significantly limits the potential for convergence in contract law. It does not prevent the application of European standards ex post to determine whether or not service providers have complied with the contractual standard of care or to provide substance to different standards such as reasonable skill and care, state of the art or satisfactory quality.[39] While for European product standards it could be argued that they should be set as the objective standard of care in services contracts to guarantee the effectiveness of the New Approach, there is no New Approach to services which would require such an application of services standards in services contracts. What remains is a purely evidential function of European standards. From the perspective of convergence, the evidential application of European standards has severe limitations. It cannot be guaranteed that the standard will be referred to—everything depends on the parties and the courts to decide whether or not to base their arguments or reasoning on a European standard. The role that the standard will play is dependent on the particular circumstances of a case. Therefore, the harmonising impact of the standard will be limited and difficult to test.

[39] U Magnus and H Micklitz, above n 29, 575.

III. EUROPEAN STANDARDS IN TORT

A. Framing Convergence in Tort

Tort has an important role to play in the regulation of liability of service providers for defective services. Unlike contract law, which provides a tool for ex ante regulation of services through an express agreement to comply with European services standards, its focus is on ex post regulation. This means that courts are required to identify after the event whether the service provider has complied with the required standard of care in tort. Private standards are frequently used to specify, or to provide substance to, general duties in tort such as 'reasonable skill and care' or 'state of the art'. As a result, tort is open to the application of European services standards. At the same time, regulation through tort has its limitations. Because of its ex post application, the success of tort as a means of regulating services is dependent on the extent to which service providers are deterred from behaving in a certain way by the possibility of liability in tort.[40] European standardisation of services could then have a deterrent effect by forcing service providers to comply with a certain set of European standards.[41] This would mean that the ex post focus of tort would be combined with an ex ante approach based on European standardisation.

An important advantage of tort in comparison with contract law is that it is more flexible about the question against which party claimants could bring an action for defective services. This also means that a broader set of standards can become applicable. This will be illustrated by looking at the PIP breast implants case. In addition to the contractual claim against the clinics where the victims received their breast implants, victims could also bring a claim against the manufacturer of the breast implants, the PIP factory. This claim would be brought in tort under the Product Liability Directive. The key issue for the courts would be to decide whether the fact that a significant proportion of PIP breast implants contained industrial silicone gel and were at a higher risk of rupture was sufficient to establish that the breast implants were defective. The Bundesgerichtshof ('BGH'), the highest civil court in Germany, referred two cases to the ECJ in which the main question was whether pacemakers were defective under the Product Liability Directive if they were part of a group of products that were at a higher risk of becoming defective, but where the risk has not yet materialised. In his Opinion, Advocate General Bot argued that such pacemakers should be regarded as defective, since they form part of a group of products in which the defect has already materialised. Therefore, the products have a higher potential to become defective and do not meet the reasonable safety expectations of

[40] On the regulatory function of tort law in general, see Part 5 of R Posner and F Parisi, *The Economic Function of Private Law* (Cheltenham, Edward Elgar, 2002) and Part II of S Shavell, *Foundations of Economic Analysis of Law* (Cambridge, Harvard University Press, 2004).

[41] F Cafaggi, above n 3, 121.

patients.[42] The CJEU agreed with the Advocate General, although its approach was more restrictive.[43] It held that, because of the specific nature and function of pacemakers, the safety requirements for such products are particularly high.[44] Moreover, it held that the products contained an abnormal potential for damage. In those circumstances, the pacemakers should be regarded as defective under the Product Liability Directive. It is clear that the concept of defect under the Product Liability Directive is being stretched. The result could also be that services which include the provision of products could be brought within the scope of the Product Liability Directive. This is in line with the CJEU's judgment in *Veedfald*,[45] in which it held that the Directive was applicable to defective medical products which were supplied in the course of medical services. In the PIP case, the European product standard for breast implants would play an important role in the determination of whether or not the implants were defective. However, the PIP factory has gone into liquidation and it has become impossible for victims to seek redress directly from the manufacturer.

Another option for claimants could then be to bring an action against the certification body that was responsible for the conformity assessment procedure of the PIP breast implants. Various claimants in Germany and France have brought cases against TÜV Rheinland ('TÜV'), which is the certification body which undertook the conformity assessment procedure for PIP's breast implants. These cases will be discussed in detail below. From the perspective of tort, it is important to note that the choice for a different defendant means that different standards become applicable. The cases against TÜV are not directly concerned with the European standard for breast implants—they are not about the substantive provisions of the European standard. Rather, it is alleged that TÜV has breached the standards that are imposed on certification bodies in the New Approach. The standards applicable to these cases are those for the conformity assessment procedure, which have been laid down in the Medical Services Directive.[46] The Medical Devices Directive provides what steps certification bodies have to take during the conformity assessment procedure. Since this procedure constitutes a service, which creates a contract for services between the certification body and the manufacturer, the EU has effectively harmonised services standards for certification bodies. The regulatory framework created by the New Approach imposes these European standards. Finally, a third possible defendant could be the public supervisory agencies that were responsible for market surveillance. Again, this would mean that different

[42] Opinion of Advocate General Bot in Cases C-503/13 and C-504/13 *Boston Scientific Medizintechnik GmbH v AOK Sachsen- Anhalt and Betriebskran kenkasse RWE* ECLI:EU:C:2014:2306. For a detailed discussion, see N Reich, 'Fehlerhaftigkeit von Medizinprodukten', (2014) 23 *EuZW* 989.

[43] *Boston Scientific Medizintechnik*, above n 42, ECLI: EU: C:2015:148.

[44] ibid, para 39–40. See B van Leeuwen and P Verbruggen, 'Resuscitating EU Product Liability Law?: Contemplating the Effects of Boston Scientific Medizintechnik GmbH v. AOK Sachsen-Anhalt and Betriebskrankenkasse RWE (Joined Cases C-503/13 and C-504/13)' (2015) 23 *European Review of Private Law* 899.

[45] Case C-203/99 *Henning Veedfald v Arhus Ambtskommune* ECLI: EU: C:2001:258.

[46] Annex II of the Medical Devices Directive.

standards would become applicable to the case. It would shift the standards from European standards for the conformity assessment procedure to European standards on market surveillance by supervisory agencies. These standards have to some extent also been laid down in the Medical Devices Directive.[47] However, it is unclear to what extent a general obligation on public agencies to supervise the market, which is imposed by EU law, enables claimants to argue that they have an individual right to damages against a public agency based on its alleged lack of adequate supervision. The judgment of the CJEU in *Peter Paul*[48] makes it difficult for victims in the PIP case to argue that they should be individually compensated by the State for its failure to take adequate actions after the discovery of the PIP breast implants scandal.

In essence, European services standards could have two different functions in tort. First of all, a European service standard could be used as a sword to establish liability of a service provider. A breach of the provisions of the European standard would result in liability on the part of the service provider. The liability would not necessarily be automatic, but the breach of the European standard would shift the burden of proof to service providers to establish that they did comply with the required duty of care in tort. For example, the European standard for Cleft Lip Surgery could provide that a cleft lip has to be closed between six months and a year after birth. If a surgeon closed the cleft lip two years after birth, this could significantly impair the child's ability to talk and could result in a claim against the surgeon in tort. The non-compliance with the European standard could then be used to establish that the surgeon had breached his duty of care towards the child. It could raise a presumption that the standard of care in tort had been breached.

Secondly, a European standard could be used as a shield against liability in tort. A service provider could rely on compliance with a European standard as a defence to a claim in tort. Although the effect would not be automatic, the fact that the service provider had complied with the relevant European standard could raise a presumption that he had also complied with the required standard of care in tort. For example, a European standard for tour operators—which does not exist—could provide that tour operators had to conduct inspections of the accommodations with which they contracted at least twice a year. If a tourist then brought a liability claim against a tour operator under the Package Travel Directive, the tour operator could claim that it had adequately fulfilled its supervision duties and had not breached the standard of care in tort on the basis that it had carried out bi-annual inspections as required by the European standard.

With both of these functions, it is assumed that the existence of a European standard has a direct impact on tort. Although it does not automatically determine whether or not a service provider should be held liable in tort, at the very least it imposes an obligation on service providers to explain why they did not comply with the European standard or why the standard did not represent the required

[47] See Articles 8, 10 and 18 of the Medical Devices Directive.

[48] See C-222/02 *Peter Paul and others v Bundesrepublik Deutschland* ECLI: EU: C:2004:606.

standard of care in tort. Moreover, courts could go beyond the requirements imposed by a European standard and impose stricter standards on service providers. However, the existence of a European standard would normally require them to justify why the standard of care should be higher than the European standard. The existence of a European standard would create an obligation both on courts and on service providers to justify why the standard did not represent the required standard of care in tort in the particular circumstances of a case. Even if European standards did not have such a strong presumptive impact on liability in tort, they could still be used as a factor to be taken into account in deciding whether or not service providers had breached the required standard of care. This would mainly be an evidential function of European standards, which would be very similar to the third function of European standards in contract law. Before these functions will be analysed in more detail, the case study on the liability of TÜV after the PIP scandal will be discussed.

B. Case Study: TÜV Rheinland in the German and French Courts[49]

As an alternative to bringing a case in contract against the service providers who implanted the breast implants, victims could also bring a case in tort against the certification body which was responsible for the certification of the breast implants on the basis of European standards.[50] In Germany and in France, cases have been brought against TÜV Rheinland ('TÜV'), which was the certification body which undertook the conformity assessment procedure for the PIP breast implants. The conformity assessment procedure has to be undertaken by a 'notified body'. Notified bodies have an ex ante regulatory function in inspecting the quality management system and design dossier of the product—their certificate is necessary to be able to place the products on the market. Once they are on the market, the Member States' public supervisory agencies, in co-operation with the Commission, are primarily responsible for the surveillance of the market.[51] But notified bodies still have a role to play—they have to undertake surveillance to ensure that manufacturers comply with the approved quality system.[52] From 1997 to 2004 TÜV has undertaken the conformity assessment procedure for PIP and has issued a number of certificates.[53] As such, it has visited the PIP factory a number of times for inspections. After the discovery of the sub-standard industrial silicone gel in

[49] This case study is based on an article which was published in the European Journal of Risk Regulation: B van Leeuwen, 'PIP Breast Implants, the EU's New Approach for Goods and Market Surveillance by Notified Bodies' (2014) 3 *European Journal of Risk Regulation* 338.

[50] In this case, EN ISO 14630:2009 Non-active surgical implants—General requirements and EN ISO 14607:2009 Non-active surgical implants—Mammary implants—Particular requirements.

[51] Article 10 of the Medical Devices Directive.

[52] Article 5.1 of Annex II of the Medical Devices Directive.

[53] For a more detailed outline of the factual background to the cases, see P Rott and C Glinski, above n 21, 137–41.

PIP breast implants in 2010, TÜV claimed it had been deceived by PIP and joined the criminal proceedings against the PIP management in Marseille with the status of victim. However, this has not prevented a number of claimants from bringing legal proceedings against TÜV. They claim that TÜV has not complied with the required standards of care for the conformity assessment procedure, as a result of which PIP could continue to be place its breast implants on the market. Therefore, they claim that if TÜV had undertaken a stricter conformity assessment procedure the harm to the victims of PIP breast implants could have been avoided or limited, because the fraud by PIP would have been discovered much earlier.

This is the first time that the certification activities of notified bodies are challenged in the context of the New Approach. It could be argued that the case is only relevant to the New Approach and as a result, not of much use to European standardisation of services. However, its implications are not limited to the New Approach. The various cases after the PIP scandal illustrate how and to what extent ex ante regulation through European standardisation combined with certification can be linked to ex post liability claims in tort at the national level. The cases against TÜV have been brought in tort and it is claimed that TÜV has breached its duty of care in that it has not complied with the provisions of the Medical Devices Directive. The claimants argue that TÜV should have paid unannounced visits and should have tested whether the products actually complied with the design dossier. If they had done this, they would have discovered the fraud committed by PIP. Proceedings have been brought against TÜV both in the German and in the French courts. While in November 2013 the Tribunal de Commerce in Toulon upheld the claim against TÜV and awarded interim damages,[54] the lower German courts have consistently dismissed the cases.[55] This approach was eventually followed by the Court of Appeal of Aix-en-Provence. In 2015, the BGH referred one of the German cases to the CJEU for a preliminary ruling.[56] Therefore, the CJEU will now have to provide the final answer. First of all, the German judgments will be discussed. Secondly, the differences with the French judgments will be analysed.

The claimant in the one of the main German proceedings received PIP breast implants in December 2008. Unlike some of the German and Austrian victims who travelled to other Member States to receive—cheaper—breast implants,[57] such as the Czech Republic or Hungary, the claimant received her breast implants in a clinic in Germany. After a number of press reports and warnings, she decided to have them removed in March 2012 and to have them replaced by new breast implants. She subsequently brought an action against TÜV before the Landgericht ('LG') Frankenthal. Her claim was dismissed on three grounds. First of all,

[54] Judgment of Tribunal de Commerce in Toulon of 14 November 2013 (N° de rôle: 2011F00517).

[55] Judgment of Landgericht Frankenthal (Pfalz) of 14 March 2013—6 O 304/12, Judgment of OLG Zweibrücken of 30 January 2014—4 U 66/13.

[56] Case C-219/15 *Elisabeth Schmitt v TÜV Rheinland*, preliminary reference made by the Bundesgerichtshof on 13 May 2015.

[57] Interview with VKI (Vienna) on 5 November 2013.

the claimant had not established any medical harm. There was no evidence that she had breast cancer or had incurred any other medical problems as a result of the PIP breast implants. The mere risk of rupture was not sufficient and there was no evidence to suggest that she was at a higher risk of breast cancer as a result of having the PIP breast implants.[58] Secondly, the claimant had been unable to prove that the specific breast implants which she had received did in fact contain industrial silicone gel. It was not sufficient for her to rely on an interview with PIP employees in which they said that industrial gel was used 'all the time'. It would have been possible for the claimant to have her breast implants tested to be able to establish the type of silicone gel which they contained. As she had not done so, her claim had to fail.[59]

Thirdly, and most importantly, the LG Frankenthal held that TÜV had not breached its obligations under the Medical Devices Directive.[60] It was the responsibility of manufacturers to ensure compliance with the provisions of the Medical Devices Directive—they did so by affixing the CE mark on their products. The obligations of a notified body were clearly set out in Annex II of the Medical Devices Directive. Firstly, TÜV had to check the conformity of the quality management system with the provisions of the Directive. This meant that it had to undertake an audit of the quality management system. However, at that point, it was under no obligation to verify whether the quality management as presented by PIP was also brought into practice.[61] Secondly, TÜV was under an obligation to check the design dossier, which gave information about the contents and design of the product.[62] Again, it was not obliged to inspect the actual products. The fact that PIP did not respect its own quality management system and design dossier could not be used to establish fault on the part of TÜV. Thirdly, as to the inspections, TÜV was under an obligation to assess whether the quality management system was put into practice.[63] While this did indeed require an assessment of the extent to which the quality management system was put into practice, there was no actual obligation to test products. The assessment of whether or not the quality management system was brought into practice was again primarily based on an assessment of the paper work.

With regard to the possibility of unannounced visits, the LG Frankenthal held that TÜV had been under no obligation to carry out unannounced visits.[64] The Medical Devices Directive used the word 'may' and an obligation would only arise if there were specific circumstances which demanded an unannounced visit.

[58] 'LG Frankenthal: Industriesilikon in Brustimplantaten—Kontrollpflichtverletzung durch die benannte Stelle', *MPR* 2013, 134–40, 135.
[59] ibid, 136.
[60] ibid, 136–38.
[61] Article 3 of Annex II of the Medical Devices Directive.
[62] Article 4 of Annex II of the Medical Devices Directive.
[63] Article 5 of Annex II of the Medical Devices Directive
[64] 'LG Frankenthal: Industriesilikon in Brustimplantaten—Kontrollpflichtverletzung durch die benannte Stelle', *MPR* 2013, 134–40, 137.

The claimants had not shown that there were any such circumstances. Overall, the LG Frankenthal made a clear distinction between the duties of notified bodies and the duties of public supervisory agencies. Notified bodies are not market surveillance agencies.[65] They do not have the same powers as supervisory agencies. Their role is limited to the conformity assessment procedure. In France, AFSSAPS was the agency responsible for surveillance. The role of a notified body vis-à-vis the manufacturer could be seen as that of a 'Begleiter'—a companion.[66]

The judgment of the LG Frankenthal was upheld on appeal by the OLG Zweibrücken on 30 January 2014.[67] However, its grounds were significantly different. The LG Frankenthal assumed that the obligations imposed on notified bodies by the Medical Devices Directive constituted the required duty of care in tort owed to women with breast implants and held that these obligations had not been breached. However, the OLG Zweibrücken went one step back to consider whether a duty of care, either in contract or in tort, was owed by TÜV to women with breast implants at all. First of all, it held that the contract between TÜV and PIP was a contract for services which did not create protective effects for women with PIP breast implants. It constituted merely a 'building block' for the manufacturers to show that they complied with the requirements of the Directive.[68] As a result, TÜV did not owe a contractual duty of care towards the women. The responsibility for compliance with the requirements of the Medical Devices Directive remained with the manufacturer. Similarly, the OLG Zweibrücken held that TÜV did not owe a duty of care in tort to women with PIP breast implants. There was no general duty of care to prevent bodily harm.[69] Such a duty of care could arise if a specific duty of care was imposed by way of legislation, but the Medical Devices Directive did not impose such a duty of care on TÜV—despite the reference to the protection of the interests of patients in the preamble of the Directive.[70] The conformity assessment procedure undertaken by TÜV did not create a legal guarantee that the products complied with the requirements of the Directive.[71] The OLG Zweibrücken reaffirmed the strong separation of duties between notified bodies and public supervisory agencies.[72] Product certification could and should not be placed at the same level as market surveillance.[73] Finally, and only in the alternative, it held that if a

[65] ibid.

[66] ibid.

[67] Judgment of OLG Zweibrücken of 30 January 2014—4 U 66/13.

[68] Judgment of OLG Zweibrücken of 30 January 2014, II 2.2 b) aa) and bb).

[69] See G Spindler, 'Market Processes, Standardisation and Tort Law' (1998) 4 *European Law Journal* 316, 331.

[70] The exact words are as follows: 'Whereas medical devices should provide patients, users and third parties with a high level of protection and attain the performance levels attributed to them by the manufacturer; whereas, therefore, the maintenance or improvement of the level of protection attained in the Member States is one of the essential objectives of this Directive'.

[71] See H Schepel and J Falke, above n 2, 237–38.

[72] Judgment of OLG Zweibrücken of 30 January 2014, II. 2.2 d).

[73] P Rott and C Glinski, 'Die Haftung der Zertifizierungsstelle im Produktsicherheitsrecht' (2014) *Zeitschrift für Europäisches Privatrecht*.

duty of care in tort was owed by TÜV to women with PIP breast implants, there had been no breach of the duty of care.[74] Here, it essentially followed the reasoning of the LG Frankenthal. Reference was made to the 'almost perfect scheme of deceit' developed by PIP.[75] Because of the public importance and of the fact that a number of German jurisdictions were dealing with the same legal questions, the OLG Zweibrücken gave permission to appeal to the BGH. The BGH has now made a preliminary reference to the CJEU.[76] Two questions were asked: first of all, is the purpose and intention of the Medical Devices Directive that notified bodies act in order to protect patients who receive goods? In other words, does the *effet utile* of the Medical Devices Directive require that notified bodies owe a duty of care in tort to recipients of products? Second, the BGH has asked whether notified bodies were required to carry out unannounced inspections and to physically inspect products under the Medical Devices Directive. The hearing of the case before the CJEU took place in May 2016.

In France, a large group of distributors and women with PIP breast implants brought a case against TÜV before the Tribunal de Commerce in Toulon ('the Toulon court'). The Toulon court delivered its judgment in November 2013.[77] Its reasoning was remarkably different from the German courts. From early on in the judgment, it put emphasis on the fact that the risks of breast implants were well known after a series of incidents in the early 1990s.[78] Furthermore, it held that the functions performed by TÜV constituted a real delegation of public services.[79] This is in direct contradiction with the reasoning of the German courts. An important factor in the French judgment was the fact that the audits undertaken by TÜV had been performed by TÜV France rather than by TÜV Germany. However, TÜV France was not a notified body under the Medical Devices Directive and, as such, was not entitled to undertake the conformity quality assessment procedures under the Directive. Therefore, the Toulon court held that TÜV had breached the provisions of the Directive.[80] Importantly, the Toulon court found that if TÜV had made an unannounced visit to the PIP factory, the fraud committed by PIP would easily have been discovered and the extent of the scandal would have been limited. It held that TÜV should have been put on notice by incidents in 2000, when PIP breast implants had temporarily been taken off the market because they contained sub-standard silicone gel. More specifically, it should have been evident to TÜV that the amount of medical silicone gel which had been bought by PIP were not consistent with the amount of breast implants manufactured in the factory.[81] Overall, the fact that TÜV had kept to an absolute minimum

[74] ibid, 2.2 e.
[75] ibid.
[76] *Schmitt*, above n 56.
[77] Judgment of Tribunal de Commerce in Toulon of 14 November 2013 (N° de rôle: 2011F00517).
[78] ibid, 140.
[79] ibid, 141.
[80] ibid.
[81] ibid.

of the obligations required by the Medical Devices Directive meant that all of its activities were focused on profit-making. The Toulon court concluded that TÜV had breached its obligations of control, surveillance and vigilance.[82] On that basis, it held that TÜV was liable to the claimants. Experts were instructed to determine the precise damages suffered by the claimants. In the meantime, the Toulon court ordered that interim damages be awarded to all claimants. TÜV has brought an appeal before the Court of Appeal of Aix-en-Provence. In January 2014, the Court of Appeal upheld the award of interim damages of €3,000 per victim.[83] However, in July 2015, the Court of Appeal essentially followed the rulings of the German courts. It allowed the appeal by TÜV and held that TÜV had complied with its obligations under the Medical Devices Directive. With similar positions now taken by the German and French courts, the judgment of the CJEU in *Schmitt* will be crucial for the victims' prospects of compensation by TÜV.

C. The Impact of PIP on Convergence in Tort

The cases against TÜV were about the certification activities of a notified body. They were about TÜV's alleged failure to undertake the conformity assessment procedure with sufficient care based on the standards imposed by the Medical Devices Directive. Although it could be argued that the standards for the conformity assessment procedure only apply to the New Approach, this discussion is also relevant to certification which has taken place outside the New Approach. The question to what extent certification bodies are under an obligation to monitor performance of certificate holders and what impact certification should have on liability in tort is also important outside the context of the New Approach. Due to the fact that certification is one of the most common ways for European standards to be applied in the services sector, the role and potential liability of certification bodies is very important. However, the important difference is that outside the New Approach the EU does not exercise direct influence over the standards with which certification bodies should comply.

The cases brought against TÜV show that it is difficult for consumers to claim that the certification of a service provider has an impact on the private law relationship between service provider and consumer. The impact of the relationship between certification body and service provider remains restricted to those two parties. Courts are hesitant to impose a duty of care in tort on certification bodies vis-à-vis the consumers of the certified service provider. The nature of certification is such that it creates a relationship between certifier and service provider.[84]

[82] Judgment of Tribunal de Commerce in Toulon of 14 November 2013, 142.
[83] See www.independent.co.uk/news/world/europe/french-legal-ruling-paves-the-way-for-compensation-for-women-with-faulty-pip-breast-implants-9075513.html.
[84] G Spindler, above n 69, 331–32.

This is very clear from the judgment of the OLG Zweibrücken.[85] It is not likely that courts will make a link between the standards used for certification and the standard of care required in tort. The ex ante regulatory framework developed through the New Approach cannot easily be applied ex post—this is what could be described as a mismatch between the ex ante regulation through European standardisation combined with certification and the ex post regulation of liability for defective products.[86] Again, this is very clear from the OLG Zweibrücken's judgment—the fact that certain requirements have been imposed on certification bodies by the Medical Devices Directive does not automatically mean that they result in the imposition of a duty of care owed to consumers in tort. Nevertheless, it is possible to use them as a basis for the imposition of a duty of care in tort. This is clear from the judgment of the Toulon court, which held that TÜV had breached its obligations of control. However, the question whether or not a duty of care should be imposed remains a question of national law. The effect of the European regulatory requirements on liability in private law is considered through the lens of national private law, which acts as a filter for its application. It is only if the regulatory requirements are consistent with the requirements of national private law that they can be applied. In the context of the New Approach, this raises questions about the extent to which Member States have to ensure the *effet utile* of the Medical Devices Directive. It could be argued that a failure to provide adequate remedies to consumers after the PIP breast scandal does not sufficiently guarantee the *effet utile* of the Medical Devices Directive. This could mean that liability has to be extended to certification bodies if the manufacturer of medical devices has gone bankrupt. The CJEU will now have to provide the final answer to the question in the preliminary reference made by the BGH. In the aftermath of the PIP breast implants scandal, the EU has already extended the obligations of notified bodies under the Medical Devices Directive.[87] Similarly, Member States are required to supervise the activities of notified bodies more strictly and to impose stricter criteria before certification bodies can become notified bodies.[88] Finally, the PIP breast implant cases raise questions about the interaction between the New Approach and the Product Liability Directive.[89] If it is not possible to protect patients or customers under the New Approach, the scope of protection of the

[85] Judgment of OLG Zweibrücken of 30 January 2014—4 U 66/13.

[86] F Cafaggi, above n 1, 217–22.

[87] Commission Recommendation of 24 September 2013 on the audits and assessments performed by notified bodies in the field of medical devices (2013/473/EU). For the background, see Commission Communication, 'Safe, effective and innovative medical devices and in vitro diagnostic medical devices for the benefit of patients, consumers and healthcare professionals', COM(2012) 540 final of 26 September 2012.

[88] Commission Implementing Regulation (EU) No 920/2013 on the designation and the supervision of notified bodies under Council Directive 90/385/EEC on active implantable medical devices and Council Directive 93/42/EEC on medical devices.

[89] Council Directive 85/374/EEC on the approximation of the laws, regulations and administrative provisions of the Member States concerning liability for defective products ('the Product Liability Directive').

Product Liability Directive could be extended.[90] It could even be argued that notified bodies should be considered as producers to be brought within the scope of the Product Liability Directive.[91]

Overall, it has been shown that the New Approach has created a framework in which convergence in tort becomes a realistic possibility. The TÜV cases illustrate that certification bodies are held accountable for their activities more broadly than just towards the manufacturer. Indirectly, through the imposition and enforcement of European standards for the conformity assessment procedure, this development could improve the effective enforcement of the European standard for breast implants. The result would be convergence in tort. However, the possible convergence is not based on the European standard for breast implants itself, but rather on the regulatory framework in which the standard is applied. Convergence is driven by the New Approach. The potential liability of certification bodies can be defended on the basis that the effectiveness of the New Approach would be compromised if certification bodies were allowed to do a lazy job without being held responsible and liable. The pressure for convergence comes from the regulatory framework in which the European standards play a role.

Outside the New Approach, and similar to the application of European services standards in contract law, there is no European drive for convergence. European services standards could also be used for certification.[92] However, there would not be a European ex ante regulatory framework that would impose the application of the European services standards and that would provide pressure for these standards to play a role in liability in tort at the national level. The pressure for convergence would not come from the EU, but would rather come from professional associations which would require certification, for example as a condition for membership. There would not be a European framework in which the certification would play a role. As a result, there would be no guarantee that the European standard would be used to determine the required standard of care in tort. It is much more difficult to expect a degree of harmonisation through such certification.

D. Convergence in Tort

After the discussion of the PIP case, we will now return to convergence in tort more generally. As a starting point, there is no European regulatory approach to

[90] G Spindler, 'Interaction between product liability and regulation at the European level' in F Cafaggi and H Muir Watt (eds), *The Regulatory Function of European Private Law*, (Cheltenham, Edward Elgar, 2009) 243–58. See also C Joerges and H Micklitz, 'The Need to Supplement the New Approach to Technical Standardization by a Coherent European Product Safety Policy' (2010) 6 *Hanse Law Review* 351.

[91] B van Leeuwen, above n 49.

[92] Interview with Chairman of Dutch Mirror Committee for Aesthetic Surgery Services (Goes) on 29 December 2012, Interview with ASI (Vienna) on 12 November 2012 and Interview with HOTREC (Brussels) on 29 November 2012.

link European standardisation of services to liability for defective services in tort. The application of European services standards in tort at the national level is not regulated or controlled by the EU. The result is that the pressure to comply with European services standards has to come entirely from stakeholders and courts at the national level. The simple adoption of a European services standard does not guarantee its application in tort. Nevertheless, the way in which European standards are applied in tort at the national level shows significant similarities across the EU.[93]

In the first section, two different functions of European standards were introduced. First of all, non-compliance with a European standard could automatically result in liability in tort or at least in a very strong presumption of liability. However, national courts have not been willing to make such a direct link between the breach of a European standard and liability. For example, while the UK courts were initially willing to make this link, they have now changed to a more flexible approach. In *Ward v Ritz*, the English Court of Appeal held that the trial judge had not given sufficient weight to a standard adopted by BSI.[94] Although they were not strictly speaking legally binding, they provided strong evidence about the professional standards to be expected. As a result, the judgment could be interpreted as supporting a clear link between a breach of a standard and a breach of the duty of care. A breach of a BSI standard at the very least would put a burden on defendants to prove that they had not breached their duty of care—it would reverse the burden of proof and result in a prima facie presumption of a breach of the standard of care. However, the Court of Appeal has since moved back from making such a direct link. Only a few years later, in *Green v Building Scene Ltd*, the Court of Appeal held that standards cannot define what is reasonably safe in all the circumstances of a particular case:[95] A breach of a European standard is not in itself sufficient to establish a breach of the standard of care in tort. It is part of a bigger picture, namely all the circumstances of a particular case. The standard is insufficient as a tool to define the precise requirements of the duty of care, which means that a breach of the standard can never automatically result in a breach of the duty of care. A similar position has been taken by the German courts.[96] That does not mean that the standard plays no role at all. Particularly in product liability law, the existence of a standard can give rise to a presumption of compliance. Non-compliance imposes a burden of proof on manufacturers to establish that they have not breached their duty of care in tort. However, the strength of the presumption will be different from case to case. Moreover, it might be that such a presumption is less strong in liability cases for services, in which a broader set of

[93] See H Schepel and J Falke, above n 2, 233.

[94] *Anthony Philip Ward v The Ritz Hotel (London) Limited* [1992] PIQR 315, 327.

[95] *Green v Building Scene Limited* [1994] PIQR 259, 269.

[96] J Falke, *Rechtliche Aspekte der Normung in den EG-Mitgliedstaaten und der EFTA—Band 3: Deutschland* (Luxembourg, Office for Official Publications of the European Communities, 2000) 349–51.

circumstances has to be taken into account.[97] The result is that the 'presumptive impact' of the standard becomes less strong. Finally, the strength of the presumption will depend on the extent to which the standard has been accepted as the professional standard in a particular sector. This will be discussed below.

The second function of European standards in tort is to provide a defence to liability. Compliance with the European standard would be a way for service providers to prove that they have complied with the required standard of care. A good example of this can be found in a judgment of the Amsterdam Court of Appeal.[98] In this case, a five year old boy, while shopping with his mother, got stuck between the end of an escalator and the floor. As a result, he suffered extremely serious injuries. In its defence, the shop claimed that it was not liable as the escalator had fully complied with the requirements imposed by the European standard.[99] However, an expert report had found that the European standard had not taken the possibility of a young child getting stuck between the end of the escalator and the floor into account. On that basis, the Amsterdam Court of Appeal held that compliance with the European standard was not sufficient to avoid liability.[100] The question was whether the escalator was safe in the circumstances of the case. Because the European standard had not taken the particular circumstances of this case into account, it could not serve as a defence to the claim against the shop.[101] The court imposed obligations that went beyond the European product standard. This illustrates a tendency for courts to consider European products standards as the absolute minimum and to increase the level of protection offered to consumers beyond what is offered by the European standard. Tort then imposes duties that go beyond the requirements of the European standard.[102]

Since European standards do not have a direct impact on liability in tort, their main function remains evidential. Essentially, this is similar to their application in contract law. The European standards can be used to specify the required professional standard of care. In the absence of a European regulatory framework, it remains for stakeholders to use the European standards in legal proceedings and for courts to decide whether a European standard adequately represents the professional standard that can be expected from the service provider. As a result, the extent to which European standardisation of services will result in convergence in tort is dependent on the extent to which European services standards are applied as professional standards in tort.[103] This is where the professional legitimacy of European standardisation of services becomes very important. It is by no means

[97] G Spindler, above n 69, 321.

[98] Judgment of the Amsterdam Court of Appeal of 24 November 2009, LJN BL4918.

[99] ibid, para 3.8.

[100] Ibid, para 3.8–3.9.

[101] G Spindler, above n 69, 320–21. See also C Joerges and J Falke, 'Die Normung von Konsumgütern in der Europäischen Gemeinschaft und die Richtlinien-Entwurf über die allgemeine Produktsicherheit' in P. Müller-Graf (ed), *Technische Regeln im Binnenmarkt* (Baden-Baden, Nomos, 1991) 159–202.

[102] G Spindler, above n 69, 321. See also G Spindler, above n 85, 250–51

[103] F Cafaggi, above n 3, 118.

certain that in liability cases, experts and courts will apply European standards. They have to obtain the status of professional standards. The professional legitimacy that is more obvious in the case of product standards adopted under the New Approach cannot automatically be assumed for European services standards.

The requirements of the state of the art could be defined by reference to professional standards or guidelines adopted in the sector.[104] There is a variety of international, European and national standards that courts can use in reaching a decision about the required standard of care. More specifically, in the healthcare sector, in some Member States, like the Netherlands, there is a presumption that doctors will comply with the relevant standards and guidelines adopted by the profession. If the doctor has not complied with the relevant standards, a duty is imposed on him to explain why he has not complied with the standards. This is called the 'comply or explain' principle.[105] However, such a presumption of compliance will only arise if it is beyond doubt that the relevant standard expresses the professional standard required from the doctor. In the healthcare sector, it is by no means certain that European standards adopted through CEN will be accepted as the professional standard. On the contrary, it has been strongly argued by the European associations of doctors that CEN standards do not constitute the professional standard.[106] It has been shown in chapter three that this opposition is based both on the European standardisation process, which is not sufficiently evidence-based, and on the representativeness of the participants in the European standardisation process, who do not adequately represent the entire profession. The European standardisation process is also considered to be too slow to adequately reflect the current state of the art in the healthcare sector.[107] Furthermore, there is no formal requirement of verification by scientific associations of medical professions.[108] Overall, for all these reasons, there is insufficient professional control by the medical profession of the making of European standards through CEN. On that basis, the associations argue that European standards do not constitute the professional standard. The lack of professional acceptance of European healthcare standards makes it less likely that they will be applied in tort.

Finally, the fact that European standards adopted through CEN are European rather than national standards might cause problems for their application in tort. Unlike with the New Approach, there is no reason for courts to assume that the

[104] E Benvenisti and G Downs, 'National courts and transnational private regulation', in F Cafaggi (ed), *Enforcement of Transnational Private Regulation* (Cheltenham, Edward Elgar, 2012) 131–46, 143. See also U Magnus and H Micklitz, above n 29, 575, and A Samanta et al, 'The Role of Clinical Guidelines in Medical Negligence Litigation: A Shift from the *Bolam* Standard?' (2006) 14 *Medical Law Review* 321.

[105] Interview with Chairman of Dutch Mirror Committee for Aesthetic Surgery Services (Goes) on 29 December 2012, interview with UEMS and CPME (Warsaw) on 19 February 2013 and interview with NEN (Delft) on 12 April 2012.

[106] Interview with UEMS and CPME (Warsaw) on 19 February 2013.

[107] ibid.

[108] J van Everdingen et al. (eds), *Evidence-based richtlijnontwikkeling: een leidraad voor de praktijk* (Houten, Bohn Stafleu, 2004).

professional standard should be a European standard. It is important to remember that European standards adopted through CEN only attempt to lay down minimum standards.[109] From the analysis above, it is clear that tort frequently adds additional requirements to European standards. As a result, compliance with a European standard is not sufficient to avoid liability. Outside the context of the New Approach, the minimum nature of European standards could not only be a reason to go beyond the requirements of a European standard. It could also be a reason to reject the standard in its entirety and to prefer a different—probably national—standard which more precisely reflects the standard of care that can be expected from service providers in a particular sector. For example, in the healthcare sector, in which professional standards are widely divergent across the EU, courts might find that the standard which is required at the national level is higher than a European standard.[110] It will be remembered that the Cross-Border Healthcare Directive 2011 expressly provides that treatment shall be provided in accordance with national standards or guidelines.[111] This is directly linked to the lack of EU competence to regulate the delivery of healthcare services at the national level. As a result, it cannot automatically be presumed that national courts will refer to European standards to determine the standard of care in tort. Their starting point is much more likely to be national standards or guidelines. A European standard would then only be relevant if there were no national standards in place. For example, this has been one of the reasons for the initiative for a European standard for Cleft Lip Services—it has been argued that there are not sufficient standards in the new Member States.[112] While this discussion has focused primarily on the healthcare sector, it is unlikely that the approach would be different in other services sectors. In the tourism sector, the strong objections to European standardisation as lacking sufficient professional legitimacy have a similar detrimental impact on the willingness of stakeholders to rely on European standards in tort.[113]

To conclude, the convergent impact of European standardisation of services on tort depends to a significant extent on their application as professional standards. At the moment, in the field of services, European standards are not considered to have the required professional legitimacy to be applied in tort. The various problems with the European standardisation process come back to bite at the moment of the application of the standards. In the New Approach, convergence is very much driven by the regulatory framework established by the EU. In this framework, as the PIP case has shown, European standardisation plays a pre-determined role, which also has an impact on tort. Without such a regulatory framework for services, the role of European standards is entirely dependent on stakeholders and

[109] See also C Joerges and J Falke, above n 101, 161.
[110] Interview with NEN (Delft) on 12 April 2012.
[111] Article 4(1)(b) of the Cross-Border Healthcare Directive.
[112] Interview with ECO (Skype) on 14 March 2012.
[113] Interview with HOTREC (Brussels) on 29 November 2012. See also U Magnus and H Micklitz, above n 29, 554.

courts at the national level.[114] At the moment, the opposition to the application of European services standards in tort is fierce, which makes the possibility of convergence in tort more difficult.

IV. EUROPEAN STANDARDS AND THE UNFAIR CONTRACT TERMS DIRECTIVE

A. Framing Convergence and the UCTD

This section on the relationship between European standardisation and the Unfair Contract Terms Directive ('UCTD')[115] is difficult to place in the structure of chapters six and seven. In essence, the UCTD provides a review mechanism to test the fairness of provisions of European standards that are incorporated in contracts between service providers and consumers. From that perspective, this section would be more appropriate in the next chapter, which analyses the role of the free movement and competition provisions as review mechanisms for the application of European standards. At the same time, the UCTD is closely connected to the application of European standards in contract law. For that reason, the role of the UCTD will be discussed in this chapter. As such, this section will serve as a transition to the next chapter.

Although the section on convergence in contract law has concluded that European standards are not frequently directly applied as contractual terms in contracts between service providers and service recipients, it cannot be excluded that such contractual application becomes more common in the future. In particular, European services standards could be applied as standard terms in consumer contracts. The application of European standards as standard terms is a kind of private regulation, since the standards are applied, most frequently by associations of service providers, to impose certain standards on service providers and their customers.[116] This means that the application of European standards as standard terms would become subject to review.[117] One of the review mechanisms could be the UCTD, which imposes standards of fairness on the inclusion of terms in consumer contracts.

In general, the review under the UCTD would be different from the free movement provisions or the competition law provisions. The free movement provisions are used to review whether European standards create obstacles to free movement, while the competition law provisions assess to what extent European standards could create obstacles to competition in the internal market. The UCTD would test specifically to what extent a European standard has an impact on the fairness of the contractual relationship between service provider and consumer. Therefore, its review is limited to the application of European standards in contract law.

114 F Cafaggi, above n 3, 119.
115 Directive 93/13/EEC on unfair terms in consumer contracts.
116 F Cafaggi, above n 27. See also H Micklitz, above n 6.
117 F Cafaggi, above n 3.

From the perspective of convergence, the UCTD has a dual function. First of all, the UCTD could create an obstacle to convergence by preventing the application of European standards in contract law. If provisions of a European standard were found to be unfair under the UCTD, courts would be obliged not to apply these provisions. The result would be that the European standard would not be effectively applied in private law. Secondly, the UCTD could provide pressure on stakeholders to adopt European standards with provisions which were fair from the perspective of the UCTD. As a result, the possibility of review under the UCTD would impose a duty on stakeholders to think about the effect of provisions in European standards on the contractual relationship between service provider and service recipient. The UCTD could encourage a process of 'fair convergence' in private law.

These two functions of the UCTD presume that a link between European standardisation and the UCTD can be made. However, this assumption has to be tested at three different levels:

(i) European standards have to be subject to review under the UCTD;
(ii) European standards have to contain provisions that would (potentially) be unfair under the UCTD; and
(iii) Consumers, consumer organisations and public authorities have to be able to enforce the UCTD.

Each of these aspects will be analysed before some conclusions will be drawn as to the ability of the UCTD to have an impact on convergence in private law through European standardisation of services.

B. The Ex Ante Abstract Review and the Ex Post Concrete Review of European Standards

A distinction should be made between two types of control under the UCTD. Firstly, European standards could be reviewed ex ante if courts found that they were recommended or made to be used as standard terms in contractual relations. This would be a more abstract review of European standards, which would not be directly linked to their application in services contracts. The review would be based exclusively on the provisions of European standards—it would not be linked to the incorporation of European standards in contracts. The adoption of European standards would be sufficient for review under the UCTD if they were recommended or made to be used in contractual relations. The actual use of European standards as standard terms would not be necessary—this kind of review would have a preventative function. This will be discussed further below.

Secondly, the specific application of European standards as contractual terms in service providers could be controlled ex post under the UCTD. This would require courts to assess in concreto the fairness of the provisions of European standards in the specific circumstances of their incorporation in services contracts. Such control would only be possible if European standards were directly incorporated in services contracts. Normally, this would require a reference to European standards in contracts.

Furthermore, Article 3(1) clarifies that the UCTD only applies to terms which have not been individually negotiated. Finally, Article 1(2) provides that the UCTD does not apply to contractual terms which reflect mandatory statutory or regulatory provisions. As a result, European standards would be outside the scope of application of the UCTD if they were regarded as individually negotiated or if they were regarded as mandatory statutory or regulatory provisions.

i. The Ex Ante Abstract Review of European Standards

Article 7 of the UCTD provides for the possibility of an ex ante review of the provisions of European services standards. This is possible if European standards are recommended or made for use as standard terms. The aim of Article 7 is prevention—it enables consumer organisations or public supervisory agencies to identify and challenge contractual terms which could potentially be unfair for consumers before they have been brought into practice.

From the perspective of European standardisation, the first question is whether European standards are recommended or made for use as standard terms. It is clear that European standards are not expressly made as contractual terms—there is nothing in the standards which states that they are made to be used as standard terms. Nevertheless, it could be argued that the adoption of a European standard constitutes a recommendation that the standards be used as standard terms in services contracts. The intention with which the standards are made is irrelevant—the test for recommending is objective.[118] Although the concrete application of European standards in contracts in the services sector is not very common, it could be argued that the purpose behind the standardisation process is to make standards for use in services contracts. At the moment, European services standards do not look very much like contract terms or standard terms. This makes it more difficult to argue that the standards are made to be applied in service contracts.

The second question is who could be said to recommend the use of European standards as standard terms? In other words, against which party would the abstract review under Article 7 of the UCTD be directed? Against which organisation could consumer organisations or public authorities bring an action to review the provisions of European standards? If actions under Article 7 were brought directly against standardisation organisations, this could have an important impact on the freedom of standardisation organisations to decide on the content of European standards. The first candidate would be CEN, which is the organisation through which European standards are made. A distinction should be made between standards which have been mandated by the EU and standards which

[118] See H Micklitz, *Bauverträge mit Verbrauchern und die VOB Teil B* (Berlin, BWV, 2005).

have been developed at the request of national standardisation organisations. For mandated standards, CEN has put in a tender to the EU and could, therefore, be said to actively promote these standards for use as contract terms. It would go beyond mere facilitation—it could be argued that CEN is the motor behind the making of European standards and that European standards are implicitly recommended by CEN as standard terms. The consequence of this would be that consumer organisations could directly bring an action against CEN to challenge the provisions of European standards. This would be a much more direct way for consumer organisations to influence the substantive provisions of European standards. However, since CEN is not directly responsible for the publication of European standards, it becomes more difficult to argue that CEN is actually recommending the use of European standards as standard terms. Moreover, in the case of mandated standards, the real initiator could be said to be the Commission, which has issued the mandate to CEN. Again, CEN's function would be primarily that of a facilitator—the initiative had been taken by the Commission.

Alternatively, an action could be brought against the national standardisation organisations. This would be most likely for standards made at the request of a particular national standardisation organisation. Moreover, it should be recalled that national standardisation organisations are responsible for the publication of both mandated and non–mandated European standards. However, it is doubtful whether the sole publication of European standards can be considered a recommendation that European standards be used as standard terms. The more likely candidates for the abstract review are professional associations—expressly mentioned in Article 7(3) of the UCTD—which might have been involved in the making of European standards for the purpose of their application as contract terms. This would mean that the abstract review would create pressure on standardisation organisations to disclose information about which parties took the initiative for European standards and which parties were involved in their making of the standards. The standardisation organisations could then seek to rely on intellectual property rights to prevent having to disclose which parties were behind a certain standard.[119] The abstract review under the UCTD would challenge the confidentiality of European standardisation. It would create a direct link with the transparency of European standardisation. In the healthcare sector, it is difficult to identify associations which are recommending the use of European standards as standard terms. Most of the associations of doctors have opposed European standardisation. In the tourism sector, professional associations in the UK require compliance with the European standard for Tourist Guide Training as a pre-condition for membership. However, this standard is not directly relevant to the contract between tourist guide and tourists, because it deals solely with the qualifications of the tourist guide.

[119] See R van Gestel and H Micklitz, 'European Integration through Standardisation: How Judicial Review is Breaking Down the Club House of Private Standardisation Bodies' (2013) 50 *CML Rev* 145, 170.

ii. The Ex Post Individual Review of European Standards

Article 1 of the UCTD provides that the Directive applies to unfair terms in contracts concluded between a seller or supplier and a consumer. European standards can be incorporated in and become applicable to consumer contracts. It has been argued above that this is not yet customary in the services sectors which have been investigated. However, if European standardisation of services becomes more common, it is possible that service providers will adopt or refer to European standards in their contracts and that they will be applied as contractual terms. It could even be the case that service providers would copy certain provisions of European standards and incorporate them directly in their contracts. European standards could be exempted from review on the basis that they are not freely accessible and have to be bought from the standardisation organisations. However, it is difficult to see why the fact that standards become products and are protected by copyright would have an impact on their coming within the scope of the UCTD. The fact that European standards have to be obtained through national standardisation organisations has an impact on their transparency as contractual terms, but it does not mean that they cannot become contractual terms and would be outside the scope of the UCTD.

iii. European Standards and Individual Negotiation

European standards would be exempted from review under the UCTD if they were individually negotiated. Since the provisions of European standards have been adopted by CEN, it is difficult to see how they could be regarded as individually negotiated. Their provisions have been laid down in advance and cannot be amended without amending the European standard itself. An argument could be made that the UCTD should not be applicable if there had been a specific discussion between service provider and consumer about whether the European standard should be made applicable to the contract. In practice, however, such a discussion is unlikely to take place. Nevertheless, the fact that European standards have not prima facie been made as standard contract terms remains important. On the basis of the legislative history of the UCTD it has been argued that these standards, which would fall in a separate category of pre-formulated terms, would require an additional element to establish that they have not been individually negotiated.[120] In such cases, consumers would have to show that they had not been able to influence the pre-formulation of the terms. This would mean that the concept of individual negotiation in the UCTD would be extended to collective bargaining. It would require an assessment of the extent to which consumers are able to influence the making of contractual terms.

In the context of European standardisation, consumers could be said to influence the adoption of European standards through their participation in the

[120] N Reich et al, *European Consumer Law* (Cambridge, Intersentia, 2014) 135.

standardisation process. ANEC is frequently involved in European standardisation processes and the same applies to consumer organisations at the national level.[121] Such collective bargaining leading to the adoption of a European standard could result in the European standard being taken out of the scope of the UCTD. For collective bargaining, it is essential that discussions take place with a view to accommodate the views of the other side and to reach a compromise on the basis of bringing two parties with opposite interests together.[122] In his Opinion in *Albany*, Advocate General Jacobs stated that in the context of collective bargaining, 'a measure of equilibrium between the bargaining power on both sides helps to ensure a balanced outcome for both sides'.[123] However, the analysis in chapter two has shown that consumer organisations are having real difficulties participating in European standardisation. Often, they are not even sitting at the table where the European standard is made. Even if they are able to participate, they only have an observer status that does not allow them to vote on the provisions of the standard. Although it could be said that they are in a position to influence the provisions of European standards through consensus-building in the standardisation process, it is clear that without the power of voting the influence of consumer organisations remains limited. Furthermore, most of the time they do not have the technical expertise necessary to influence the formulation of the substantive provisions of European standards. As a consequence, European standardisation cannot be considered as collective bargaining between service providers and consumers, since it is essentially a process controlled by businesses. Consumers might be consulted in the process, but the standardisation process does not involve negotiations between two sides which each have equal bargaining power. The equilibrium mentioned by Advocate General Jacobs in *Albany* does not exist in European standardisation. As a result, it is unlikely that the involvement of consumer organisations in European standardisation would result in European standards being exempted from review under the UCTD.

iv. European Standards and Mandatory Statutory or Regulatory Provisions

Finally, European standards would fall outside the scope of the UCTD if they constituted mandatory statutory or regulatory provisions as provided by Article 1(2). The correct interpretation of Article 1(2) has been the subject of discussion by the CJEU in a number of cases. In *Cofidis*,[124] it was held that that the contractual terms did come within the scope of the UCTD because the terms went beyond the requirements imposed by the relevant French legislation. On that basis, they

[121] Interview with ANEC (Brussels) on 4 April 2012.

[122] In the context of employment law, see C Barnard, *EU Employment Law* (Oxford, OUP, 2012) 709–10.

[123] Opinion of AG Jacobs in Case C-67/96 *Albany International BV v Stichting Bedrijfspensioenfonds Textielindustrie* ECLI: EU: C:1999:28, para. 181.

[124] Case C-473/00 *Cofidis SA v Jean Louis Fredout* ECLI: EU: C:2002:705.

could not escape review under the UCTD. In *RWE Vertrieb*,[125] the CJEU held that if it is absolutely clear that a term was imposed by legislation, this would mean that the legislature has already performed a balancing exercise between the rights of the seller and the consumer. The result of the balancing exercise was that a fairness review under the UCTD was no longer possible and the exception under Article 1(2) applied. However, it has to be absolutely clear that the contractual term which is disputed comes within the scope of the national legislation. If there is any uncertainty about this, as was the case in *Cofidis*, the UCTD will be applicable. Most recently, in *Barclays Bank*,[126] the CJEU held that Article 1(2) applied to contractual terms imposed by statutory legislation if no other arrangement had been made between the parties and the only applicable terms were those imposed by the legislation.

Without the application of European standards in legislation, the main question with respect to their application in consumer contracts is whether these standards are mandatory regulatory provisions. In other words, are European standards adopted in a regulatory framework which makes compliance with the standards mandatory? In the context of the New Approach, which is clearly a European regulatory framework, it could at least be argued that European standards become de facto mandatory. Although it is clear from the construction of the New Approach that European standards provide but one way of showing compliance with the essential requirements of a directive, in reality the New Approach puts significant pressure on manufacturers to comply with European standards.[127] It is made much more difficult for manufacturers to show that they comply with the essential requirements of a directive if they want to use standards other than the European standards made through CEN. On that basis, it is arguable that European standards are mandatory regulatory provisions under Article 1(2). However, following *RWE Vertrieb*, the main question is whether the legislature has performed a balancing exercise between the rights of the seller and the consumer. In European standardisation, it is difficult to identify such a balancing exercise. The balancing would have to take place in the context of the standardisation process—the general set-up of the New Approach is not sufficient. Because it is difficult for consumers to participate effectively in the standardisation process, and it is unlikely that businesses participating in European standardisation could be relied on to perform this balancing exercise. As a result, it is much more difficult to guarantee that the required balancing exercise takes place. This would mean that European standardisation, also in the context of the New Approach, should not benefit from the statutory exemption in Article 1(2).

Furthermore, even if European standards were considered as mandatory regulatory provisions under Article 1(2), the contractual application of European

[125] Case C-92/11 *RWE Vertrieb AG v Verbraucherzentrale Nordrhein-Westfalen e.V* ECLI: EU: C:2013:180.

[126] Case C-280/13 *Barclays Bank SA v Sara Sánchez García and another* ECLI: EU: C:2014:279.

[127] See also Case C-171/11 *Fra.bo SPA v Deutsche Vereinigung des Gas- und Wasserfaches EV* ECLI: EU: C:2012:453.

standards in consumer contracts itself would not be mandatory. Although compliance could be considered mandatory ex ante, since manufacturers would have to declare or prove that they complied with the European standard before they could place their products on the market, the New Approach does not impose the application of European standards in the contract between manufacturer and consumer. Therefore, it becomes more difficult to make an analogy with *Barclays Bank*, since the contractual inclusion of European standards would not be imposed by the legislation under the New Approach.

Outside the New Approach, which includes European services standards, it is even clearer that European standards do not become mandatory regulatory provisions. This is because European standardisation of services is not incorporated in a regulatory framework and compliance with the standards does not become mandatory. Article 26(5) of the Services Directive 2006 does not create a regulatory framework for European standardisation of services. The mere encouragement of the making of European services standards does not establish a regulatory framework in which European standards are adopted. Although the Standardisation Regulation 2012 has formalised the possibility for the Commission to issue mandates for standards in the services sector, this is still quite far away from imposing legally binding obligations on service providers through European standardisation. European standards are not legally binding and do not obtain the status of law. Therefore, European services standards, whether they have been mandated by the Commission or not, cannot be considered as mandatory regulatory provisions and come within the scope of the UCTD. The next question is to what extent the provisions of European services standards could be regarded as unfair terms under the UCTD.

C. Unfair Terms in European Standards

In essence, there are three ways for the provisions of European standards to be regarded as unfair under the UCTD:

(i) The provisions could be covered by the indicative list of terms which might be regarded as unfair provided in the Annex to the UCTD;
(ii) The provisions could breach the transparency requirement imposed by Article 5 of the UCTD;
(iii) The provisions could cause a significant imbalance in the parties' rights and obligations to the detriment of the consumer under Article 3(1) of the UCTD.

To consider the potential fairness of European standards, it is necessary to take a close look at their provisions. If we look at a number of standards which have been adopted in the healthcare and tourism sectors, it becomes clear how difficult it is to link the UCTD to the provisions of European standards. In chapter one, various elements of the service process which could be dealt with by way of European standardisation were set out. Hans Micklitz has suggested a number of subjects which are usually covered in European standards, such as education, equipment or facilities, pre- and post-contractual obligations and monitoring.[128] Many of these subjects can be found in European standards. For example, the Aesthetic Surgery Services standard has provisions on competences, facilities and communication with patients. The European standard for Recreational Diving Services has provisions on information, training and education. However, from the perspective of the UCTD, it is problematic that the way in which these provisions are set out in the European standards does not look like a contract at all. It is clear from the introduction of many of the European standards that they intend to provide a number of recommendations for service providers. They do not set out the mutual rights and obligations of service providers and consumers. The recommendations in the standards have not been adopted with a view to impose contractual obligations on service providers. If a comparison is made with some of the standard terms and conditions which are used by private clinics for plastic surgery, there are numerous important differences. The standard terms set out precisely what patients are entitled to under the contract and how they should pay for it. The key difference is that these standard terms are based on the mutual rights and obligations of the parties to the contract. This mutuality of obligations, which is the foundation of a contract, is missing in European standards. They remain recommendations for service providers which are not intended to be binding on them and certainly not on consumers or patients. As a result, before the provisions of European standards could be regarded as standard terms, it would be necessary to include a provision in European standards to link the European standards directly to a contract for services.[129] This is an important proviso for the discussion that follows below, which is based on the assumption that European standards can be regarded as standard terms per se.

Returning to the three possible ways to regard provisions of European standards as unfair, the first possibility would be to find that they came within the scope of the indicative list of unfair terms in the Annex to the UCTD. This requires an assessment of the contents of European standards adopted in the healthcare and tourism sectors. In both sectors it is difficult to find provisions of European standards which could potentially be regarded as unfair. The main reason for this is that the European standards contain provisions which are primarily focused on the delivery of the service—they are standards which are directly linked to the service process. Furthermore, it could be argued that, since most provisions of European standards are directly about the service process, they should be excluded from the

[128] H Micklitz, 'The Service Directive: Consumer Contract Law Making via Standardisation', in A Colombi Ciacchi et al. (eds), *Liability in the Third Millennium (Liber Amicorum Gert Brüggemeier)* (Baden-Baden, Nomos, 2009) 439–64. For a detailed assessment, see H. Micklitz, *Services Standards: Defining the Core Consumer Elements and their Minimum Requirements*, Study Commissioned by ANEC, Brussels, April 2007.

[129] As suggested by H Micklitz, above n 128.

scope of the UCTD because they are essentially about the definition of the main subject matter of the contract as provided by Article 4(2).

Nevertheless, it is possible to identify some terms which could come within the scope of the indicative list. For example, both the Aesthetic Surgery Services standard and the Recreational Diving Services standard contain provisions which define procedures for risk assessments.[130] These provisions include a definition of what constitutes an 'adverse event' and guidance on how to deal with complications and emergencies. These provisions could potentially be regarded as attempting to exclude or limit the legal liability of a service provider 'in the event of the death of a consumer or personal injury to the latter resulting from an act or omission of that seller or supplier' as provided in 1(a) of the Annex to the UCTD.[131] Moreover, the provisions of European standards could be regarded as 'irrevocably binding the consumer to terms with which he had no real opportunity of becoming acquainted before the conclusion of the contract' as provided in 1(i) of the Annex. European standards are covered by copyright, which means that they become products that have to be bought from the national standardisation organisations. This has a real impact on the ability of European consumers to become aware of the provisions of European standards. The applicability of Article 1(i) of the Annex would depend on the extent to which consumers would be able to obtain the provisions of European standards and to what extent they could reasonably be expected to buy European standards.[132] This is closely linked to the transparency requirement imposed by Article 5 of the UCTD.

Secondly, Article 5 of the UCTD provides that contractual terms 'must always be drafted in plain, intelligible language'. In *Commission v Netherlands*,[133] the CJEU held that a service provider has to ensure that the consumer is in a position to obtain sufficient knowledge *before* the contract is concluded. A distinction should be made between the plainness of contractual terms and their intelligibility. Terms have to be written in plain language so as to enable the consumer to understand their implications. Furthermore, they must have been set out in such a way that they are intelligible to the consumer. This could also mean that they must have been drafted in the consumer's language. For European standards, it could be problematic that they have been drafted by stakeholders. Although most of the time they have been adopted with the intention of improving the protection of the consumer, they have not always been drafted in a language which is easily understandable to the consumer. This could be particularly problematic for the healthcare sector. For example, the Aesthetic Surgery Services standard contains very detailed descriptions of medical treatments, which are then linked to

[130] See Article 5.1 of prEN 16372:2012 Aesthetic Surgery and Aesthetic Non-Surgical Medical services and Article 4.2 of prEN 14467:2002 Recreational Diving Services—Requirements for Recreational Scuba Diving Service Providers.

[131] The author is grateful to Federico Della Negra for this suggestion.

[132] This is essentially the private law mirror dispute from the public law dispute in the Dutch *Knooble* case, discussed in R van Gestel and H Micklitz, above n 119.

[133] Case C-144/99 *Commission v Netherlands* ECLI: EU: C:2001:257.

different categories of risk. Such provisions are inevitably difficult to understand for consumers, because they are primarily intended for practitioners in aesthetic surgery. However, it could again be argued that they come within the scope of Article 4(2) of the UCTD because they define the subject matter of the contract.

The transparency requirement goes beyond the mere wording or language of the terms. It is ultimately based on enabling competition in the market.[134] A proper understanding of the contractual terms enables consumers to make decision about whether to conclude a contract with a competitor who might be using other contractual terms. It is clear from the CJEU's judgment in *RWE Vertrieb*[135] that a positive obligation is imposed on service providers to provide sufficient information to enable consumers to prefer a competitor. Such an onerous obligation could be problematic for European standardisation. It would connect European standardisation directly to competition law. Article 5 could be interpreted in such a way as to impose an obligation on service providers who apply European standards to provide more background information about the standards.[136] If consumers have to be able to make an adequate assessment of the role that a European standard plays in the services market, it might be necessary to disclose information about why and by whom it has been made. In other words, consumers might have to receive information about which parties are behind the making of European standards. The implications of such an obligation for European standardisation would be serious. After all, the European standardisation process is entirely confidential. Information about the negotiations leading to the adoption of a European standard is not accessible to outsiders. This includes the names of participants in the European and national technical committees. In its judgment in *Schulz*,[137] in the context of a contract for the supply of gas which was not directly governed by the UCTD, the CJEU imposed a very far-reaching obligation to disclose information on service providers—including the grounds for adjustment of the price of the contract.

In the context of European standardisation, this obligation to disclose could have serious consequences. The Aesthetic Surgery Services standard could be an interesting example. One of the main aims of the standard is to set out what qualifications practitioners in aesthetic surgery should have before they can perform certain treatments. One of the provisions states that practitioners should not make misrepresentations to patients about their qualifications. However, it could be argued that they are under a positive obligation to inform patients about their precise qualifications. This is particularly important since the European standardisation process was started with a view to limit the amount of treatments that could be performed by medical practitioners who do not have sufficient

[134] N Reich et al, above n 120, 144–45.

[135] *RWE Vertrieb*, above n 125.

[136] H Micklitz and N Reich, 'The Court and Sleeping Beauty: The Revival of the Unfair Contract Terms Directive' (2014) 51 *CML Rev* 771.

[137] C-359/11 *Alexandra Schulz v Technische Werke Schussental GmbH* ECLI: EU: C:2014:2317.

qualifications.[138] As a result, another link between the transparency of the European standardisation process and the application of European standards has been identified. The lack of knowledge about the background to European standards could be a reason for courts to refuse to apply the provisions of European standards on the basis that they did not comply with the transparency requirement imposed by Article 5. It could even be argued that consumer organisations should be able bring an action against service providers who rely on these terms and could indirectly obtain access to European standards on the basis of the positive obligations imposed by the transparency requirement in the UCTD.[139]

Finally, the provisions of European standards could be regarded as unfair on the basis that they cause a significant imbalance in the parties' rights and obligations to the detriment of the consumer. This is covered by Article 3(1) of the UCTD. There have been few cases at the European level in which the CJEU has had the occasion to interpret this general fairness clause. Recently, in *Aziz*,[140] the CJEU seemed to interpret this test as very much linked to the specific circumstances of a case. This would suggest a test based on an abuse control of unfair terms.[141] This test would be very much linked to the national legal order in which the contract terms would be applied. Because of the *in concreto* application of the test under Article 3(1), it is difficult to assess what its implications for the provisions of European standards will be. However, similarly to the indicative list in the Annex, it would seem unlikely that the provisions of European services standards, which are primarily aimed at providing standards for the service process, would be considered as unfair on the basis of Article 3(1). They are not sufficiently focused on the contractual rights and obligations of service providers and consumers. Therefore, to conclude, the transparency requirement in Article 5 would be the most likely candidate to cause problems for European standards.

D. The Role of the Injunction and the Impact of the UCTD on Convergence

Finally, assuming that European standards come within the scope of the UCTD and could contain potentially unfair terms, the next question is how consumers, consumer organisations or public authorities could enforce the UCTD against service providers. Here, an important role could be played by the injunction. Article 7(1) makes clear that Member States have to provide adequate remedies to prevent the continuing application of unfair terms. Furthermore, the UCTD is one of the Directives to which the Injunction Directive[142] applies. This means that, under

[138] Interview with NEN (Delft) on 11 April 2012 and interview with Chairman of Dutch Mirror Committee for Aesthetic Surgery Services (Goes) on 29 December 2012.

[139] See also R van Gestel and H Micklitz, above n 119, and H Micklitz and N Reich, above n 136, 786.

[140] Case C-415/11 *Mohammed Aziz v Caixa* ECLI: EU: C:2013:164.

[141] H Micklitz, 'Public Interest Litigation before European Courts', in E Terryn et al (eds), *Landmark Cases of EU Consumer Law: In Honour of Jules Stuyck* (Cambridge, Intersentia, 2013) 633–52.

[142] Directive 2009/22/EC on injunctions for the protection of consumers' interests.

Article 7(2) of the UCTD, Member States have to acknowledge and facilitate the possibility of public authorities and consumer organisations seeking injunctions in consumer disputes.

From the perspective of the UCTD, the CJEU delivered an important judgment in *Invitel*.[143] Invitel was a Hungarian telecom provider whose standard terms included a term which enabled the provider to change the rates without explaining the basis on which this would happen and the reasons for it. The key question was whether a finding of unfairness in court proceedings brought by a consumer organisation or a collective group of claimants would also be applicable to parties which did not take part in the proceedings—in other words, if a ruling of unfairness would have an *erga omnes* effect. The CJEU held that the UCTD did not prevent an *actio popularis* which would have *erga omnes* effect. However, it did not actually have to rule on whether the effective application of the UCTD required such an *erga omnes* effect of a finding of unfairness. Nevertheless, the judgment gives a clear impetus to public authorities and consumer organisations to challenge the fairness of contractual terms without having to worry about whether such proceedings would actually be effective in protecting consumers.

From *Invitel* and from the wording of Article 7, it is clear that the UCTD has a preventive function—it enables organisations to bring actions against service providers to prevent the use of unfair contract terms. This also means that the injunction is not limited to the concrete application of standard terms in particular contracts. Although the action in *Invitel* was directed against the application by a Hungarian telecom provider of standard terms which were applied in its contracts with customers, the review could also be extended to the recommendation of contract terms. In *Commission v Italy*,[144] the CJEU held that the abstract review under Article 7 of the UCTD would be deprived of its effectiveness if it could not be aimed at standard terms which are recommended or which have been made for use but which have not yet been brought in practice. Therefore, it also applies to the future use of standard terms which contain unfair terms.[145] In practice, the possibility of an injunction is often used by consumer protection organisations in ex ante negotiations with service providers or associations. They could then be forced to remove the terms from the contracts before they are actually brought into practice. This has important consequences for European standards, which are often not directly incorporated in contracts. It means that consumer organisations could bring actions for injunctions against standardisation organisations simply on the basis of the adoption of European standards which contain unfair contract terms. Alternatively, an action could be brought against an association of service providers if they recommended the use of European standards as standard terms. Once again, this raises the question whether the standards should be made publicly available to facilitate the abstract review. It could be argued that the abstract

[143] Case C-472/10 *Nemzeti v Invitel* ECLI: EU: C:2012:242.

[144] Case C-372/99 *Commission v Italian Republic* ECLI: EU: C:2002:42.

[145] For a discussion in English law, see *Office of Fair Trading v Foxtons Ltd* [2009] EWCA Civ 288.

review would not be effective if consumer organisations or public authorities were required to buy standards from the national standardisation organisations.[146] It should be reminded that actions against standardisation organisations would only be successful if it could be shown that European standards adopted through CEN were recommended or made for use in contractual relations. It is uncertain if European standards in the healthcare and tourism sector could be said to fall in this category.

In conclusion, the UCTD could have a similar function to the free movement provisions and the competition law provisions, which will be discussed in chapter seven. It could prevent the application of European standards in contract law if they were regarded as unfair. As such, the UCTD could act as an obstacle to convergence—convergence would only occur if European standards complied with the fairness and transparency requirements imposed by the UCTD. However, it is clear from the way in which European services standards are made that they do not have a focus on contractual rights and obligations. In the absence of a contract in which European standards could be incorporated, there is little evidence to suggest that they would contain potentially unfair terms. In the healthcare and tourism sectors European standards do not resemble a contract.[147] Although this does not preclude the abstract review of European standards, the role that the UCTD is likely to play in the review of such standards is limited. Moreover, it means that the function of the UCTD to impose a process of 'fair convergence' on European standardisation—meaning that stakeholders are encouraged to include fair terms in their standards—is limited as well. At the moment, the connection between European standardisation of services and contract law is too tenuous for the UCTD to have an important impact on European standardisation of services.

V. A PRELIMINARY CONCLUSION

The previous chapters have shown that it is complicated and difficult to make European standards in the healthcare and tourism sectors. The conclusion has to be along similar lines for the application of these standards in private law. Even if European services standards have successfully been adopted, they still face a lot of difficulties at the moment of their application in private law. Although there are differences between contract law and tort, in essence both suffer from the lack of a European regulatory framework which links European standardisation to private law. Convergence does not come out of nowhere—there has to be a certain pressure to increase convergence in private law across the EU. At the European level, there is no such pressure for European standardisation of services. Given the concerns that have been raised by the Commission about the direction European standardisation of services is taking, it is surprising that it has not taken matters

146 See R van Gestel and H Micklitz, above n 119.

147 See H Micklitz, above n 6.

more strongly into its own hands. Although it would like European standardisation of services to develop in a certain direction, namely to become more facilitative of free movement, it is not willing to provide that direction itself. Article 26(5) does no more than to encourage European standardisation and cannot be considered as pressure for convergence in private law. A New Approach to services could provide the necessary pressure, but there are no indications that such a regulatory framework will be created.

In the absence of a European regulatory framework, the pressure for convergence has to come almost entirely from the stakeholders. However, it is difficult to rely on stakeholders to apply European standards in practice. The direct application of European standards in private law is uncommon. European standards are not frequently applied by way of ex ante regulation in contract law. Similarly, their ex post regulatory function is limited to providing evidence to specify the required standard of care. This is essentially similar in contract and tort law.[148] No automatic effect is achieved by the adoption of a European standard—its function remains purely evidential. Convergence is difficult to achieve with such an evidential function, since there is no European co-ordination. The precise impact of the standard will be dependent on national private law and will be different from case to case. In addition, the various problems with the making of European services standards also have an impact on the application of European standards in private law. The strong objections to European standardisation of services in the healthcare and tourism sectors make it less likely that the standards will be applied in contract law or tort. In general, it is not possible to identify co-ordinated pressure on the part of the stakeholders to increase convergence in private law. Although they develop European services standards for certain reasons, these reasons are not sufficiently linked to their application in private law. Stakeholders do not really seem to care about what happens with a European standard after its adoption. The result is that the application of European standards in private law remains uncertain and fragmented. As a consequence, the role of the UCTD as a review mechanism for the application of European standards in contract law will remain limited.

[148] See U Magnus and H Micklitz, above n 29, 516.

7

The Application of European Standards in Free Movement Law and Competition Law

AFTER AN ANALYSIS of the application of European standards in contract law and tort, this chapter moves on to discuss the interaction between European standardisation, free movement law and competition law. The first part focuses on the impact of the free movement provisions on convergence in private law. The second part addresses the impact of the competition law provisions. The structure that is followed is essentially similar to the previous chapter. Both parts start with explaining the impact of free movement law and competition law on convergence, followed by a case study. They conclude with an analysis of the impact of the free movement and competition provisions on the potential for convergence in private law through European standardisation of services.

I. FROM THE APPLICATION OF EUROPEAN STANDARDS TO THEIR REVIEW

The application of European standards in free movement and competition law is conceptually different from their application in contract law and tort. Free movement and competition law do not constitute separate fields of private law in which European services standards could be applied. Rather, they impose certain requirements on the application of European standards in private law. They provide a 'frame' for convergence in which European standards have to fit. The application of European standards in contract law or tort will only be successful if they are compatible with the free movement and competition provisions. They are used as a review mechanism to review the provisions of European standards. If they contain provisions which breach the free movement or competition provisions, these provisions will not be enforced in private law.

The result is that convergence in private law through European standardisation becomes conditional on compliance with the free movement and competition provisions. At the same time, the possibility of review imposes a process of convergence itself, since it provides pressure on European standardisation organisations to adopt standards which are compatible with the free movement and competition provisions. Even if convergence in contract law and tort is relatively limited, it could still be that the free movement and competition provisions have a strong convergent impact on private law.

II. EUROPEAN STANDARDS IN FREE MOVEMENT LAW

A. Framing Convergence in Free Movement Law

Two different functions of the free movement provisions can be identified. These two functions are not mutually exclusive—they supplement each other. First of all, the free movement provisions can be used by a court to refuse to apply a European standard in a private law dispute. It can be illustrated by the following fictitious scenario:[1] a Dutch health insurer offers its customers the possibility, for a monthly supplement, to be insured for a limited number of cosmetic interventions. For this purpose, the health insurer concludes contracts with a number of private cosmetic clinics in the Netherlands and Belgium. These contracts expressly provide that the clinics will comply with the requirements imposed by the European standard for Aesthetic Surgery Services. Mrs Houben lives in Rotterdam, but she would like to get some Botox treatment from COSMOBILE, a private clinic based in Belgium which occasionally sends its cosmetic surgeons to the homes of their customers to treat them at their homes. Under the contract with the health insurer, they are not allowed to do this as it would be in breach of the European standard. COSMOBILE claims that this contractual provision constitutes a breach of its right to freely provide services and refuses to comply with it. It sends a 'mobile doctor' to Mrs Houben to treat her at her home and sends an invoice to the health insurer. The health insurer refuses to reimburse COSMOBILE for the treatment and COSMOBILE brings an action for payment against the insurer. If the Dutch court finds that the provision of the European standard breaches COSMOBILE's right to freely provide services, it could refuse to enforce this provision in the contractual relationship between the health insurer and COSMOBILE. The result would be that the health insurer would become liable to COSMOBILE in contract law on the basis of the non-compliance of the European standard with the free movement provisions. As a consequence, the application of the free movement provisions would create an obstacle to convergence in private law because the European standard is not compatible with free movement law.

To illustrate the first function more broadly, a second fictitious example will be provided.[2] An English private certification body certifies tourist guides who want

[1] This example can also be found in B van Leeuwen, 'Free movement of services, European standardisation and private law', in H Micklitz, Y Svetiev and G Comparato (eds), 'European Regulatory Private Law: The Paradigms Tested' *EUI Working Papers Law* 2014/04, 27–40.

[2] ibid.

to provide tourist guide services in the UK. The European standard for Tourist Guide Training requirements is used as the basis of its certification activities. It refuses to certify Mr Von Amsberg, a German tourist guide who wishes to provide his services in Oxford, because he has not spent 240 hours in Oxford as part of his practical training. Mr Von Amsberg studied Classics in Oxford 40 years ago and claims that this requirement constitutes an obstacle to the exercise of his right to freely provide services in the UK. He brings an appeal against the refusal to provide him with a certificate claiming that the 240 hours requirement is incompatible with free movement law. If a court found that the requirement breached Mr Von Amsberg's right to freely provide services, the court would refuse to apply the standard. The certification body would be liable to Mr Von Amsberg in contract law because the European standard breached the free movement provisions. The requirement of certification based on the European standard prevented Mr Von Amsberg from offering his services in the UK and from concluding contracts with possible customers in the UK. If Mr Von Amsberg had suffered damages as a result of his lack of certification, he could also bring a claim for damages against the certification body. Overall, this second example illustrates the market access dimension of the free movement provisions. The refusal of the court to apply the European standard for Tourist Guide Training would enable the service provider to have to access the UK market for tourist guides.

The second function of free movement law is more indirect. The examples above have shown that European standards are unlikely to be applied in private law if they do not comply with the free movement provisions. This puts pressure on standardisation organisations and on stakeholders to adopt European standards which are compatible with free movement law.[3] It would be useless for stakeholders in the services sectors to adopt and apply European standards if they were not applied in private law because they breached the free movement provisions. In effect, the free movement provisions themselves stimulate a process of convergence. However, this convergence is not based on European standardisation, but on the requirements which free movement law imposes on European standardisation. As a result, the application of free movement law provides a regulatory tool to control the compatibility of European standardisation with the free movement provisions. It could be exercised ex post, by courts refusing to apply European standards in contractual disputes. The effectiveness of this ex post tool would be dependent on the willingness of national courts to scrutinise the compatibility of European standards with free movement law. Similarly, it could be exercised ex ante, by putting pressure on stakeholders to adopt standards which respect the free movement provisions. This is also where the Commission could play a more prominent role in ensuring that stakeholders understand the obligations imposed on them by free movement law.

[3] See L Azoulai, 'The Court of Justice and the Social Market Economy: The Emergence of an Idea and the Conditions for its Realization' (2008) 45 *CML Rev* 1335.

The success of the two functions of free movement law is dependent on the extent to which private parties are bound by the free movement provisions. The two examples discussed above assume that private parties are bound by free movement law and that the free movement provisions are applicable in contractual disputes between private parties. In other words, it is assumed that the free movement provisions have horizontal direct effect. However, this issue is far from fixed. Therefore, the judgment of the CJEU in *Fra.bo* will be analysed to determine the scope of horizontal direct effect of the free movement provisions.

B. Case Study: *Fra.bo*[4]

Fra.bo SpA ('Fra.bo') is an Italian manufacturer of copper fittings.[5] Such copper fittings are used to connect two pieces of piping for water or gas. They have sealing rings made of malleable material at the ends to make them watertight. Fra.bo wanted to sell these copper fittings on the German market. They were not covered by the New Approach, which meant that there was no harmonised European standard with which Fra.bo could comply. In Germany, the Deutsche Vereinigung des Gas- und Wasserfaches eV ('DVGW') made standards that laid down the technical requirements with which copper fittings had to comply.[6] It was an association established under private law. The applicable German legislation provided that products in connection with the supply of water could be lawfully brought on the German market if they had a CE mark. If they did not have a CE mark, the alternative was for products to be certified by DVGW. Therefore, DVGW was given an important a role in the German regulatory framework. Because Fra.bo's copper fittings did not fall under the New Approach, Fra.bo was dependent on certification by DVGW. This certification would take place in accordance with standards which had been developed by DVGW itself. The German State did not exercise any influence on the standardisation process and the certification process—in that respect, DVGW was independent.[7]

In 1999, Fra.bo applied for certification by DVGW. In 2000, it was awarded a certificate for the duration of five years. The certification assessment procedure itself had been sub-contracted by the German laboratory that was normally used and approved by DVGW to a non-approved Italian laboratory. During the five year period in which the certificate was valid DVGW received complaints by third

[4] This case study is to a significant extent based on a case note published in the European Journal of Risk Regulation: B van Leeuwen, 'From Status to Impact, and the Role of National Legislation: The Application of Article 34 TFEU to a Private Certification Organisation in *Fra.bo*' (2013) 3 *European Journal of Risk Regulation* 405.

[5] Case C-171/11 *Fra.bo SPA v Deutsche Vereinigung des Gas- und Wasserfaches EV* ECLI: EU: C:2012:453. For a more detailed discussion of the factual background, see H Schepel, 'Case C-171/11, *Fra.bo SPA v Deutsche Vereinigung des Gas- und Wasserfaches*' (2013) 9 *ERCL* 186.

[6] *Fra.bo*, above n 5, paras 6–7.

[7] ibid, para 24.

parties, which resulted in a re-assessment procedure directly undertaken by the approved German laboratory. In 2005, DVGW informed Fra.bo that its fittings had not passed the ozone test, but that it was free to submit its own assessment report within three months. Fra.bo then had another assessment done by a non-approved Italian laboratory, which found that its fittings did pass the ozone test. However, DVGW refused to recognise this report because it had not been undertaken by one of its approved laboratories.[8] As a consequence, it cancelled Fra.bo's certificate in June 2005. Therefore, Fra.bo was no longer able to place its copper fittings on the German market.

After the cancellation of the certificate, Fra.bo brought an action against the cancellation before the Landgericht Köln, which dismissed its claim.[9] It appealed to the OLG Düsseldorf, which decided to stay the proceedings to make a preliminary reference to the CJEU. Its main question was whether Article 34 TFEU, which provides for the right to free movement of goods, was applicable to the standardisation and certification activities of DVGW.[10] On a first impression, this case seemed to be a good occasion for the CJEU to clarify to what extent the right to free movement of goods had horizontal direct effect. While it was already clear that the rights to free movement of persons, services and establishment had—at least in certain situations—horizontal direct effect, the situation was significantly less clear for the right to free movement of goods.[11] According to Advocate General Trstenjak, there was no justification to maintain a different approach for the free movement of goods. Therefore, she invited the CJEU to recognise that all free movement provisions were horizontally directly effective.[12] In the previous decades, the CJEU gradually moved from an approach based on the public or private status of regulators to an approach based on the impact of their actions on the internal market.[13] Whether a regulator was private or public is no longer decisive for the applicability of the free movement provisions. Given that DVGW had obtained a position of significant power in the certification market as a result of the German legislation, it was virtually impossible to place the fittings on the German market without a certificate awarded by DVGW.[14] This effect was reinforced by the fact that the referring court had found that the copper fittings were not covered by a harmonised European technical standard, which meant that this was not a case in which Fra.bo could obtain a CE mark. Certification by DVGW was then the only alternative. AG Trstenjak argued that given this de facto competence

[8] ibid, para 12.

[9] Judgment of Landgericht Köln of 5 March 2008–28 O (Kart) 529/07.

[10] *Fra.bo*, above n 5, para 16.

[11] C Krenn, 'A Missing Piece in the Horizontal Effect Jigsaw: Horizontal Direct Effect and the Free Movement of Goods' (2012) 49 *CML Rev* 177.

[12] Opinion of AG Trstenjak in *Fra.bo*, above n 5, ECLI: EU: C:2012:176, para 43.

[13] H Schepel, 'Constitutionalising the Market, Marketising the Constitution, and to Tell the Difference: On the Horizontal Application of the Free Movement Provisions in EU Law' (2012) 18 *European Law Journal* 177.

[14] Opinion of AG Trstenjak in *Fra.bo*, above n 5, ECLI: EU: C:2012:176, para 25.

to decide which products could lawfully be placed on the market, which had been granted to DVGW by the German legislation, its activities had to be caught by Article 34 TFEU.[15]

Unlike AG Trstenjak, the CJEU did not provide a clear answer about the potential horizontal direct effect of Article 34 TFEU.[16] It decided not to use any conventional formulas about the horizontal or vertical direct effect of the free movement provisions. No reference was made to its case law based on *Walrave and Koch*,[17] which could certainly have been applied to this case.[18] In this line of cases, the free movement provisions were applied to private parties that were involved in collective regulation on the basis of the exercise of legal autonomy. These two functional criteria were not referred to. Rather, the CJEU decided to rely on three factors which collectively justified the application of the free movement of goods provision to DVGW. First of all, German legislation had provided that goods certified by DVGW would be compliant with national law and could be lawfully brought on the market.[19] Secondly, DVGW was the only body that certified copper fittings in Germany. As a result, the only possibility for businesses to obtain a certificate of compliance was through certification by DVGW.[20] Thirdly, a lack of certification by DVGW would result in serious difficulties to place products on the German market.[21] Almost all German consumers bought copper fittings which had been certified by DVGW.

On the basis of these three arguments, the CJEU held that 'a body such as the DVGW, by virtue of its authority to certify the products, in reality holds the power to regulate the entry into the German market of products such as the copper fittings at issue in the main proceedings'[22] and that Article 34 TFEU was applicable to its standardisation and certification activities. When the case returned to the OLG Düsseldorf, it held that the specific ozone test requirements imposed by DVGW constituted a restriction to Fra.bo's right to free movement of goods which could not be justified.[23] DVGW had to pay compensation to Fra.bo. Permission was given to appeal to the BGH.[24] However, the case was settled before the BGH could decide on it. Therefore, it has not been decided which party would under free movement law ultimately be responsible for the breach of Fra.bo's right to free movement of goods and which party is liable to pay damages

[15] ibid, para 50.

[16] H van Harten and T Nauta, 'Towards Horizontal Direct Effect for the Free Movement of Goods? Comment on Fra.bo' (2013) 38 *EL Rev* 677, 689.

[17] Case C-36/74 *Walrave and Koch v Association Union cycliste internationale and others* ECLI: EU: C:1974:140.

[18] H Schepel, 'Case C-171/11, *Fra.bo SPA v Deutsche Vereinigung des Gas- und Wasserfaches*' (2013) 9 *European Review of Contract Law* 186, 189.

[19] *Fra.bo*, above n 5, para 27.

[20] ibid, para 28.

[21] ibid, para 30.

[22] ibid, para 31.

[23] Judgment of Oberlandesgericht Düsseldorf of 14 August 2013, VI-2 U (Kart) 15/08.

[24] ibid, para 42.

to Fra.bo—would this be the private certification body that adopted a standard which contained provisions in breach of the free movement of goods, or would it be the State, which provided the legislative framework that protected the activities of DVGW?[25]

C. The Impact of *Fra.bo* on Convergence in Free Movement Law

First of all, it is necessary to determine the scope of application of the CJEU's judgment in *Fra.bo*. There has been a substantial amount of discussion about whether the application of the free movement provisions to DVGW in *Fra.bo* really constituted horizontal direct effect or whether the judgment was in fact directed against the German legislation.[26] The fact that the relevant German legislation had granted an important role to DVGW was no doubt an important reason to extend the application of the free movement provisions to DVGW. This is also clear from the final ruling of the CJEU, in which it held that 'Article 28 EC must be interpreted as meaning that it applies to standardisation and certification activities of a private-law body, where the national legislation considers the products certified by that body to be compliant with national law and that has the effect of restricting the marketing of products which are not certified by that body'.[27] On that basis, the fact that the German legislation had provided a clear role and effect to DVGW's standardisation and certification activities was one of the foundations of the judgment.

In the traditional line of case law based on *Walrave and Koch*, the horizontal applicability of the free movement provisions was determined by the question whether a private regulator was involved in collective regulation on the basis of the exercise of legal autonomy. As far as collective regulation is concerned, the collective dimension in *Fra.bo* was primarily vertical—the important nationwide effect of DVGW's activities was the result of the German legislation.[28] It is not likely that DVGW would have enjoyed the same market power if the German legislation had not given such an important role to it. Although it could be argued that DVGW should not be held responsible for being the only certification body in the market, this exclusive position was probably the result of the reference to DVGW in the German legislation. At the same time, from the perspective of the exercise of legal autonomy, the role of the German legislation was not so important.[29] It was expressly stated in the judgment that the German State did not exercise any decisive influence over DVGW's activities. Through its legislation,

[25] B van Leeuwen, 'Private Regulation and Public Responsibility in the Internal Market' (2014) 33 *Yearbook of European Law* 277.

[26] See H van Harten and T Nauta, above n 16; H Schepel, above n 18; B van Leeuwen, above n 4.

[27] *Fra.bo*, above n 5, para 34.

[28] B van Leeuwen, above n 4, 407.

[29] ibid, 408.

the German State had effectively given DVGW a carte blanche to exercise its activities in accordance with its own standards.[30] On that basis, the case against DVGW would seem to be more horizontal in nature. The actual measure that was challenged was of a private nature, but the impact of that measure had been reinforced by public legislation. Overall, this interaction and tension between the collective regulation aspect and the legal autonomy aspect in *Fra.bo*, in combination with the ambiguous approach of the CJEU, means that it is difficult to determine whether the case concerned horizontal or vertical direct effect of Article 34 TFEU.

However, these difficulties do not mean that it is impossible to make more general observations about the scope of the judgment. The structure of the judgment reveals that in determining whether the free movement provisions are applicable the CJEU has adopted an approach based on the *impact* of private regulation on the internal market.[31] The three arguments set out above that were used to justify the application of Article 34 TFEU to DVGW were provided *after* the CJEU referred to the definition of a restriction of the right to free movement of goods based on the *Dassonville*[32] formula.[33] Traditionally, the determination of the applicability of the free movement provisions preceded the determination of a restriction. In this case, the issue of applicability is determined on the basis of the identification of a restriction. To put it in simple terms, Article 34 TFEU was held applicable to DVGW *because* its actions constituted a restriction of the free moment of goods.[34] Therefore, it is clear that Article 34 TFEU was applied to DVGW's activities because of the impact its activities had on the internal market—not because of its public or private status as regulator. Moreover, it means that while in *Fra.bo* the German legislation played an important role, it cannot be excluded that Article 34 TFEU will be applied to certification bodies which enjoy significant market power without them having been given a special role by public legislation. It should equally be possible for standardisation or certification bodies to obtain an important position in the market independently from the State. In such circumstances, there is no good reason to maintain that the free movement provisions would not be applied to their activities. On the contrary—it is submitted that *Fra.bo* provides authority for the argument that the impact of the exercise of private regulation on the EU's internal market determines whether they will be held accountable under the free movement provisions. As a consequence, the impact of free movement law on convergence depends on the extent to which European standardisation has an impact on the market and to what extent it creates obstacles to the ability of service providers to offer their services in the internal market.

[30] H Schepel, above n 18, 190–91.
[31] See H Schepel, above n 13. See also B van Leeuwen, above n 25.
[32] Case C-8/74 *Procureur du Roi v Benoit Dassonville and another* ECLI: EU: C:1974:82.
[33] B van Leeuwen, above n 4, 407.
[34] ibid.

D. Convergence in Free Movement Law

Finally, the analysis of *Fra.bo* will be linked to the two functions of the free movement provisions introduced above. The impact of free movement law on three different actors involved in European standardisation will be analysed: (i) the (European) standardisation organisations; (ii) certification organisations; and (iii) service providers and their customers.

First of all, organisations such as CEN and national standardisation organisations are engaged in collective regulation on the basis of their legal autonomy. The aim of European standardisation is to have a collective impact on a particular services sector. On that basis, it is likely that the free movement provisions will be applicable to standardisation organisations, since they satisfy the *Walrave and Koch* criteria. However, in the context of the application of European standards in private law, it is unlikely that cases will be brought directly against standardisation organisations. Although CEN facilitates and administers the European standardisation process, the simple adoption of a European services standard does not achieve an important effect in law. A second step is necessary to apply the European standard in private law. For European services standards, it is more likely that cases will be brought directly against parties which apply a European standard in their regulatory conduct. It is at this point that the European services standard will actually start to have an impact on the internal market. Nevertheless, the second function of free movement law is important for standardisation organisations. Knowing that European standards might not be enforced because of their incompatibility with the free movement provisions will make stakeholders more cautious during the standardisation process.[35] It also provides an incentive for standardisation organisations to raise awareness among stakeholders about the necessity of compliance with the free movement provisions. If they want to be able to effectively use and apply their standards, they had better ensure that their standards were free movement proof. An important role here will be played by the Commission.[36] They should provide clear guidance to parties involved in European standardisation to ensure that they do their best to make European standards compatible with the free movement provisions. However, this becomes difficult if one of the main purposes of the standardisation process is market restriction, such as in the example of the Tourist Guide Training standard.[37] In such cases, the Commission should be alert from the moment of the submission of the proposal to ensure that parties do not embark on the making of such a standard, or that they are made fully aware of the likely impact of the standard on the internal market.

[35] Interview with DG Enterprise of the European Commission (Brussels) on 29 November 2012.

[36] See F Cafaggi, 'Private Regulation in European Private Law', in A Hartkamp et al (eds), *Towards a European Civil Code* (Alphen aan de Rijn, Kluwer, 2011) 91–126, 111–12.

[37] Interview with the Guild, ITG and APTG (London) on 21 January 2014.

Secondly, the free movement provisions can have an impact on the activities of certification bodies. This is also where a link can be made to the PIP case analysed in chapter six. After *Fra.bo*, it could be argued that the free movement provisions are applicable to certification bodies if the requirement of certification could create an obstacle to free movement. However, if one lesson is to be drawn from *Fra.bo*, it is that one has to carefully scrutinise the impact of certification activities on the market. The key question is whether a lack of certification constitutes a real obstacle to provide services in a particular Member State. Again, the European standard for Tourist Guide Training provides a good example. In the UK, the professional associations for tourist guides require guides to be certified. This certification can be obtained by passing an exam. However, the tourist guide profession is not regulated in the UK—there is no 'tourist guide police'.[38] There is no State control on whether a tourist guide is certified. It could be possible that the standard is de facto enforced by the market.[39] The question then is how seriously certification is taken by the market. At the moment, attractions like Westminster Abbey and St Paul's Cathedral only allow access to tourist guides who have been certified by ITG.[40] As such, a lack of certification would have a serious impact on the ability of tourist guides to offer their services in London. Moreover, it would have an indirect impact on the ability of tourists guided by uncertified tourist guides to visit these attractions. However, there are signals that, after significant market pressure, attractions will no longer require tourist guides to be certified.[41] This would open up the market to uncertified tourist guides. As a result, it could be argued that, in this case, the market itself is able to correct and to overcome obstacles to free movement created by private parties through the application of European standards. It would seem that in this example the ability of the market to overcome a lack of certification is higher than for the copper fittings in *Fra.bo*, in which a lack of certification made it virtually impossible to bring products on the German market.[42] This was the result of the protective effect granted to certification by DVGW by the German legislation. In the absence of such a protective effect, a lack of certification would not have the same impact on the right of service providers to freely offer services in another Member State. On that basis, it would seem less likely that the free movement provisions were applied to such cases. In conclusion, the free movement provisions are likely to be applied to certification organisations if a lack of certification constitutes a real obstacle to free movement which cannot be overcome or remedied by the market.

Thirdly, another scenario in which free movement problems could arise would be the application of a European standard in the contract between service provider and service recipient. In such cases, the provisions of the standard would

[38] ibid.
[39] ibid.
[40] ibid.
[41] ibid.
[42] *Fra.bo*, above n 5, para 30.

obtain contractual force. In free movement law, the approach of the CJEU towards contractual terms has been ambiguous and it is unclear in which circumstances contractual terms come within the scope of the free movement provisions. While the CJEU held in *Sapod Audic*[43] that contractual agreements between private parties can never be reviewed under the free movement provisions, in *Haug-Adrion*[44] it seemed willing to review the impact of the provisions of a private insurance contract on the ability of a customer to exercise his rights to free movement. Gareth Davies has argued that the correct approach is to ask whether a contractual term intervenes in the ability of parties to conclude contracts with third parties—in other words, whether the term has a third-party effect outside the contractual relationship between contractor and contractee.[45] Another approach could be to see whether the party which is insisting on the contractual term is in a position of dominance vis-à-vis the other party.[46] With such an approach, market dominance would be a decisive criterion for the application of the free movement provisions. The result of the application of the free movement provisions to the contractual terms could be that a term in the contract between service provider and customer would not be enforced by the court on the basis of its incompatibility with the free movement provisions. There could then also be a damages claim on the basis of the breach of the free movement provisions. After the judgment of the Swedish Labour Court in *Laval*,[47] it is clear that a breach of the free movement provisions in a case between two private parties could also result in horizontal liability.[48] In that case, Swedish trade unions were held liable for a breach of the right of a Latvian company to freely provide services in Sweden. This is also what is happening after the CJEU's judgment in *Fra.bo*—the Italian company has successfully claimed damages against DVGW in the German courts.[49] It is unclear to what extent DVGW would be able to reclaim these damages from the State.[50]

Similarly, in the context of European standardisation, private parties which have had to pay damages to other private parties because of their application of European standards which breached free movement law could also bring a claim for damages against the standardisation organisation that had made the standard.

[43] Case C-159/00 *Sapod Audic* ECLI: EU: C:2002:343.

[44] Case C-251/83 *Eberhard Haug-Adrion v Frankfurter Versicherungs-AG* ECLI: EU: C:1984:397.

[45] G Davies, 'Freedom of Contract and the Horizontal Effect of Free Movement Law' in D Leczykiewicz and S Weatherill (eds), *The Involvement of EU Law in Private Law Relationships* (Oxford, Hart Publishing, 2013) 53–71.

[46] ibid.

[47] *Arbetsdomstolens domar* (Judgments by the Labour Court) 2009 No 89 of 2 Dec 2009. Unofficial English translation by L. Carlson: http://arbetsratt.juridicum.su.se/Filer/PDF/ErikSjoedin/AD%20 2009%20nr%2089%20Laval%20English.pdf.

[48] U Bernitz and N Reich, 'Case comment: The Labour Court Judgment in the Case Laval et Partneri' (2011) 48 *CML Rev* 603. See also N Reich, 'Horizontal Liability in EC Law: Hybridization of Remedies for Compensation in Case of Breaches of EC Rights' (2007) 44 *CML Rev* 705.

[49] Judgment of Oberlandesgericht Düsseldorf of 14 August 2013, VI-2 U (Kart) 15/08.

[50] B van Leeuwen, above n 25.

This raises the difficult question to what extent standardisation organisations are under an obligation to stakeholders to adopt European standards which are compatible with the free movement provisions. In principle, there seems to be no objection against stakeholders, such as the Dutch health insurer in the scenario discussed above, claiming damages from the standardisation organisation which was responsible for the adoption of the European standard. This would increase the pressure on standardisation organisations to guarantee compliance with the free movement provisions in the standardisation process.[51]

Finally, it is important to analyse to what extent, and in what way, parties involved in European standardisation can avail themselves of the justifications provided by the Treaty. The CJEU held in *Bosman*[52] that private regulators can rely on the same justifications for restrictions on free movement as the Member States. This should also apply to regulation through European standardisation. However, in the case of European standardisation of services, a distinction should be made between the standardisation process and the application of the standard in private law. Although there might be very good justifications for stakeholders to make a European standard which contains provisions that could potentially be restrictive of free movement, such justifications should be kept separate from the application of the standard in private law. In order to justify a potential breach of the free movement provisions, service providers have to show how their decision to apply the European standard to the case in question could be justified. This has a particular impact on the reasoning on proportionality.[53] While a European standard might have sought to strike a balance between health protection and free movement, the relevant question is whether the *application* of the standard in private law was proportionate. This requires a case-by-case approach. As a result, private parties that have applied European standards in their regulatory conduct cannot hide behind the general aims of a European standard—what matters is the impact of the standard on the case in question.

In conclusion, there is a direct link between convergence and the horizontal application of the free movement provisions. In the context of European standardisation of services, the free movement provisions are most likely to be applied to parties which are applying European standards in their regulatory activities than to standardisation organisations. However, they still put pressure on standardisation organisations to comply with free movement law. Moreover, it cannot be excluded that stakeholders who have been held liable for the application of European standards in breach of the free movement provisions will seek damages from the standardisation organisation which was responsible for the adoption of the standard. As such, free movement law has a dual function for convergence—on the one hand, it prevents convergence through European standardisation if

[51] L Azoulai, above n 3.
[52] Case C-415/93 *Union Royale Belge des Sociétés de Football Association ASBL v Jean-Marc Bosman and others* ECLI: EU: C:1995:463.
[53] F Cafaggi, above n 36, 105–06.

European standards do not respect free movement law; on the other hand, it stimulates convergence by putting pressure on European standardisation to comply with the free movement provisions. However, the potential for convergence ultimately depends on the impact of European services standards on the market. The free movement provisions will only be applied to European services standards if they really have an impact on the market. Without a New Approach to services, it is unlikely that European services standards are able to create real obstacles to free movement.

III. EUROPEAN STANDARDS IN COMPETITION LAW

A. Framing Convergence in Competition Law

The functions of competition law with respect to European standardisation and the application of European standards in private law are similar to those of the free movement provisions. First of all, competition law could be used to challenge the European standardisation process itself. Secondly, it could be used to review the provisions of a European standard and to prevent standards from being applied in private law. Thirdly, they could put pressure on standardisation organisations and stakeholders to comply with the competition law provisions in the adoption of European standards.

The functions of the competition law provisions are distinct, because Article 101 TFEU focuses on anti-competitive agreements between businesses, while Article 102 TFEU focuses on the exercise of regulatory power by a business which has a position of dominance in the market. As a result, both articles are likely to have different functions in reviewing the application of European standards in private law. Since the adoption of a European standard constitutes an agreement between businesses, Article 101 TFEU provides a direct tool for stakeholders to challenge the standardisation process itself—including its aim, transparency and inclusiveness. In that respect, it also has a different function from the free movement provisions, which are more likely to focus on the impact of European standards on the internal market. Article 102 TFEU could also be applied to the standardisation process, for example if stakeholders claimed that one of the participants in the process had abused its position of dominance in the market by forcing the inclusion of certain requirements in the European standard. However, Article 102 TFEU is more likely to be applied to the application of European standards in private law.

The different functions of the competition law provisions can best by illustrated by a few examples. First of all, the competition law provisions could be used to challenge the adoption of a European standard. For example, tour operators could claim that the adoption of the European standard for Tourist Guide Training constituted an anti–competitive agreement between associations of tourist guide associations with the sole purpose to exclude tour managers from the tourist guide market. The possible non–compliance with Article 101 TFEU would be used to challenge the adoption of the European standard in competition law. This could also lead to a claim for damages against the tourist guide associations. In *Courage v Crehan*,[54] the CJEU held that a breach of the competition law provisions can result in a claim for damages between private parties.[55] As such, the validity of a European standard would be challenged on the basis of the aim of the standardisation process. Similarly, a European standard could be challenged on the basis that the parties which had made the standard had conspired to exclude a particular party from the standardisation process. This will be illustrated below by the case study of *EMC Development*.

Secondly, the competition law provisions could be used to challenge the application of European standards in private law. For example, a number of professional associations of tourist guides in the UK have created a body which examines and certifies tourist guides who want to offer their services in the UK. Mr Von Amsberg, whose case was already discussed above, could also challenge the refusal to provide him with a certificate on the basis that the creation of a certification body that applied the European standard constituted an agreement under Article 101 TFEU to exclude non-local tourist guides from the market. The challenge would then be more directly linked to the substantive provisions of the European standard. The application of the European standard by the certification body meant that Mr Von Amsberg was unable to offer his services in the UK market and to conclude contracts with tourists. Similarly to the free movement provisions, the application of competition law would facilitate market access by ensuring that anti-competitive provisions of European standards would not be applied. Mr Von Amsberg could also choose to base his claim on Article 102 TFEU, if the certification body was the only one in the market. He would then base his challenge directly on the exercise of regulatory power by the certification body.

The third function of the competition law provisions would be to provide pressure on standardisation organisations and stakeholders to adopt European standards which complied with competition law. Convergence in private law would only take place if European standards were compatible with the requirements imposed by the competition law provisions. Furthermore, the competition law provisions have horizontal direct effect which makes them directly applicable to private law disputes. However, the potential of competition law to influence convergence in private law is dependent on the extent to which standardisation organisations and stakeholders fear that competition law would really bite and prevent the effective application of European standards in private law. This will be discussed after an analysis of the *EMC Development* case.

[54] Case C-453/99 *Courage Ltd v Bernard Crehan* ECLI: EU: C:2001:465.

[55] N Reich, 'Horizontal Liability in EC Law: Hybridization of Remedies for Compensation in Case of Breaches of EC Rights' (2007) 44 *CML Rev* 705.

B. Case Study: EMC Development

EMC Development ('EMC') is a Swedish business which is involved in the development, making and exploitation of a particular kind of cement which is energetically modified. Cement is a construction product which is covered by the New Approach. The essential requirements for construction products have been laid down in the Construction Products Directive[56] while the technical specifications have been laid down in a harmonised European standard.[57] This European standard sets out the various types of cement that are produced in the EU. Products which comply with the European standard can carry the CE mark, which is required to place them on the market.

A European standard for cement was adopted by CEN in 2000. EMC was not happy with the provisions of the standard. It claimed that the standard was designed in such a way as to exclude its own type of energetically modified cement and that the cement industry had formed a cartel in the standardisation process to favour current manufacturers. The result was that EMC was unable to offer its type of cement on the market. Therefore, it claimed that there had been a breach of Article 101 and Article 102 TFEU. The businesses involved in the standardisation process had abused their dominant position—not just during the standardisation process but also afterwards. In 2001, EMC decided to complain to the Commission. The Commission replied that it did not consider the European standard to be a regulatory barrier to entry to the cement market. Therefore, the competition law provisions had not been breached. EMC then submitted a formal complaint to the Commission in 2002. The Commission subsequently assessed EMC's complaint on the basis of its Guidelines on the Applicability of Article 101 TFEU to Horizontal Co-operation Agreements ('the Guidelines'). In these Guidelines, there is a specific section on standardisation agreements.[58] A significant part of this section is devoted to the impact of standardisation on intellectual property rights and to standard terms adopted through standardisation. It states that the 'European standardisation bodies recognised under Directive 98/34/EC of the European Parliament and of the Council of 22 June 1998 laying down a procedure for the provision of information in the field of technical standards and regulations and on rules on Information Society services are subject to competition law to the extent that they can be considered to be an undertaking or an association of undertakings within the meaning of Articles 101 and 102'.[59] In the Guidelines, the Commission states that standardisation agreements usually produce significant

[56] Council Directive 89/106/EEC on the approximation of laws, regulations and administrative provisions of the Member States relating to construction products.

[57] The current version of this standard is EN 197-1:2011 Cement—Part 1: Composition, specifications and conformity criteria for common cements.

[58] Commission Communication, 'Guidelines on the applicability of Article 101 of the Treaty on the Functioning of the European Union to horizontal co-operation agreements' (2011) *OJEU* C/11, 55–72.

[59] ibid, 56.

positive economic effects and increase competition. According to the Commission, '[s]tandardisation agreements which do not restrict competition by object must be analysed in their legal and economic context with regard to their actual and likely effect on competition. In the absence of market power, a standardisation agreement is not capable of producing restrictive effects on competition'.[60] The effect on competition is determined by reference to criteria that focus on the standardisation process: whether participation in the standardisation process is unrestricted; whether the standardisation process is transparent; whether there is an obligation to comply (the binding nature of the standard) and whether access to the standard is on fair, reasonable and non–discriminatory terms.[61] It is also important to assess whether there is a possibility to develop other standards. If it is found that European standards restrict competition under Article 101(1), it is still possible that Article 101(3) provides an escape route. According to the Commission, standardisation agreements frequently give rise to efficiency gains.[62]

In *EMC Development*, the Commission reviewed the standardisation process leading to the adoption of the European standard for cement and concluded that there had not been any breach of the Guidelines. The complaint was formally dismissed in 2005. EMC then brought a case for annulment of the Commission's decision before the General Court. This case provided an occasion for the General Court to decide to what extent European standardisation under the New Approach was covered by the competition law provisions and what the legal status of the Commission's Guidelines was. EMC had made a number of complaints which focused directly on the standardisation process. First of all, it complained that the standardisation process had been controlled by Cembureau, an association of cement producers who were already well established in the cement market. Secondly, it submitted that the Chairman of the Technical Committee responsible for the making of the standard was biased and had a conflict of interests, because he worked for one of the main cement producers. The Commission should have ensured that the Chairman was neutral. As a consequence, the process had not been non–discriminatory. EMC also complained that the Commission should have supervised the standardisation process more closely. Finally, the process had not been sufficiently transparent. The interests of parties which had not been directly involved in the Technical Committee had not been taken into account and the Commission was under an obligation to inform and consult more broadly than just among the national standardisation organisations.

In 2010, the General Court rejected EMC's claim in its entirety.[63] The involvement of the Cembureau had not gone beyond normal lobbying activity. EMC

[60] ibid, 59.
[61] ibid, 59–60.
[62] ibid, 64.
[63] T-342/05 *EMC Development v European Commisison* ECLI: EU: T:2007:152.

had not provided sufficient evidence to substantiate its claim that the Chairman had been biased. The European standard had been developed in accordance with CEN's own guidelines, which ensured that a sufficiently broad range of interests was taken into account in the standardisation process. Furthermore, the Commission had not made any error in deciding that the evidence submitted by EMC was insufficient to establish a lack of transparency in the procedure leading to the adoption of the European standard. More generally, the General Court approved the Commission's application of its own Guidelines. This could be considered to be a judicial endorsement of the Commission's Guidelines.[64] An appeal to the CJEU was dismissed in 2011.[65] The result of this case is that if the Commission Guidelines have been complied with a European standard developed through CEN does not constitute a restriction to competition and falls outside the scope of Article 101 TFEU. Even if there has been a breach of the guidelines, a breach of Article 101 could still be avoided if the Commission found that the standard could be justified on the basis of Article 101(3).

C. Convergence in Competition Law

Since the primary purpose of European standardisation is to conclude an agreement between businesses—in the form of a European standard—that is intended to have an impact on the market, it could be expected that European standardisation and competition law would regularly interact and perhaps even clash.[66] However, this has not been the case. European standardisation appears to have a privileged position in competition law.[67] It has enjoyed this privilege for some time and it has been questioned whether this is entirely deserved. Harm Schepel already argued in 2001, on the basis of the Commission's Guidelines adopted in that year, that the European Commission's approach towards standardisation was suspiciously lenient.[68] Furthermore, he noted that the CJEU had been unwilling to get involved by discussing the interaction between European standardisation and competition law.[69] This unwillingness to scrutinise standards for their compatibility with the competition law provisions can most recently be observed in the CJEU's judgment in *Fra.bo*.[70] The CJEU was asked two questions—one on the free movement provisions and the other on the competition law provisions. The German court had only asked the competition law questions as an alternative if

[64] R Schellingerhout, 'Standard Setting from a Competition Law Perspective' (2011) *Competition Policy Newsletter* 3. See also S Sattler, 'Standardisation under EU competition law rules' (2011) 32 *European Competition Law Review* 343.

[65] C-367/10-P *EMC Development v Commission* ECLI: EU: C:2011:203.

[66] H Schepel, *The Constitution of Private Governance* (Oxford, Hart Publishing, 2005) 309.

[67] ibid, 313.

[68] ibid, 310–13.

[69] ibid, 310.

[70] *Fra.bo*, above n 5.

the reply to the first question was negative. The CJEU did not find it necessary to discuss the applicability of the competition law provisions, although it could still have been relevant.[71]

It is not surprising that the Commission is protective of European standardisation, which is one of the foundations of the New Approach. This would not be effective if constant challenges were being made against European standards on the basis of the competition law provisions.[72] The very adoption of the New Approach itself means that the Commission puts a lot of faith in European standardisation. This is also reflected in the Guidelines. After the CJEU's judgment in *EMC Development*, it is possible to conclude that the Guidelines have now obtained judicial approval.[73] However, although reference is made to the role of standardisation in the New Approach, the Guidelines also apply to European standardisation outside the New Approach—including European standardisation of services.

In general, it is clear that the assessment criteria laid down in the Guidelines are very much focused on the standardisation process—on the procedure. This is not surprising, particularly for standards adopted under the New Approach, since the impact of these standards after their adoption is significant. From that perspective, it is important to focus on the standard-making process.[74] This is not necessarily the case for European standards adopted outside the New Approach. They have to gain their impact through a second regulatory step, such as the application of the standard in contracts or in certification. It has been argued above that the free movement provisions have been applied in such a way as to concentrate on the impact of the standards on the market. As such, it could be argued that competition law is more likely to play a role for standards adopted under the New Approach, while the free movement provisions are more likely to be applied to standards that need a second step to have a regulatory impact on the market. The procedural focus of the competition law review under Article 101 TFEU would not be suitable to test that impact.

Furthermore, there might be a practical reason why parties are more likely to rely on the free movement provisions than on the competition law provisions. For competition law cases, there is quite a burden on claimants to show that conduct has an anti-competitive effect. This requires a substantial amount of work, statistics and economic analysis. There is more flexibility with the free movement provisions. Here, the CJEU is more likely to assume a breach on the basis of hypothetical impact on the market. In other words, with the free movement provisions it is easier for claimants to shift the burden of proof to defendants. This could be a reason, for example in *Fra.bo*, why the free movement provisions

[71] See also B Lundqvist, *Standardization under EU Competition Rules and US Antitrust Laws* (Cheltenham, Edward Elgar, 2014) 213–14.

[72] H Schepel, above n 66, 320.

[73] R Schellingerhout, above n 64.

[74] R Werle and E Iversen, 'Promoting Legitimacy in Technical Standardisation' (2006) 2 *Science, Technology and Innovation Studies* 19.

were preferred by the claimants, which meant that the CJEU did not have to rule on the compatibility of DVGW's certification activities with the competition law provisions.[75]

While the focus of Article 101 TFEU has been more on the standard–setting process, Article 102 TFEU is more likely to be used to challenge the application of European standards. From that perspective, it is surprising that the German court did not ask any questions about the potential applicability of Article 102 TFEU to the dispute in *Fra.bo*. However, despite the theoretical possibility of Article 102 TFEU being applied, it is unlikely to be of much relevance to European standardisation of services. Certification activities would only be caught if the certification body itself enjoyed a dominant position in the certification market. The creation of a certification body by a number of businesses in a particular market would probably come under Article 101 TFEU. Secondly, and even more importantly, there are very few businesses which enjoy a dominant position in the market in the healthcare and tourism sectors. This finding can be extended to services more generally, with the exception of services that were previously owned by the State and that have now been liberalised in many Member States. In such services sectors, such as telecom and energy, there are still a lot of former incumbents with significant power in the market. With the exception of postal services,[76] there have been no European standardisation initiatives which deal with the delivery of services in these markets. This can be explained by the fact that the EU itself has adopted a lot of instruments with the aim of encouraging competition in the market. These instruments have had an important impact on the private law relationship between service provider and consumer and have focused on the contractual standards of care.[77] As a result, both the need for and scope of European standardisation in these sectors is limited. In the healthcare sector, there are very few businesses which enjoy a dominant position. This is firstly because there are very few businesses in this sector anyway, and in those Member States in which healthcare insurance has (to some extent) been privatised there is a significant amount of competition among insurers. In the tourism sector some tour operators might have a dominant position, but most of the service providers are SMEs and small businesses.[78] Therefore, it is unlikely that Article 102 TFEU will be frequently applied to the conduct of businesses in the healthcare or tourism sectors.

In conclusion, the competition law provisions are unlikely to play a prominent role in European standardisation of services. This means that there is little pressure

[75] The author is grateful to Jan Trommer for this suggestion.

[76] For a list of the CEN standards which have been developed for postal services, see https://ec.europa.eu/growth/single-market/european-standards/harmonised-standards/postal-services_en.

[77] M Cantero, 'Towards the Self-Sufficiency in European Regulatory Private Law (I)—The Case of European Telecommunications Services Law' in H Micklitz and Y Svetiev (eds), 'A Self-Sufficient European Private Law—A Viable Concept?' *EUI Working Papers, LAW 2012/31*, 165–94.

[78] Interview with HOTREC (Brussels) on 29 November 2012.

from competition law to adopt standards which are competition law proof. In a way, they are in competition with the free movement provisions which, now that the CJEU is moving to an effects-based approach, are more easily able to focus on the impact of regulatory conduct on the market. The current approach towards European standardisation adopted by the Commission remains protective of the standardisation organisations. However, this protection is very much based on the dependency of the Commission on European standardisation in the New Approach. It cannot be guaranteed that the Commission will be equally lenient to European standardisation outside the New Approach. There are indications—and the *EMC Development* case is one of them—that European standardisation is used by groups of stakeholders to impose a particular type of product or service on the market. While this could be justified in the context of the New Approach, in which the EU is directly asking stakeholders to impose standards on the market, a more critical approach could be adopted outside the New Approach.

Case studies such as the Aesthetic Surgery Services standard and the Tourist Guide Training standard provide evidence that it is possible for stakeholders to argue that European standardisation would have anti-competitive effects and that the intention of European standardisation was to restrict access to particular services markets. If the EU and the standardisation organisations do not respond to these concerns, it is possible that the stakeholders will increasingly seek to challenge European standardisation initiatives and the application of these standards on the basis of the competition provisions. However, they are only likely to do so if standardisation has a real impact on their ability to access particular markets. While it was clear that in *EMC Development* the standardisation process had a real impact on the company's ability to participate in the cement market, this does not necessarily have to be the case for European services standards. For such standards, their regulatory impact is left entirely to the market.

IV. A PRELIMINARY CONCLUSION

Even if European standards have been applied in private law, it cannot be guaranteed that they will lead to convergence in private law. The free movement provisions and the competition law provisions each impose certain conditions on convergence. In the absence of a regulatory framework for European standardisation of services such as the New Approach, they could provide European pressure on standardisation organisations and stakeholders for European standards to be developed and applied in a way which guarantees compliance with the requirements imposed by EU law. However, the extent to which this pressure will be successful depends on whether European standards come within their scope of application.

The free movement provisions and competition law provisions are more likely to play a role in the application of European standards than the UCTD, which was discussed in the previous chapter. However, European standards will only come under their review if the standards have an impact on the market. The application of European standards must be regarded as an obstacle to free movement or competition in the market before courts will apply the free movement or competition provisions. The cases which have been discussed in this chapter suggest that European standards might not have such an impact on the market without them being protected or reinforced by public legislation—*Fra.bo*—or by a European regulatory framework—*EMC Development.* Without such protection, services markets are able to overcome the potential obstacles created by European standards without having to rely on free movement law or competition law. As the Tourist Guide Training example illustrates, the market is able to eliminate the protective effects of European standards.

8

Paradoxes of Convergence

AFTER THE ANALYSIS of the making of European services standards in the healthcare and tourism sector and the application of European standards in private law, this final chapter will now return to the theme of convergence. Its intention is to make some broader comparisons between European standardisation in the healthcare and tourism sectors and to link these discussions to the possibility of convergence in private law. The same will be done for the application of European standards in private law. This analysis will enable us to draw conclusions about the potential of convergence in private law through European standardisation of services.

I. RETURNING TO THE THEME OF CONVERGENCE

In chapter one, the process of convergence in private law through European standardisation was set out. This test for convergence has two limbs. First of all, European services standards have to be made. The European standardisation process has to lead to the successful adoption of European standards in the healthcare and tourism sectors. Secondly, these European standards have to be applied in private law. Through their application in practice, the European standards have to have a convergent impact on private law at the national level. There must be a link between the adoption of a European standard and the liability of service providers in private law. If one of these two steps does not take place, the process of convergence in private law through European standardisation encounters difficulties. The previous chapters have shown that there are in fact serious problems at both stages of the process of convergence. Very few European standards for services have been adopted so far. Although it has to be acknowledged that European standardisation of services is a relatively new phenomenon, the reluctance to get involved in European standardisation of services highlights some fundamental problems. Furthermore, the low number of European services standards makes it more difficult to assess their ability to be applied in private law. Comparisons have had to be made with European standards for products. It is clear that the application of European services standards in private law is complicated. The European standards suffer from a legitimacy problem—both from the point of view of professionals in the sector and from the perspective of consumers, who have limited access to the process and to European standards. If European standards are applied in private law, the manner in which they are applied makes it difficult for them to realise convergence. Therefore, convergence in private law through European standardisation of services remains, at the moment, ambition rather than reality.

Convergence is dependent on the interaction between European standardisation, (free movement of) services and private law. The comparisons and analysis made in the next sections show that there are a number of obstacles that act as an obstacle to convergence. The causes of these difficulties can ultimately be traced back to two paradoxes that have been uncovered in the analysis in the previous chapters. The first is the European paradox: the EU would like European standardisation of services to develop in a certain direction, which is compatible with the internal market and free movement of services, but it is not taking control to ensure that European standardisation is really developing in that direction. The second paradox is that of the stakeholders who are involved in European standardisation of services: they would like European standardisation to be applied in private law and to play a role in the legal framework which regulates their services. However, at the same time, they do not really care about private law and about the legal framework in which European standards would have to play a role. These two paradoxes have to be resolved before convergence becomes a more realistic possibility. However, before these paradoxes will be analysed in more detail, the main problems in the interaction between European standardisation, services and private law will be discussed.

II. EUROPEAN STANDARDISATION AND SERVICES

A. Outsiders and European Standardisation: Who Initiates Convergence?

Who are the stakeholders who take the initiative for European standardisation of services? In both the healthcare and the tourism sector European standardisation is often initiated by outsiders. While outsiders is a general term, in the context of European standardisation it means standardisation is started by stakeholders who are not sufficiently representative of a particular sector and who are having difficulties obtaining a more prominent role in that sector. This also explains the fierce opposition to certain initiatives for European standardisation of services. European standardisation provides a platform to outsiders to set standards which would become applicable to the entire sector. In the healthcare sector, the Aesthetic Surgery Services standard provides a good example. Medical practitioners who practise in aesthetic surgery do not necessarily belong to any of the existing medical specialties. Their attempts to be recognised as a separate specialty have been unsuccessful after a rejection by the European associations of medical specialists. European standardisation provides an alternative route to them to establish a form of recognition vis-à-vis the rest of the medical profession. The result of such a strategy is that they also embark on territory which is traditionally held by other medical professions. European standardisation is not a common means of setting standards for medical practice, but it provides a way which enables medical practitioners in aesthetic surgery to set standards without direct interference by the rest of the profession. In the tourism sector, the Tourist Guide Training standard was initiated by a group of tourist guides who sought to protect and impose their own definition of what a tourist guide should be like—a locally trained guide with local qualifications. This interpretation was in stark contradiction to the interpretation of tour operators and travel agencies, who prefer to use tour guides who travel with tourists and who are not based at the location where they offer their services.

In both examples, European standardisation was used by groups that were not representative of the sector. However, they were at least service providers in the relevant sectors. The example of the European standard for Cleft Lip Surgery was initiated by a patient organisation. The European Cleft Organisation had been campaigning for years for a European standard on Cleft Lip Surgery. However, it did not have a way to make standards which would have a certain authority in the sector. Again, European standardisation provided a means to work on a standard that could not be made through traditional routes for medical standardisation. It enabled patient or consumer organisations to try and promote higher quality standards. As such, it would enable a broader interpretation of the term 'stakeholders' to include organisations which have historically had difficulties getting involved in European standardisation. However, these organisations are struggling to get the support of service providers in the sectors. For example, the Cleft Lip Surgery project was not supported by the main European associations for medical professionals. Similarly, in the tourism sector, hotel owners fear that European standardisation would be used by certification bodies to impose standards on their hotels. European standardisation would enable them to extend their market because more standards for certification would be available at the European level.

Overall, it is clear that the process of convergence is frequently initiated by parties which represent a minority (view) within the profession. They are having difficulties being effective within the sector. European standardisation constitutes their attempt to embrace the entire profession and to reach broader consensus on difficult issues. The problem is that the initiation of European standardisation does not have a convergent impact, but rather provokes divergence. The European standardisation process forces the insiders to distinguish themselves from the outsiders and to put renewed emphasis on the differences in approach between them and the outsiders. The problem is that the procedure for European standardisation has no way to deal with such representation problems. There is no way for CEN to avoid it being used as a vehicle by an unrepresentative minority that tries to impose standards on other stakeholders in a sector. The only formal requirements are that five national standardisation organisations must participate in the European standardisation process and that a 71% weighed majority of the organisations must have voted in favour of the standardisation project.[1] However, CEN

[1] Article 6 of CEN Internal Regulations, Part 2 (2013).

cannot impose requirements on which parties should or should not participate in a European standardisation process. It is entirely dependent on parties that are willing to invest and participate in European standardisation of services. Because CEN ultimately has to make its money out of standardisation projects, one cannot realistically expect CEN to refuse to start a particular standardisation project on the basis of a lack of adequate representation.[2] Moreover, there is also the problem of resources—European standardisation is more accessible to stakeholders who have the financial resources to participate in the process. This again enables a particular group of outsiders—such as certification bodes in the tourism sector—to impose their standards through European standardisation.

The dominance of outsiders in European standardisation is more of a problem for services than for product standards made under the New Approach. This is because in the New Approach the Commission directly controls which parties participate in the standardisation process. Even if it is argued that this control might not always be effective, there is much more incentive for a broader range of stakeholders to participate in European standardisation. After all, they know that in the framework of the New Approach a European standard will obtain a quasi-legal effect. As a consequence, it becomes much more important for them to participate in the standard-setting process.[3] These incentives do not exist for European standardisation of services. Moreover, the limited impact of European services standards might be a reason for stakeholders not to participate in European standardisation. The attempts of outsiders to impose standards on the entire sector could then be considered futile, since their effect in law will remain limited.

B. Triggers for European Standardisation: What are the Drivers for Convergence?

Without a New Approach to services, the EU is unable to effectively control the aims of European standardisation initiatives in the services sector. In the New Approach to goods, European standardisation has a clear market-facilitative purpose. The primary purpose of the New Approach is to facilitate free movement and to improve the internal market for goods. Standardisation has been made an instrument to increase the functioning of the internal market.[4] The absence of a clear regulatory framework for European standardisation of services means that the same impetus cannot be given for standardisation of services. The result is that many of the European standards for services have had very little to do with the improvement of the internal market for services. On the contrary, a substantial number of the European services standards that have been developed could

[2] M Egan, 'Regulatory strategies, delegation and European market integration' (1998) 5 *Journal of European Public Policy* 485.

[3] R Werle and E Iversen, 'Promoting Legitimacy in Technical Standardisation' (2006) 2 *Science, Technology and Innovation Studies* 19.

[4] H Schepel, *The Constitution of Private Governance* (Oxford, Hart Publishing, 2005).

better be described as obstacles to free movement. The motivation for stakeholders to start a European standardisation process for services was certainly not focused on the facilitation of free movement. The European standard for Tourist Guide Training was a clear counter–reaction to the liberalisation of the profession brought about by the judgments of the CJEU in the 1990s. Its aim was to protect the position of local tourist guides in the dynamic and transforming tourism sector. Similarly, although the Aesthetic Surgery Services standard may have the improvement of the quality of aesthetic surgery as its primary aim, it is at the same time vigorously criticised on the basis that it constitutes an attempt to protect or reserve the market to a particular group of medical professionals. Market fragmentation and market protection are commonly used terms to describe the motivation behind European standardisation of services. This is not at all what the Commission and the EU foresaw when they included European standardisation in Article 26 of the Services Directive. However, the Commission has very limited means to do something about it. It could be argued that the Commission should raise more awareness among CEN and stakeholders about the potential impact of European standards on the internal market. The fact that the application of European standards which obstruct free movement might be more difficult after the gradual extension of the application of the free movement provisions to private parties could serve as an indirect stimulus to stakeholders and to CEN to focus more on market–facilitative European standards for services.

If the healthcare and tourism sectors are compared, it is clear that the potential function of European standardisation would be different in each sector. With the adoption of the Package Travel Directive,[5] the EU has created rules on the information which tourists should be provided with before the conclusion of a contract. When it comes to performance, Article 5 of the Directive expressly provides that tour operators or travel agents are liable for the proper performance of the contract. This means there has been European harmonisation of the existence of liability—including a limited number of defences—which could be supplemented by European standards which would lay down standards for service providers in the tourism sector. The Package Travel Directive provides an incentive for the creation of such European standards, which would primarily focus on the extent to which tour operators are required to check the safety of the service providers at the destination of the holiday. Standardisation would fulfil a clear market-facilitative role in the European regulatory framework for package travel. The fact that very few standards have been made that give substance to Article 5 of the Directive shows that stakeholders cannot be relied on to take the initiative for the adoption of safety standards. The result is that these standards remain to be identified ex post via litigation at the national level. Furthermore, standards are likely to remain national standards. The situation is different in the healthcare sector. Although the Cross-Border Healthcare Directive 2011 lays down standards on the information

[5] Council Directive 90/314/EEC on package travel, package holidays and package tours.

that should be provided to patients,[6] the Directive clearly provides that the standards of treatment remain national.[7] There is no European harmonisation of liability for medical negligence in a cross-border context. Therefore, there is less impetus for European standards on medical treatment to be adopted—there are no European legal standards which could be supplemented or specified through European standardisation. While it is true that an increased level of cross-border movement of patients could encourage the creation of European standards in the healthcare sector, there is no European legal framework that encourages the adoption of such standards.

Convergence works well if there is a common—or uniform—driver to initiate the process.[8] In the EU, the common driver behind convergence has always been the building of the internal market. Although convergence might have more than one purpose, its central aim is to facilitate free movement within the internal market. This requires European control of the direction in which the process of convergence is going. At the very least there has to be a degree of European co-ordination about the purposes of convergence and its role in the internal market.[9] Such control or co-ordination is missing for European standardisation of services. Article 26 of the Services Directive is insufficient as a tool to provide a frame in which it can be guaranteed that European standardisation of services contributes to the internal market for services. The same applies to the Standardisation Regulation 2012.[10] Although the Standardisation Regulation recognises European standardisation of services, it does not establish something like a New Approach. Such a New Approach to services would be a possible means for the EU to ensure that European standardisation for services would contribute to the functioning of the internal market. However, if this is considered to be one step too far, the Commission should at the very least take more control of the purposes of European standardisation of services and should check that standardisation projects are compatible with the free movement provisions. This would be a less drastic way of trying to impose a common drive for convergence. At the moment, convergence through European standardisation of services is fragmented. Stakeholders in the healthcare and tourism sectors start to work on European standards for all sorts of reasons, but they do not share a common motivation behind the initiation of European standardisation of services.

[6] Directive 2011/24/EU of the European Parliament and of the Council on the application of patients' rights in cross-border healthcare.

[7] Article 4(1)(b) of the Cross-Border Healthcare Directive.

[8] W van Gerven, 'Bringing (Private) Laws Closer to Each Other at the European Level' in F Cafaggi (ed), *The Institutional Framework of European Private Law* (Oxford, OUP, 2006) 37–78.

[9] W van Gerven, 'Private Law in a Federal Perspective', in R Brownsword et al (eds), *The Foundations of European Private Law* (Oxford, Hart Publishing, 2011) 337–51.

[10] Regulation 1025/2012 of the European Parliament and of the Council on European standardisation.

C. Quality of Services and European Standardisation: What is the Impact of Convergence on Quality?

Quality is an inherently personal concept. Because of the strong subjective nature of quality, it is normally left to the market. Tourists can choose the hotel they would like to stay in on the basis of their own definition of what standards and characteristics a hotel should have. Patients, in the ideal scenario, can choose their own doctors on the basis of what qualities they should possess. In both sectors, ex ante regulation imposes certain requirements that service providers have to fulfil before they can provide their services on the market. Hotels usually have to obtain a licence, while doctors have to obtain qualifications through training and examinations. Once the service providers have complied with these requirements, they are allowed to enter the market and to distinguish themselves so as to enable consumers to make an assessment of the quality of their services.

The various case studies in this book show that, from the perspective of the quality of services, there are essentially two categories of convergence through European standardisation. The first category, to which the Aesthetic Surgery Services and Cleft Lip Surgery initiatives belong, includes standards which aim to identify a minimum level of quality above which competition in the market can take place. The intention behind these projects is that competition on quality is only really possible if a certain minimum quality level is guaranteed. This minimum level of quality is very close to the identification of a minimum level of safety. Certain safety standards have to be imposed to enable consumers to make safe choices about the kind of treatment they would like to receive. This additional layer of regulation through European standardisation is necessary because the market is not sufficiently transparent and because consumers suffer from a lack of information. The PIP breast implants scandal provides good evidence of the failures of the market for aesthetic surgery services.[11] European standardisation is then used as a tool for consumer protection. In the healthcare sector, the problem is that European standardisation is not accepted as a tool to identify a minimum level of quality of healthcare. The medical profession claims that it will lead to a process of de-professionalisation, which will ultimately lead to a lowering of the quality of healthcare. There are insufficient guarantees that European standardisation in the healthcare sector is an evidence-based activity. It would open up the healthcare sector to market forces. This process would not result in a higher quality of care. As a result, it is not in the best interests of patients to contribute to European standardisation. However, the medical profession does not deny that it is necessary for a minimum level of quality of healthcare to be identified. The criticism is directed against European standardisation as a tool. Moreover, it is argued

[11] B van Leeuwen, 'PIP Breast Implants, the EU's New Approach for Goods and Market Surveillance by Notified Bodies' (2014) 3 *European Journal of Risk Regulation* 338.

that the minimum level of care should not be identified at the European level, but should rather be left to the Member States.

The second category of convergence includes European standards which attempt to impose one particular type of quality on the market. This is the main objection against European standardisation in the tourism sector. The Tourist Guide Training standard provides the best example. It constitutes an attempt to impose one particular kind of tourist guide on the market—those who are locally established and who have received local training. As a consequence, European standardisation would lead to a reduction in diversity, which is undesirable from the perspective of consumers. This kind of standardisation is not necessary to identify a minimum safety level for services, but it rather restricts the market. Its aim is inherently protectionist—the European standard is intended to protect locally established tourist guides from the market. The possibility of European standards for hotels raises similar objections. European standardisation of hotel services would seek to put hotels in a particular European frame, which would reduce the diversity of hotels. As such, the objections in the tourism sector are even more fundamental than in the healthcare sector. While in the healthcare sector European standardisation is not considered to be the right tool to regulate quality of healthcare, in the tourism sector the very regulation of quality itself is not considered to be desirable. The tourism market is highly transparent and there is plenty of information available for consumers to make well-informed choices.

These examples also provide evidence of the fundamental differences between standardisation of goods and services. For European standardisation of goods, quality becomes almost synonymous with compatibility. However, the delivery of services has more dimensions than the three dimensions of a product. Standardising services means standardising human interaction. In the healthcare sector, European standardisation is rejected as a tool. In the tourism sector, the very necessity of European standardisation is denied. European standardisation means that consensus has to be reached at the European level about the kind of quality which should be offered to consumers. However, this kind of consensus could also be considered as fundamentally inconsistent with the foundations of an internal market in which different services with different levels of quality are offered. There have to be good justifications to attempt to realise convergence in that internal market. For products, convergence through European standardisation is justified on the basis that it makes the internal market for goods much more effective through the harmonisation of product requirements. However, for services, European standardisation will only improve the internal market if it contributes to the safety of services in the internal market. There is a serious risk that European standardisation will lead to a reduction of the diversity of services or that it will facilitate market protectionism. At the moment, there is little evidence to suggest that European standardisation of services is able to improve free movement of services.

III. EUROPEAN STANDARDISATION AND PRIVATE LAW

A. Convergence Without a European Regulatory Framework: Linking European Standardisation to Private Law

European services standards do not obtain a clear legal effect after their adoption. They have to rely on public or private law to obtain binding force in law. While stakeholders cannot exercise direct control over the application of European standards in public law, they could have a direct influence over the application of European standards in private law. From the perspective of the EU, there is no European framework to provide for or to encourage the application of European services standards in private law. This is different from European product standards which have been made under the New Approach. These standards obtain a clear legal effect after their adoption—they provide substance to the essential requirements laid down in European legislation. Furthermore, there is a clear link between European standardisation and product liability. Although the PIP breast implants scandal illustrates that the New Approach does not have a direct impact on the application of European product standards in private law, the argument could be made that their application in private law is necessary to guarantee the effective application of the New Approach. If European standards were not applied in private law, this could create obstacles to the free movement of goods, which would indirectly endanger the effectiveness of the regulatory framework that has been created with the New Approach. In other words, the regulatory framework itself requires convergence in private law. For services, there is no European regulatory framework that requires or even encourages the application of European standards in private law. As a result, there is no European driver for convergence. Convergence becomes entirely dependent on the willingness of national private law to apply European standards as the standard of care in contract or tort cases. This is similar in both the healthcare and the tourism sector.

The judgments of the German courts in the cases brought against TÜV Rheinland after the PIP breast implants scandal show the difficulties with relying on national private law to create convergence through European standardisation. In the absence of a European regulatory framework, national courts will apply national private law principles to determine the legal impact of European standardisation. This is not necessarily consistent with a process of convergence, since there is no guarantee that a uniform European approach will be taken to the application of European standards. Moreover, national courts show a reluctance to make an automatic link between ex ante regulation through European standardisation and ex post regulation through the determination of liability in private law. In the New Approach, the extent to which the effectiveness of EU law requires this link to be made is uncertain. The situation is even more unclear for European standardisation of services, for which there is no European regulatory framework. This means that the application is not only dependent on national private law, but also on the willingness of stakeholders to create a link from European standardisation to private law. The various governance problems that affect European standardisation have a negative impact on the application of European standards by stakeholders. This is not only caused by the problems with guaranteeing adequate representation in European standardisation, but also by the limited transparency and accessibility of the European standardisation process. In the tourism sector, SMEs are having real difficulties exercising influence on European standardisation. The result is that, because they have not played any part in the making of the European standards, they are unlikely to apply them in their services activities. Similarly, the fact that European standards become products that have to be bought from the national standardisation organisations means that consumers are unlikely to become acquainted with European standards. As a consequence, the extent to which consumers can expect compliance with European standards becomes more limited.

Without European control, convergence is entirely dependent on European standardisation and private law to establish a link between them. At the moment, the conclusion has to be that European standardisation of services and private law do not sufficiently match for convergence to be effective. In effect, this is a fundamental cultural problem. Where Pierre Legrand argued that the differences in legal culture prevented the possibility of convergence,[12] this book has highlighted a clash in culture between European standardisation and law. The world of law and the world of European standardisation do not sufficiently talk to each other for them to jointly initiate and bring about a process of convergence in private law. As a result, the co-ordination which takes place at the European level through standardisation of services does not result in convergence in law.[13] There is insufficient awareness among standardisation organisations and stakeholders who are participating in European standardisation of services of the role that European services standards should play in the legal regulation of services and the extent to which their standardisation projects are consistent with the existing legal framework. This lack of legal expertise in the making of European standards and the ignorance of the legal regulatory framework result in an inability to connect European standardisation to private law. It is not just limited to private law, but it applies in a similar way to the free movement provisions. A process of convergence through European standardisation has to improve the internal market for services. This can only be guaranteed if the European standards that are made, actually facilitate free movement of services. The obligations imposed by the free movement provisions have been extended to private parties who are involved in collective regulation and whose regulatory activities have an impact on the internal market.[14] As such, compliance with the free movement provisions is a precondition for convergence in private law. Therefore, there has to be compatibility

[12] P Legrand, 'European Legal Systems Are Not Converging' (1996) 45 *ICLQ* 52.

[13] Cf. W van Gerven, above n 9.

[14] H Schepel, 'Constitutionalising the Market, Marketising the Constitution, and to Tell the Difference: On the Horizontal Application of the Free Movement Provisions in EU Law' (2012) 18 *European Law Journal* 177.

between European standardisation of services and the free movement provisions. The non-compliance of European standardisation with free movement law will prevent convergence in private law.

B. Convergence Through Standardisation: The Impact of European Standards on the Liability of Service Providers

Once a European standard has been adopted in a services sector and there is willingness on the part of courts and stakeholders for the standard to be applied in private law, the next question is what impact the European standard could have on the determination of liability of service providers. In chapter one, this was introduced as the procedural dimension of convergence. The question is whether the adoption of a European standard encourages a transformation from an *obligation de moyens* towards an *obligation de résultat*. Traditionally, service providers were expected to provide their services with the necessary level of care, but it could not be claimed by service recipients that they were entitled to a certain result. European standardisation has the potential to transform this if service providers were legally required to comply with the provisions of a European standard. If such a development took place, it would mean that service recipients could claim compliance with a European standard as an *obligation de résultat*. However, the analysis in chapter six has shown that European standardisation does not have this impact on the obligations of service providers. Courts are unwilling to make a direct link between the breach of a European standard and liability in private law. The primary reason for this is that European standards have not been made with the idea that a breach will immediately lead to liability in private law. The possible liability of service providers depends on a whole range of circumstances. European standardisation is unable to encapsulate all these circumstances in one single instrument. This is particularly important for the provision of services, which is a process.

All of this would be solved if European standards were directly incorporated in services contracts. This does not happen frequently in the services sector. It could become more common if more European services standards were made in the future. The result would be that the contract provided the bridge from an *obligation de moyens* to an *obligation de résultat*—the service provider would become contractually bound to comply with the provisions of a European standard. However, the empirical research has shown that there is resistance among stakeholders to make compliance with (European) standards contractually binding. In the healthcare sector, the objection is mainly based on the protection of professional autonomy. Medical professionals must be able to exercise their professional judgment and to act in the best interests of patients. Strict compliance with standards would not always be in the best interests of patients.[15] As a result, although

[15] E Freidson, *Profession of Medicine: A Study of the Sociology of Applied Knowledge* (Chicago, UCP, 1988).

standards will always play a role in the determination of liability, they should not have an automatic impact. A similar position is taken in the tourism sector. Here, the emphasis on professional autonomy is less prominent. The tourism sector relies more on the market and considers the application of standards as restrictive of market freedom. Regulation through European standardisation is considered neither necessary nor desirable. Overall, therefore, it can be said that the objections to the application of European standards in both sectors are relatively similar to the objections to the making of European standards.

If courts and stakeholders are not willing to apply European standards directly in private law, this does not mean that European standards have absolutely no role to play in private law at all. They could still have an evidential role in the determination of liability of service providers. The PIP breast implant group litigation in the UK provides a good example. The possible non-compliance with the European standard for breast implants is used to establish that PIP breast implants were not of satisfactory quality. European standardisation is used to specify an existing objective standard of care in private law—in this example, the requirement of satisfactory quality. Similarly, European standards could be used to provide substance to open standards such as the state of the art or reasonable skill and care.[16] The evidential use of European standards in services sectors could also result in convergence in private law. However, such a process would be extremely difficult to measure. Again, there would be no control at the European level about the precise impact that European standards would have. Furthermore, their effect would be very dependent on the extent to which they could be connected to the particular circumstances of a case.

Most importantly, this evidential strategy for convergence requires stakeholders to use European standards in liability cases. In chapter one, it was explained that convergence would be very much based on the bottom-up application of European standards in practice. The practical application of European standards would constitute a bridge from the making of European standards to their application in private law.[17] European standards would obtain the status of professional standards through their application in practice. This is exactly where the difficulties arise and the bridge from practice to private law collapses. In the healthcare and the tourism sectors there are strong objections to European standards being applied as the professional standard. When a product standard has been adopted in the New Approach, there can be little doubt that this European standard constitutes the standard with which these goods have to comply. When a European services standard has been adopted, there is no guarantee that this standard will be accepted as the professional standard in that services sector. A European services

[16] See E Benvenisti and G Downs, 'National courts and transnational private regulation' in F Cafaggi (ed), *Enforcement of Transnational Private Regulation* (Cheltenham, Edward Elgar, 2012) 131–46.

[17] Similar to the application of CESL in business transactions: V Reding, 'The Next Steps Towards a European Contract Law for Businesses and Consumers' in R Schulze and J Stuyck, *Towards a European Contract Law* (Munich, Sellier, 2011) 9–22.

standard would not enjoy authority in a sector simply on the basis of its adoption. There are clear indications that stakeholders would be reluctant to apply European standards in practice. This reluctance could be based on the methodology for the making of European standards—for example, the medical profession could refuse to follow European standards because they were not sufficiently evidence-based. Alternatively, the application of a standard could be refused on the basis of the parties which had been involved in the making of that standard—for example, SMEs could refuse to apply European standards which had been made without their involvement.

Finally, convergence through European standardisation suffers from the fact that the strategy for convergence would involve a combination of what Roger Brownsword has described as soft convergence and medium convergence.[18] The initial European standardisation process would only result in soft convergence at the European level. Medium convergence, the introduction of mandatory minimum standards, would be realised through the application of European standards in private law. The link from soft convergence to medium convergence will only be made if the introduction of European mandatory minimum standards is considered desirable. This is a particular problem for the healthcare sector, in which standards across the EU are widely divergent. For both cultural and financial reasons, some Member States have much higher standards of care than other Member States. In these Member States, there would be resistance to make European minimum standards mandatory, because this would result in lower standards of care. They even resist soft convergence at the European level, since it would provide an incentive to public authorities and health insurers to cut costs and for lower mandatory standards to be introduced at the national level. This why the European standard for Cleft Lip Surgery is so strongly opposed by some of the Member States with well-functioning healthcare systems. They do not object to providing assistance to some of the new Member States to help them to improve quality of healthcare, but they fear that the adoption of European standards would lead to pressure to lower standards at the national level. Soft convergence through European standardisation would not improve the quality of care, but would rather result in the lowest common denominator.

IV. PARADOXES OF CONVERGENCE

A. The EU Paradox

One of the recurrent themes of this book is that the lack of a European regulatory framework is making it much more difficult for convergence in private law through European standardisation of services to take place. Such a regulatory

[18] R Brownsword, 'Convergence: What, Why, and Why not?', in H Micklitz and Y Svetiev (eds), 'A Self-Sufficient European Private Law—A Viable Concept', *EUI Working Paper LAW* 2012/31, 77–82.

framework would be able to provide a driver for convergence, which is necessary to give it direction and to improve the process. The Commission has made it very clear that it is worried about how European standardisation of services could develop and that it would like to push European standardisation of services in a direction that would help it to improve the internal market for services. However, while it has certain means at its disposal to guarantee more directly that European standardisation of services is compatible with the free movement provisions, it has not taken any steps to do this. This is what could be described as the EU paradox of convergence. There is a gap between the EU's rhetoric and its actions.

There are two possible explanations for this paradox. The first could be uncertainty. The Commission is not convinced that European standardisation of services is necessarily a useful tool to regulate the internal market for services. As such, it is uncertain about European standardisation as a tool for convergence. The reason for this is that very few European standards have been made and that it has been difficult to measure their impact. It does not want to create a European regulatory framework without knowing that European standardisation of services would actually help to improve free movement of services. However, in a way, this argument could be considered circular. The Commission might never discover the full potential of European standardisation of services unless it actually embraces it in its regulatory strategy for services. Its uncertainty is also based on the position of stakeholders. A European regulatory framework for standardisation of services would provide more top-down legitimacy to European standardisation, but it would still be reliant on stakeholders to make standards for services. The Commission has received signals that stakeholders do not support European standardisation of services. This has reaffirmed its uncertainty and has made it necessary for the Commission to take the initiative for further research and orientation on what European standardisation of services could do for the internal market.[19]

A second explanation for the paradox, which is to some extent linked to the first, could be disinterest. The limited impact of European standardisation of services on the internal market so far could mean that the Commission is not too worried about it. Although there is little evidence to support the argument that European standardisation of services is really able to improve free movement of services, it is not possible to conclude either that it constitutes a serious obstacle to free movement. The impact of European standardisation on the market has been marginal, which could also prove that the market has a natural ability to overcome obstacles created by European standardisation. The tourist sector could be evidence of this ability of the market, now that the requirement for licensed tourist guides is being abolished for some of the major attractions in London. This significantly reduces the impact and market-restrictive effects of the European standard for Tourist Guide Training. Therefore, it could be said that there is no real reason for the Commission to be worried about European standardisation of services. Its

[19] M/517 Mandate addressed to CEN, CENELEC and ETSI for the Programming and Development of Horizontal Service Standards of 24 January 2013.

impact has been marginal and the way in which it has been used is fragmented and incoherent. As a result, there is no urgency or pressure for the Commission to get involved. European standardisation of services has not proved that it requires more attention.

B. The Stakeholders Paradox

The second paradox which has been identified focuses on the role of stakeholders in European standardisation of services. They decide to start with European standardisation because they want to change something in their services sector. There is always a plan or an aim behind European standardisation. The problem for European standardisation is that it will always need law to have a real impact on how a particular service is regulated. European standardisation of services could be described as soft law, but it is definitely softer than law. Although the legal impact could be based on the practical application of the standards, which would mean that the stakeholders would to a certain extent be in control of the legal application of standards, the simple adoption of European standards is not enough. European standardisation of services needs private law to have an impact. At the same time, stakeholders seem to be ignorant of the requirements that the law imposes on them and on the role that their European services standard would play in the regulation of that service.[20] One of the key findings of this book is that European standardisation of services does not care enough about the legal environment in which the standard will be received. The paradox can be formulated very clearly: European standardisation of services needs private law, but European standardisation does not care about private law. This is particularly ironic from the perspective of private law, since private law could facilitate convergence through European standardisation of services. It would enable stakeholders to make the link from standardisation to legal regulation. However, before this can be successful, stakeholders have to be aware of the requirements that are imposed on them by private law. This includes the compatibility of European standards with the free movement, the competition law provisions and the UCTD.

Again, two possible explanations for the paradox will be offered. The most logical explanation would be inability. Most stakeholders who are involved in European standardisation of services are not lawyers. They do not approach the problems they would like to resolve from the perspective of law. The same is true for the European and national standardisation organisations. Employees of these organisations often have a technical or scientific background. This is a direct consequence of the fact that standardisation organisations have historically become prominent through the technical standardisation of products. As a result, they did

[20] H Micklitz, 'The Service Directive: Consumer Contract Law Making via Standardisation' in A Colombi Ciacchi et al. (eds), *Liability in the Third Millennium (Liber Amicorum Gert Brüggemeier)* (Baden-Baden, Nomos, 2009) 439–64.

not need to have legal expertise. Moreover, under the New Approach, the mandate of the stakeholders in European standardisation remains very technical. The legal framework has been taken care of by the EU. For European standardisation of services, the situation is different. Stakeholders themselves become responsible for the application of European services standards in the legal framework. At the moment, they are unable to take up this responsibility. More involvement of lawyers in the development of European services standards would be desirable. These lawyers should have knowledge and experience of the European regulatory framework for services. Furthermore, stakeholders should be educated about the demands that are imposed on them by the legal framework. It has to be admitted that lawyers are already frequently sitting around the table in European standardisation of services. However, their role has often been to protect national legislation and to resist convergence, rather than to facilitate convergence through matching European standardisation to the legal framework in which it should play a role.

Another more difficult explanation for the paradox could be disconnection. This would be closely linked to the disinterest explanation provided for the EU paradox. It could be that stakeholders understand that legal regulation is necessary in their sector, but that they do not see European standardisation of services as intrinsically linked to that legal regulation. Standardisation would be more of a publicity or promotion exercise to establish the position of stakeholders in a particular sector, which could then encourage the start of a similar convergent process in law. Stakeholders would not need to worry about law, because law would do a different job, which would probably take over or overrule European standardisation of services. This is also where we can see a clear clash between public and private regulation. For example, in the Aesthetic Surgery Services standardisation project, the stakeholders are working under the constant threat of their project being overruled by national, and possibility even European, legislation. In a way, they would not be unhappy with this, because the standardisation project is intended to provoke stricter legal regulation of aesthetic surgery services. The European standardisation project could then be seen as a prelude to legislative action. It would mean that the European standardisation project would remain disconnected from legal regulation.

C. Trying to Resolve the Paradoxes

Towards the end of this thesis, it is clear that the picture which has been painted of convergence in private law through European standardisation of services is rather pessimistic. If convergence through European standardisation is to be successful, a number of improvements are necessary—both at the level of the standard–making and at the level of the application in private law. It does not seem likely that the Commission will move towards a New Approach to services any time soon.

This book has discussed the complicated relationship between the EU,—in particular, the Commission—CEN and national standardisation organisations. In the New Approach, the EU and the Commission have a dominant role vis-à-vis national standardisation organisations. Initiatives for European standardisation are taken at the European level and their scope and purpose are strictly controlled by the EU. CEN acts as an intermediary and co-ordinates the work. Without a New Approach for services, national standardisation organisations are much more powerful in European standardisation of services. The co-ordination and control at the European level is missing. As a result, national standardisation organisations do not act in a co-ordinated way and do not necessarily act in the interests of the EU's internal market. So far, CEN has chosen the side of the national standardisation organisations. If European standardisation of services is to make a successful contribution to the internal market, the Commission will have to rebalance the relationship with CEN and the national standardisation organisations. More control at the European level is necessary.

Stricter control of European standardisation of services by the Commission would ensure that standardisation activities were consistent with free movement law and that they would contribute to the functioning of the internal market. It would also facilitate the application of European standards in private law. At the same time, it could increase the tension between national standardisation organisations and the EU. Moreover, national law could be resistant to too much top-down Europeanisation through standardisation. Therefore, the main challenge for the Commission will be to find a balance between ensuring that European standardisation of services is used to improve the internal market for services and guaranteeing that stakeholders are sufficiently involved in standardisation so that European standards will be successful in private law. The involvement and support of stakeholders remains crucial for the successful application of European standards in private law.

Finally, two recommendations will be made. First of all, the Commission should take a more prominent role in European standardisation of services. This should start with stricter supervision of European standardisation of services. This supervision should take place from the moment that a proposal for a European services standard is submitted until the final adoption of the standard. The Commission should take the role of educator to teach stakeholders how European services standards can be made compatible with free movement law. Moreover, it would be helpful if the Commission started to issue more mandates in the field of services standardisation. Even without a New Approach to services, such mandates could provide a certain direction to European standardisation of services and could be an incentive for convergence.

Secondly, CEN should reconsider the requirements for the start of a European standardisation process. Changes have to be made to ensure that European standardisation of services is initiated by stakeholders who are sufficiently representative of a services sector. Furthermore, the process has to be made more accessible and transparent. Although it would be a serious threat to its current business model, CEN should seriously think about making more standards freely accessible to the public. This will ultimately improve the potential for European standardisation of services to obtain a more prominent role in the regulation of services. Moreover, CEN will have to make internal changes. This also applies to national standardisation organisations. For a real impetus to standardisation of services, more expertise in the services sector is required within standardisation organisations. CEN will have to become more embedded in the services sector.

Annex: List of Interviews

I. RECORDED INTERVIEWS

1. CEN (Comité Européen de Normalisation) (Brussels) on 4 April 2012
2. ANEC (European Association for the Co-ordination of Consumer Representation in Standardisation) (Brussels) on 4 April 2012
3. NEN (Netherlands Standardisation Institute) (Delft) on 12 April 2012
4. ASI (Austrian Standards Institute) (Vienna) on 12 November 2012
5. HOTREC (Association of Hotels, Restaurants and Cafes in Europe) (Brussels) on 29 November 2012
6. DG Enterprise of the European Commission (Brussels) on 29 November 2012
7. Chairman of Dutch Mirror Committee for Aesthetic Surgery Services (Goes) on 29 December 2012
8. UEMS (European Union of Medical Specialists) and CPME (Standing Committee of European Doctors) (Warsaw) on 19 February 2013
9. VKI (Consumers Association of Austria) (Vienna) on 5 November 2013
10. Guild (Guild of Registered Tourist Guides), ITG (Institute of Tourist Guides) and APTG (Association of Professional Tourist Guides) (London) on 21 January 2014
11. UK barrister (London) on 28 January 2014

II. NON-RECORDED INTERVIEWS

1. ECO (European Cleft Organisation) (Skype) on 14 March 2012
2. ECO (European Cleft Organisation) (Skype) on 2 May 2012
3. General Osteopathic Council (UK) (Telephone) on 8 May 2012
4. KNMG (Royal Dutch Medical Association) (Utrecht) on 28 June 2012
5. NZA (Dutch Healthcare Authority) (Utrecht) on 3 July 2012
6. Kwaliteitsinstituut voor de Zorg (Quality Institute for Healthcare) (Diemen) on 23 August 2012
7. Orde van Medisch Specialisten (Dutch Order of Medical Specialists) on 30 August 2012
8. Inspectie voor de Gezondheidszorg (Dutch Health Care Inspectorate) (Telephone) on 31 August 2012
9. NOB (Dutch Underwater Sports Federation) (Telephone) on 29 January 2013
10. Professor Klaus Tonner (Rostock) on 13 August 2013

Index

9 781509 908332

Printed by Libri Plureos GmbH in Hamburg,
Germany